Light in Darkness

An Exploration into God

ANTHONY J. KELLY, CSsR

Paulist Press
New York / Mahwah, NJ

Cover image by estevez / Shutterstock.com
Cover and book design by Lynn Else

Library of Congress Cataloging-in-Publication Data
Names: Kelly, Anthony, 1938– author.
Title: Light in darkness : an exploration into God / Anthony J Kelly, CSsR.
Description: New York / Mahwah, NJ : Paulist Press, 2020. | Includes bibliographical references and index. | Summary: "No question, argues theologian Anthony Kelly, is more important than God and our relationship to God (individually and collectively). He explores these issues while integrating science, theology and philosophy. Kelly offers a fresh perspective on Aquinas as an aid to modern spiritual seekers. Trinitarian theology, he suggests, integrates private devotion with our social obligations. Finally, he approaches the Liturgy as a way to collectively explore into God"—Provided by publisher.
Identifiers: LCCN 2019056797 (print) | LCCN 2019056798 (ebook) | ISBN 9780809154692 (paperback) | ISBN 9781587688652 (ebook)
Subjects: LCSH: God (Christianity)—Knowableness. | God (Christianity)—Attributes. | God (Christianity)—History of doctrines.| Spiritual life—Catholic Church. | Catholic Church—Doctrines.
Classification: LCC BT103 .K445 2020 (print) | LCC BT103 (ebook) | DDC 231—dc23
LC record available at https://lccn.loc.gov/2019056797
LC ebook record available at https://lccn.loc.gov/2019056798

ISBN 978-0-8091-5469-2 (paperback)
ISBN 978-1-58768-865-2 (e-book)

Published by Paulist Press
997 Macarthur Boulevard
Mahwah, New Jersey 07430
www.paulistpress.com

Printed and bound in the
United States of America

To esteemed colleagues of the new generation,
Joel Hodge and Christian Jacobs Vandegeer

CONTENTS

INTRODUCTION

The subtitle of this book, like any number of others, is reliant on Christopher Fry's *A Sleep of Prisoners*:

> The human heart can go to the lengths of God.
> Affairs are now soul-size:
> The enterprise
> Is exploration into God.[1]

For the poet, "the human heart can go to the lengths of God," since "affairs are now soul-size," so that human "enterprise" becomes "exploration into God." These phrases have already served in many books and essays. They evoke a major concern, indeed, the "ultimate concern," as writers following Paul Tillich have termed the question of God.[2] I have opted for *An Exploration...*, since it is neither possible nor desirable to conceal the highly personal and limited standpoint of anyone embarking on an exploration of this kind. All such explorations are, in fact, a response to the mystery hidden in the existence of the universe and of everything and everyone in it. It is also a response within the tradition of the lived experience of what is acclaimed and celebrated as God's own self-revelation. This has come to narrative and provocative expression in the sacred writings of Israel and the Church, a process that can be tracked over thousands of years, which reaches its culmination in Christ: "Long ago God spoke to our ancestors in many and various ways by the prophets, but in these last days he spoken to us by a Son" (Heb

1:1–2)—further specified as "the reflection of God's glory and the exact imprint of God's very being" (Heb 1:3).

An exploration into God? I think the *into* is important. That preposition connotes both focus and movement—compared to simply being about God. Any suggestion of an exploration of God risks giving the impression of some kind of controlling knowledge of what exceeds all finite intelligence—as though the divine mystery is simply there for inspection like any other object. If, indeed, affairs are now "soul-size," that does not mean reducing the infinities of the divine mystery to our human size measured by the soul, human intelligence, or anything else. It does imply, however, that knowing, loving, and being united with God are the fulfillment of the constitution and orientation of all created beings, especially in the consciousness of spiritual beings.

Despite this God-ward orientation of our being, a strange kind of amnesia can come into cultures and even creep into theological and scriptural studies, Church communication, and affect interreligious dialogue. It is not overstating this tendency to call it a forgetfulness of God, a forgetfulness of the major issue implicit in all discussion of meaning and value. Needless to say, I make no judgment on anyone's personal relationship with God—just as I have every reason not to call into question God's personal relationship to each one of us. Whether we think much about it or not, God's relationship to us, theologically speaking, is the permanent underpinning of personal existence, individually and communally. I dare not make any judgment about that as though standing outside it or just watching religious behavior, spectator-fashion, uninvolved or arrogantly self-satisfied. Still, there is something worth talking about in what is the all-important issue. True, good people may well have rather vague ideas of God, and yet do the will of God in their search for justice and decency. That may well be a normal state of affairs, the heart being well ahead of the mind—and even the hand, healing and giving, outstripping even the feelings of the heart.

Now, that might seem all too obvious and generally taken for granted. We writers on theological, spiritual, or philosophical topics can be appalled at the new popular atheism and be bemused by its low standard of argument, even while grateful for the scientific ingredients of its various positions. The great classic atheisms of our time, deriving from Darwin, Nietzsche, Marx, and Freud, have done their work well, and had a good effect, in many ways, on religious discourse—a shock therapy, but a necessary one. The prestige of science, and its accompanying scientific mythology, is very high. Religious expression by contrast seems a musty brocade of quaint notions. In the general cultural conversation, God-talk is drowned out and anyone advancing theological positions is rowing against the tide. But here is the odd point: our very familiarity with religious observances and even religious thinking can lead into isolated and eerily abstract places where no breath of life stirs. We can find ourselves thinking, acting, and even praying without a great deal of awareness of the drama enacted in human history, and in the Western world, above all. What is going on between us, each one of us, and God—the ocean of life and love and goodness from which we have our being and future—has dropped from consideration. The sense of original wonder and adventure has disappeared. At funerals, for instance, apart from a few conventional phrases, say, of how the dear departed has gone to God or received a reward for a good life, there is little mention, and, indeed, little capacity to mention, the moment of truth to which life leads, and the radiance of the "perpetual Light" that now shines, as St. Augustine says: "After this life God is our life."[3] That statement might seem too bleak or abstract for those who have enjoyed life in its present form. But the great religious traditions have never wavered in their conviction that following the ways of God leads to life's fullness and bliss. The problem is that our notion of God has become so limited and abstract that seeing God face-to-face promises no excitement. God as our destiny and bliss is a hard topic to sell.[4]

In the course of writing this "exploration," a number of matters crystallized for me—and perhaps will be of value for readers if this book comes their way. The first is the drastic, mutual impoverishment that has occurred in separating theology from philosophy, for both are aspects of the one, original love of wisdom (*philosophia*). Indeed for most of Christian history, the greatest thinkers were quite happy to think of themselves as "philosophers," strenuously engaged both in contemplative and philosophical activities. Philosophers of this kind were usually members of communities, either monastic or something similar, suggesting a shared experience and practice of the love of God with mind and heart. That incited further exploration into the mystery of God through prayer, meditation, liturgical practices, and, of course, study of the classic sources of wisdom in Scripture, and in the writings of all the wise, to say nothing of disputation and discussion, and even spiritual counsel and direction. Predictably, it would not be long before some philosophers, deprived of a larger sense of life and human experience, started declaring that theology was a weak-minded version of philosophy, and lacking all objectivity. Consequently, the topic of God could be addressed only obliquely, as in, say, a consideration of the validity of Aquinas's five "proofs" (not that he ever so described them). Philosophy was tempted to purify itself from any association with religion and to defend itself from the pious encroachments of faith, and so declared theological statements to be lacking the support of reason. Theology also suffered from an increasing isolation and intellectual timidity. It tended to stay close to the comfort and uniqueness of its own biblical sources, sacred scriptures, and its venerable traditions. But at the price of papering over questions needing an answer was higher if theology was to maintain (or win) intellectual respectability in the contemporary world of science and scholarship. A collaborative method based on the structure of the human consciousness and enabling a partnership among science, philosophy, and theology in all its different operations was needed. It could promote the authentic development of human culture, and of the human minds and hearts it affects, in their acts of intelligence, moral responsibility, and even religious faith. Bernard Lonergan's *Method in Theology* is a good example of what has been achieved in a new collaborative setting. But that, and similar works, were a long time coming, and the hoped-for integration of all aspects of an exploration into God has not yet been fully realized. But writers like Lonergan on theological method and, quite differently, Bruno Latour on anthropology suggest the stirrings of a new collaborative approach, and new ways of moving toward a new frontier.

Compared to classical and early medieval times, the present age is starkly different. Knowledge has exploded and expanded unimaginably after the foundation of the great universities. Expansion meant specialization and consequent fragmentation. Different faculties now had their designated and well-defended area of competence, and if you taught philosophy, say, in a designated school or faculty of philosophy, you were not doing theology. That, in turn, had been specified as dealing only with religious matters in a way that neither Augustine nor Aquinas would have understood, for basic philosophical issues were inevitably implied in all theological questions. Accordingly, "explorations into God" suffered. Brilliant individuals, trapped in the monodimensional achievements of science, lost the ability to move in a larger horizon and became seemingly atrophied in an incapacity to feel the force of larger questions. Scientific achievements can result in tunnel vision. If faith and intelligence called for a larger point of view, religion was quickly declared to be the enemy of progress and diagnosed as a social illness infecting culture with alien concerns and primitive methods.

There is no point, for the theologian—or for the religious person for that matter, in getting "hot and bothered" over the situation. Science dominates culture, and its achievements, theoretic and practical, deservedly provoke wonder and gratitude. Attempting to refute genuine science would not only be mean spirited, but it would also be seen as resisting the truth and undermining trust in the integrity of scientific intelligence. We live in the digital age and possess the means to communicate in ways without parallel at other times. We may in some circumstances argue against the monodimensional outlook of science, but only to suggest a larger horizon in which the fullness of our humanity, in the scope of its experience and in the reach of its intelligence, can anticipate, however dimly, absolute truth, goodness, and beauty. The experience of the Church through history and the effect of major world-forming religions could be contemplated by the historian as an immense social experiment. It is still being conducted after thousands of years, and in the consciousness of millions of people. How that can be assessed apart from personal witness can never be a definitive judgment; nor can it be separated from the scandals that dim the radiance of faith and compromise what religions stand for in the witness of their followers. Any kind of exploration into God can seem disconcertingly inconclusive. For the history of faith can never, of its nature, be a controlled experiment. The wisdom, love, and mercy of God cannot be tested in laboratory conditions. For many of a scientific outlook, God is the great placebo, leaving life and the world unchanged by masking the need for scientifically respectable and properly tested remedies for what ails our human condition. The faithful might rightly respond that the crucial test is to be found in the intersubjective relationship involved, between God and the believer. But such a personal kind of knowledge is hardly a laboratory experiment when it expresses love for and faith in "what no eye has seen nor ear heard nor the human heart conceive." Though reducing this immense history of experience to an experiment governed by a scientific protocol would be impossible, for there is no point in seeking control and verification in matters as large as life and in issues as soul-size as the mystery of God. There can never be a definitive proof so as to leave believers right and their adversaries wrong in a knockdown confrontation. In such cases, we must leave something to the grace of divine inspiration. Only God can impress and win the human heart. But how this happens and in what measure, I, for one, am in no position to tell—although it is clear that acrimonious arguments don't seem ever to do much good.

Still, wherever one might be, there is a sense of something lost—a lessening of the sense of God in the cultural atmosphere we breathe. Human beings in this scientific age have become all too knowing, and all too inclined to occupy center stage in assessing the universe, and even consigning God a place within it. Despite the problems, there is also a new opportunity—a sense of something to be gained in the world of today and for the world of tomorrow. Hence, this little exploration.

There are eight chapters in what follows. The first, "Where Is Your God? The Absent Frontier," starts with a reference to Psalm 42, and goes on to consider in a number of ways the frontier at which human life touches on the mystery of God. We are either invited to move further into the region of the absolute Other, or sent back to the familiar world of more of the same, undisturbed by godly considerations. The culture is in a state of flux. It has entered into a postmodern situation in which "God is dead" sounds all too certain, while affirming the opposite in this pluralist age has value only as a personal conviction that leaves the wider world untouched. The problem of evil is oppressive, but then, the problem of the good is a continuing surprise. It inspires from time to time new attempts to prove the existence of God, both from science and philosophy. Such intimations of the absolute Other suggest new horizons in which all genuine forms of knowledge can operate and ideally collaborate.

But two topics are important since they pervade our exploration. The first is the special character of analogical language by which words and ideas born of the experience of our routine world can be stretched, as it were, toward what is other. A literal-minded age may not recognize the flexibility and range of possible reference in language attempting to name all dimensions of reality. When the evocative and creative character of language wanes, words drown in the flood of advertising and media chatter.

There is a second aspect. It is commonly understood that theology as the consideration of God is, according to the hallowed formula, "faith seeking understanding." It might be thought that an odd kind of knowledge is implied until it is realized that a form of faith—and love, too—pervades all our efforts to understand. In a paradoxical sense, the more self-involved in mind, heart, and imagination, the more we come to know realities beyond our routine scope. Think how the love of nature has informed ecological and environmental sciences. At the highest instances in the history of faith, consider how loving God with all one's heart and mind and soul and strength has resulted in a special kind of knowledge of God as it is expressed in the Bible and in the great mystics.[5] That kind of knowledge may not be immediately available to those of us of more flickering spirituality, but it does indicate a different kind of knowing that the scholastic tradition called "connatural knowledge." The philosopher of science Michael Polanyi described this way of knowing as "personal knowledge"—in contrast to the impersonal, objective, analytical approach to knowledge usually attributed to science—especially in its dealing with nonpersonal or prepersonal realities. There is room, then, for knowledge of a more participative kind—a knowing born of action, self-involvement, and personal experience. To describe any exploration into God and not to mention the special personal kind of knowledge involved, could hardly prove convincing.

The second chapter, "The Be-ing of God: Limitless Mystery" is more of a synthesis and could no doubt be mystifying to some modern readers because of its philosophical and Scholastic tone. The purpose, however, is not to mystify, but simply to make a clearing space in which talk about God and the exploration into God become possible. It aims to challenge the prevalent assumption that God is merely a big being among many beings, in effect, something like a superior angel or an elusive factor or most forceful agent of some kind. By retrieving the great medieval tradition as represented in various aspects of the work of Aquinas, we emphasize that God is not *a* being, but the sheer original act of Being, *Ipsum Esse*, as the Scholastics would say. God is therefore unlimited, unconditioned, and absolute "To Be"—termed in the present context, "Be-ing itself." True, there is recognizable danger in this. If God is Be-ing, how then is everything that is, not identified with God? If that question is to find an answer it needs first to recognize the gifted character of being, and the consequent independence of each being under the creative hand of God. Each being *is*, and thereby participates in the radical perfection of being that is essentially realized in God, since the very essence of God is "to Be," Be-ing. To that degree, God is "No-thing" compared to all the things that make up the world, even though the world is held in being by the all-actual Be-ing that God is. The universe, and everything in it, exists by the sheer gift of Be-ing. Only God essentially is; all else, having no essential claim on being, receives its being as a gift. This perspective will be especially important in the next chapter, for not only do all beings participate in the sheer Be-ing of God, but the more so do conscious beings, in their knowing and loving, participate in consciousness of God through knowing truth and loving the good.

This third chapter, "The God of Human Consciousness," attempts to combine a number of perspectives and so to refresh our "exploration into God" in new ways, above all by bringing out the role of consciousness—or what philosophers might call "intentionality." The individual points can be itemized as the phenomenon of consciousness, the meaning of creation, consciousness within and of creation, and consciousness of the God of creation in an emergent and evolutionary world. In elaborating this topic, we particularly emphasize that the human being is not a spectator, but a participant in the unfolding of creation. The human is a microcosm in which all the energies of spirit and matter combine in a unique field of relationships. In this context, we raise the largely forgotten question of the human soul, the principle of not only openness to the whole of creation but also of a dialogical relationship with the Creator. Such considerations open the way to a fresh collaborative outlook based on the creative presence of God in every aspect of the universe—which gives depth and breadth to this exploration into God. I note that recent discussion of "intelligent design" cannot long ignore the question of the design—and dynamics—of intelligence, as a conscious activity opening onto the universe and participating in the boundless creativity of God.

The fourth chapter is entitled "Trinitarian Connections: Inside Knowledge." It aims to enlarge the trinitarian frame of reference while at the same time intensifying the distinctive Christian experience of God in Christ and the Spirit. To this end, we refer to basic scriptural sources—especially in John's Gospel—on which the subsequent classic trinitarian doctrine and theology rely. With its implications of the primacy of relationality and communion, a trinitarian sense of God is well attuned to a contemporary understanding of the dynamics inherent in the character of the emergent universe. It is likewise a fertile source for promoting interfaith dialogue. A renewed trinitarian vision can prove a precious resource in the present era. It is presented as "inside" knowledge of God: believers are drawn into the movement of the life of God and are conformed to each of the divine persons.

The fifth chapter, "Creator and Father Almighty," treats of crucial aspects of the Creator-creation relationship. It considers and reemphasizes the presence of God in every aspect of the created universe, while at the same time stresses the "gifted" character of creation. When creation has its origin in the divine freedom, and in a love unconditioned by anything outside itself, we can understand more fully the meaning of God's creation "out of nothing." Indeed, it is the equivalent of saying God creates "out of love." This love is dependent on nothing outside of God who freely calls and sustains all things in being. We mention, too, an implicit trinitarian dimension in that creation is most deeply understood as emerging from the inner life of the Trinity. It is therefore made possible by the self-expression of God in the Word and in divine ecstasy of love in the Spirit. Given these divine origins, the created universe is a unified whole—heaven and earth, the visible and the invisible—as the creed expressed it—thus giving rise to a particular biblical realism in which God is known through the material of creation and contemplated as such. Against this background, we delay briefly on two potential blockages to understanding creation, that of invoking God as "Father" in a postpatriarchal world, and the acclaiming of God as "almighty"—in a world jealous of its freedom. As regards the first, we stress that God is invoked and confessed as Father only in relation to his self-gift in the Son and the Spirit—so that a critical understanding of the trinitarian order is called for. In the order of our coming to know the Father, the Holy Spirit can be more justly referred to as the "first divine person," leading faith to Christ and, through him, to the Father. Second, the omnipotence of the Creator is not reducible to divine caprice: for all the works of God are tempered by an infinite wisdom and intelligence, just as the self-giving love of God is the subversively omnipotent factor in regard to the goal and manner of God's creative and providential action.

"By Way of Negation: Biblical and Philosophical Perspectives" heads the sixth and shorter chapter. This negative character of our knowledge of God in both its biblical and philosophical versions does not amount to a denial of the possibilities of this exploration into God. Rather, the aspect of negation intensifies and amplifies, in a positive manner, the inevitable (and desirable) dimension of light-in-darkness when referring to God. Theologically speaking, there can be no negativity in the Light that God is, that is, in the divine intelligence and intelligibility. But the human mind unaided cannot in this life be exposed to that Light, but is rather bat-like in its experience and understanding of who and what God is. The negative character of our knowledge of God has been remarked on in several situations within the present "exploration." It is implicit in all analogical thinking, yet it may come as a surprise to find this negative dimension woven into the biblical sources arising from those who were utterly convinced of divine revelation and of the positive truth so disclosed. The way of negation, therefore, is not merely a mystical option, but belongs intrinsically to all cultivated knowledge of God, both in philosophy and theology.

The seventh chapter, "God and Dialogue"—which, arguably, could have been first or at least earlier—draws attention to the mysterious and novel character of dialogue as a unique event. Genuine interfaith dialogue is an authentic disclosure of the transcendence of God. While the formal implementation of such dialogue is a major current commitment in the mission of the Church, it is worth recalling the imperatives original to the Christian tradition that point in this direction, such as the mission to all nations, the practice of intercession, the love of neighbor and even of enemies. In all this, *dialogue* is not primarily a noun, but a verb. It expresses a conscious, intersubjective activity, a passing over to the other, and a return to oneself, in an expanding sense of the *We* of all humanity in God, an inexhaustibly promising event within God's communication to human history.

Chapter 8, "Exploration Unending: An Open Conclusion," rounds off the exploration so far. It offers a summary, and then a number of remarks on the following topics:

- The orientation to transcendent mystery as the field in which religious language makes sense
- The problem of evil—and of the good
- The philosophical experience of "letting go" (Heidegger's *Gelassenheit*)
- The gifts of the Holy Spirit
- Liturgical enactment

All these are pointers to the further journey, the exploration into God, ever inexhaustible and ever incomplete.

Chapter 1

WHERE IS YOUR GOD? (PSALM 42:3)

The Absent Frontier[1]

A verse from Psalm 42 introduces what is to follow:

> My soul thirsts for God, for the living God.
> When shall I come and behold the face of God?
> My tears have been my food day and night,
> while people say to me continually, "Where is your God?"
> (vv. 2–3)

Expressed here is the ardor and agony of thirsting for God, along with the patient hope that the face of God will finally be revealed. In the meantime, there is the time of tears, of waiting, pain, and loss in the face of all the world's evils, and the ever-recurring taunt, "Where is this God of yours?"

A COUNTERCULTURAL CONTEXT

Witnessing to God in a culture for which "God is dead," non-existent, or usurped by more accommodating idols, promises little comfort.[2] The situation for those who seek God can be described as "countercultural," even if that is too weak and vague a phrase.

Cultural indifference to the God of faith is one thing, but a radical disaffection from God because of what is often called "the problem of evil" is another. Evil is a huge parasitical influence affecting all that is good not only in individual lives, but also in families, communities, and societies—national and global. No matter how virulent the experience of evil, hope rests in God. Only from God can the final answer be given, with all its implications of healing, release, forgiveness, liberation, and the fullness of life....But when will that answer be given? When will this problem of evil, wrapped in impenetrable darkness and weighted with all the sadness of the world yield to the luminous bliss and goodness of God, when "death will be no more; mourning and crying and pain will be no more" (Rev 21:4)?

A peculiar aspect of the influence of evil is to reduce everything to its own terms so that no other problems remain, or if they remain, they are hidden from consideration. Most of all, the parasitical character of evil is unnoticed while evil itself is promoted into consideration as an evil principle, or a reality in its own right. As a result, the problem of evil cannot be placed where it most belongs, at the heart of the blazing mystery of God, in the great sweep of the divine, all-merciful, and creative will.

References to this "problem of evil" demands that we ask also, Whose problem is it? Presumably if it is possible for some at least to live lives untroubled by religious or transcendent considerations. If that is the case, there would be no problem for them in the first place; evil would be part of the violent and generally desperate state of affairs, but managing: *that* is the challenge. If you have the good luck of being comparatively sheltered from what so characteristically afflicts the larger world—violence, disease, war, hunger, poverty, natural calamities—the only sane response would be to maximize the advantages and let the rest sort itself out, either through random interactions, market forces, or good luck! But once values begin to enter into calculation, the situation changes. There is a hierarchy of values extending from the material, the vital, through the social, political, and up to cultural and transcendent considerations. At each level, evil tends to be understood with a different force and menace.

If vital values of health and fitness are dominant, then evil tends to be understood only in terms of sickness, disease, and incapacity. If the transcendent value of living in union with God is uppermost, then the greatest evil would be loss of God. If it is realized that moral evil can lead to a fundamental lovelessness in the sight of God, the only response is prayer for mercy and an effective change of heart. Once the goodness of God becomes the overriding consideration, while evils will come, it will be clear that no one is alone in suffering them, even those we have caused: before, within, and ahead of the present situation is the infinite mercy and absolute goodness of God. Furthermore, the more the commandment to love God with all one's heart and soul and mind and strength resonates in one's life, the more one is exposed to the force of evil, and the more troubling and provocative the power of evil becomes. Where is God? Why is God silent? Why is the future so dark and undecided even as the name of God is dishonored and idols are raised up in the service of human obsessions? Though the crucified Jesus is resurrected, though this is the event designed to inspire hope through all generations, how long must hope wait and suffer the waiting in patience? Why, after the resurrection, does history take so long?

For their part, believers must not talk God to death. The mystery eludes all human language and does not encourage religious chatter. Nonetheless, the words of faith reach forward in adoration and love: "Beloved, let us love one another, because love is from God; everyone who loves is born of God and knows God...for God is love" (1 John 4:7–8). To have faith is to be plunged into the depths of the Mystery we can never objectify nor stand back from. To exist, to live, and finally, to love, is to be drawn into the homeland of our hearts, a region immediately recognized as more real than the air we breathe.

On the other hand, commitment to God is vulnerable and exposed to the full blast of these words from Nietzsche's *Antichrist*:

> The Christian conception of God—God as god of the sick, God as a spider, God as spirit—is one of the most corrupt conceptions of the divine ever attained on earth. It may even represent the low-water mark in the descending development of divine types. God degenerated into a

> *contradiction* of life, instead of being its transfiguration and eternal Yes! God as the declaration of war against life, against nature, against the will to live! God—the formula for every slander against "this world," for every lie about the "beyond"! God the deification of nothingness, the will to nothingness pronounced holy.[3]

Through this powerful denunciation, Nietzsche unwittingly provides the key to unlock a large box of questions. Is the God of Jesus and of Israel a contradiction of life, or the source of life transfigured and eternally affirmed? Has our cultural denial of death fabricated a god made in our sickly image? Have the tiny preoccupations of a consumerist culture deadened the capacity to experience the true glory of life? On the other hand, where is the true generative force of history and culture to be found? Must the engines of history be mendacity, murder, and violent exclusion of the other? Moreover, has the religious search for life's deepest meaning become too associated with a necrophiliac adjustment to the status quo?[4] Might it not be that the real God, truly adored and intelligently explored, will inspire courage and a limitless hope in the infinities of love and mercy? It is as though language about God has too long been in a deep freeze, and now needs to be defrosted if it is to bring new energies into an exploration into God.

These are some of the large questions in the current cultural context. Any searching for God is not helped by an all-too knowing Christian fundamentalism intent on purveying a narrowly rigid notion of God. Perhaps the biggest problem of all is what David Bentley Hart refers to as the bad habit of thinking of God as a very big thing in the world of things, a big actor in a world of many agencies, without any idea of the actual reality of God as transcending all modes of being or acting or doing.[5]

BEGINNING AFRESH

Yet there are possibilities in the new situation as well. By responding to the harsh criticisms arising from today's atheism, believers in God can find their faith purified.[6] Believers can no longer enjoy a free ride on the cultural religiosity of the past. The "masters of suspicion" have rightly unmasked much conventional religiosity as either a psychological or social subterfuge. If Marx dismissed religious belief as an ideology of economic privilege, faith in the true God places believers in solidarity with the poor of the world. If Freud sought to unmask religion as infantile projection, an authentically adult faith is a spiritual force for freedom and liberation from oppression. If science is often intent on replacing the God of faith with what can be measured, controlled, and analyzed, a purified faith finds immeasurably higher values in the universe as God's creation. Although Nietzsche bitterly reproached Christianity as a resentful belittling of humanity, a freshly humanized faith finds in God a foundation for a new inclusive humanity, animated by love, justice, and mutual service. The true God is newly revealed when idols are toppled—the gods of the group, of psychological projection, or of social security—the many gods of human presumption and consumption.

Though faith enlists its own range of images, it must learn to employ them precisely *as* images, not as idols or as mere fabrications of human sentiment. To that degree, such images are not idols but icons—images of faith, designed to let the mystery disclose itself on its own terms. Faith is indeed illumined and focused by the Scriptures, sacraments, and authoritative teachings of the Church—ultimately, through the whole incarnate reality of Christ himself. All of these are images, be they words or symbols, and necessarily contain elements of creative human expression. Still, they are not merely the products of human creativity. A deeper inspiration is at work. The images of faith shine with a light from beyond them; they bespeak the infinity of the mystery that has expressed itself in our world. The images of faith are not projections onto the blank screen of human aspiration, for they are backlit, as it were, by the revelation of a love not of this world. In short, an authentic faith is intent on letting God be God!—in the scandal of the cross; in a humble invocation of the Spirit; in the shared celebration and witness of those who make up the people of God, saints and sinners alike.

A purified faith can refresh our notion of God, even in what appears as a postreligious and "godless" phase of culture. The myth, not the science, of evolution tended to undermine human dignity and to rob the world itself of its mysterious depth and direction. As naive notions of how God acts in nature are surpassed, faith is free to explore how God is ever creative, the great attractor drawing the immense, groaning, manifold totality of the world toward its goal.

In this respect, Israel's invocation of the Lord as *YHWH* was a kind of gracious riddle. God gave his name as "I will be who I will be" (see Exod 3:14). Subsequent generations of faith have invoked God in such terms and found the mystery of God self-revealed in Christ and the Spirit. However unreserved God's communication, it can be received only through the gift and in the receptivity of faith. The Word of God is spoken from a great silence into the listening of the human heart. The attentive heart is ever searching for words, the better to serve the truth revealed. The Word of God and the Spirit of God cannot be contained or constricted, nor reduced to anything less than the self-communication of inexpressible mystery. With the great prophet, Elijah, all believers must struggle against the false gods, to know the one, true God only in humble self-surrender to the "sound of sheer silence" (1 Kgs 19:12). Such is the awesome silence of the mystery within which the whole world groans, hopes, and prays for fulfillment (see Rom 8:18–27).

In the silence and darkness of the mystery, God is experienced as "No-thing"—for God is not like anything else occurring within the horizon of our knowing. God is beyond the range of our words and outstrips all ideas and concepts. Gregory of Nyssa, one of the great mystical doctors of the Church, has written,

> The unlimited divine nature cannot be accurately contained by a name. Rather every capacity for concepts and every form of words and names, even if they seem to contain something great and befitting God's glory, are unable to grasp God's reality. But starting from certain traces and sparks, as it were, our words aim at the unknown, and from what we grasp we make conjectures by a kind of analogy of the ungraspable.[7]

However intimately present to the heart of faith, the one God infinitely surpasses all human capacities of understanding and expression. Speech about God, therefore, must always favor the language of analogy.[8] Religious expression shuffles between what is known within our experience, and the unknowable, inexpressible reality of God. All our words lead into the divine silence, just as the holy darkness surrounds what little clarity we have. In comparison with the clearly defined world of particular realities, God is "No-thing" and "No-where," never contained within any category or concept or image. Although the Creed certainly intends to affirm the reality of God, no formula of faith can disclose it. Every creed, every formula of belief, alike await the evidence that only God can give.

Awareness of God is not a soft option for an elusive transcendence, in contrast to the down-to-earth, definable realities that can be inspected by scientist or scholar. And yet, the conscious experience of God is the vital datum from which the thinking of faith emerges and to which it returns. The meaning of God constitutes an excess over-brimming any discipline, every pattern or method of exploration, even the capacities of the human mind itself. As Aquinas put it eight centuries ago, God is outside any genus of classification.[9] Despite the problem of the unclassifiable excess of what God is, faith must maintain its clear focus and expression. The focus is concentrated at the point where maximum light and darkness meet. There is the light of intelligence and revelation, while, at the other extreme, there are the darkness and silence of what can never be mastered or expressed. In that play of light and darkness, particular expressions, utterances, rituals, and practices of faith breathe a surplus of meaning, so as to inspire adoration, thanksgiving, and continuous and eager searching. All this makes for a God-sized horizon without which the words and deeds, the beliefs and celebrations of faith cannot but appear flat and trivial.

Admittedly, theology is always on the edge of defeat. Theology knowingly accepts that its intelligence can never be complete. It needs to be patient with its groping conceptions.[10] On the other hand, the love of the heart needs to show no such patience, for love reaches toward the divine reality itself, beyond the clouded and fragmented mode of our human conceptions and judgments.[11]

As known and loved, God indwells the consciousness of lover. To the measure theological intentionality is animated by the love of God, it cannot be content with a superficial or monodimensional understanding of the divine Other. The mind of love seeks to appreciate the beloved Other in its every aspect, and to penetrate it more deeply—just as the Holy Spirit searches the depths of God.[12]

Great saints or mystics speak of God out of a living and luminous sense of divine presence in themselves and others. That ideal is, however, rare in the mundane business of theological communication. On the other hand, even theologians and indeed everyone, from time to time, whatever their religious convictions, has a sense, however faint, of the attraction of something Other, inviting to a more full and blessed life. Such special moments are not at one's command. Even the greatest mystical writers seem to expect darkness and aridity as they move forward in a "cloud of unknowing." In this respect, faith in God is far from being a crutch for the intellectually undeveloped. It is more the willingness to be exposed to the unfathomable Truth that alone judges and satisfies, despite the ignorance, fragility, guilt, failure, and inconclusiveness of our existence. Faith is not a "crutch" for the weak—or, if there is a crutch involved, it is to be found in the timidity of unbelief and its conformity to a culture that has lost its sense of transcendence. Faith is surrender to God, and to the exploration of the infinities of love and mercy, beauty and truth of this God, and in solidarity with all. Unbelief at this stage of cultural history seems more like capitulation to a banal consumerist ideology, ignorant of history and intolerant of everything that might disturb its cultural composure.

Surrender to God, however, does not allow the intelligence of faith to escape the humble and always frustrating effort of trying to put into words what is most deep and inexpressible in human experience. Inevitably, that entails being burdened with all the limitations of language and vocabulary, just as it means facing the meagerness of one's own wit and skill when faced with a challenge to speak of God—especially in today's world.

A CURIOUS NEGLECT

There is a more curious aspect of the problem. Christian biblical scholarship has been oddly silent in this area. Indeed, Larry W. Hurtado, in his *God in New Testament Theology*,[13] cites the words of another eminent and earlier scholar, Nils Dahl:

> For more than a generation, the majority of NT scholars have not only eliminated direct references to God from their works, but have also neglected detailed and comprehensive investigation of statements about God. Whereas a number of major works and monographs deal with the Christology (or ecclesiology, eschatology, etc.) of the NT, it is hard to find any comprehensive or penetrating study of the theme "God in the NT."[14]

Perhaps it is because scholars were wary of being ensnared in philosophy and sought merely to give an account of how God's action was perceived in history; or, even more specifically, because they sought to concentrate on what makes Christianity unique, namely, Christ. As a result, a christocentric, rather than a theocentric, concentration of theology occurred. It slowly emerged that a deeper, theocentric appreciation of Christ was needed—Christ in the Godward and Father-ward connection of his identity and mission.[15]

A gradual separation of theology from spirituality and a God-directed way of life within community of praxis has taken place. The birth of the university and its different faculties occasioned a rupture between theology and contemplative dimensions of life. Contemplative communities took for granted that successive conversions would be experienced in a God-centered life, as its members moved through the phases of purgation, illumination, and union.[16] Such historical contexts are not irrelevant to the present imperatives for Christian faith regarding interreligious dialogue.

The God question is being posed in more urgent and concrete terms. We cannot but agree with Karl Rahner's judgment that the "experience of God really constitutes the very heart and center of Christianity itself, and also the ever-living source of that conscious manifestation which we call 'revelation.'"[17] In Bernard Lonergan's *Method in Theology*, religious believers are described as undergoing a conversion—an event that dismantles and abolishes the horizon in which their knowing and choosing went on and sets up a new horizon in which the love of God will transvalue our values and the eyes of that love will transform our knowing."[18] Hans Urs von Balthasar further specifies a relation to God as "the movement away from myself, the preference of what is other and greater."[19] Such approaches find solid support in biblical accounts of the experience of the prophets and in the Gospel's narrative of the challenges faced by Jesus's disciples in proclaiming the kingdom of God.

One aspect of the problem is the artificial separation of theology from philosophy as it occurs in the Scholastic manualist theological tradition. It supposed, for instance, a division in its treatment of the topic of God into *de Deo Uno* and *de Deo Trino*, as though the former was the domain of reason and the latter that of faith. In Aquinas's originally integrated theological exposition, however, the order of presentation begins with "the unity of God" and then proceeds to the "Trinity of persons." Questions relating to the unity and the Trinity of God are interwoven and directed to the one theological reality. "God" is never less than the God of revelation, and always includes the conviction that God is the fullness of being, truth, goodness, and beauty.

In the long history of thinking about God, *philosophy*, in fact, has been the preferred general term including what today we would refer to as *theology* and *philosophy* (with all their respective divisions and subdivisions).[20] The search for wisdom and its cultivation were necessarily conducted in a godly way of life combining prayer, community, and spiritual discipline. In the development of a Christian intellectual tradition, philosophy was not one discipline among many, but a search underpinning all areas of learning and illumined by them. The observation of nature; the instruction in grammar, rhetoric, and dialectic; or in the sciences of philosophy and sacred teaching, all converged on the one truth. In all this, resources deriving from the pagans Plato and Aristotle were gratefully received, even if there was no pagan philosopher present to pose objections on the grounds of content or method.

Indeed, the promotion of all knowledge in the various monastic or academic communities in this period was in the hands of those professing Christian faith—though this would be eventually affected by the influence of the pagan philosophers and the Jewish and Muslim translators and commentators on the works of Aristotle.[21] This early medieval period was marked by the influx of new knowledge, even if it was still possible in that emerging world for the human mind to be familiar with all available knowledge, and thereby to relate it to the spiritual quest of faith.

There occurred, however, a gradual differentiation of modes of knowledge with the rise of the university and its division of faculties. Accordingly, a faculty of philosophy could go about its work at a safe distance from theology or "sacred doctrine."[22] A necessary division of labor was never far from a fragmentation and break down of an integrated body of knowledge in the service of God. The ground was laid for the well-known binary oppositions of nature and grace, science and wisdom, philosophy and theology, Scripture and dialectic, and so on.[23]

Socrates, as Plato presented this great "lover of wisdom" to the ancient world, declared that "genuine philosophers continually practice dying...for they will be of the firm conviction that only there in the other world will they find the knowledge they are seeking."[24] In contrast, the biblical experience of God demands a continual practice of *living*, not in search of a knowledge reserved for another world, but in the light of truth that has been revealed within the history of this world. For Aquinas, theology (or "sacred doctrine") is akin to a primal kind of wisdom, *sapientia*, in which faith and love savor the divine reality, even in an intellectual register.[25] Hence, it is never a matter of seeing or comprehending the divine mystery, but rather of developing a discerning taste for it—a point to bear in mind in the inevitably abstract discussions of the existence and character of God.

In the cultivation of this wisdom, the heart's surrender to God is a gifted experience associated with "the gift of faith." Faith entails an experience of being found by God that at once brings the peace of homecoming and spurs a further searching into the One who found us. However faith might be defined, it is a particular form of consciousness unfolding within this vast, intelligible, but increasingly mysterious, universe. God is recognized as the fulfillment of the spiritual search for the ultimately meaningful, the absolute good and beauty. Faith, as it gives rise to theological thinking, inspires a higher form of thinking about the wonder of existence itself. It includes awareness of such a gift, the manner of its giving, and the character of the giver—and the response it invites. Aristotle had classically reminded us that the love of wisdom—"philosophy," in its original sense—begins with wonder. The mind expands in wonder at existence, in the wonder of anything existing, in the wonder of making sense of anything—and even more, the wonder of being conscious in a universe inviting us to wonder at what the explanation of all our explanations might be. To that degree, any deep reflection begins and ends in wonder, so much so that the activity of thinking and the act of faith are respectively ways of wondering, inciting endless questions and the restless attraction toward what can never be fully grasped, although simply, radiantly, and unsettlingly *given*!

Theology is classically defined by St. Anselm as "faith seeking understanding"—seeking to understand in so many different domains, be they philosophical, psychological, mystical, social, aesthetic, political, or religious and interreligious. It is unavoidable that each step forward is accompanied by increasing dissatisfaction. Libraries of texts can appear to be so much pitiable verbiage when confronted with the great question: What is God? Who is God? The answer is always missing, slipping out of the structures of language and the reach of ideas, the lines on the page and the shelves of books. On the other hand, we must be patient with who and what we are. There is no point in straining to such a degree of spiritual intensity that the very idea of God becomes oppressive. It may seem better to make peace with the settled world of religion despite its tendency to reduce God to the familiar, and to impose a manageable sense of proportion on the searching spirit. It is possible, however, that while believers can always have too much religion, they can never have too much of God, the *You* who is the form and source of life, love, wisdom, and beauty. Confusing God with religion, therefore, is deadly. It does nothing for the glory of God and even undermines the great social and cultural virtue of religion, traditionally understood as a part of the social virtue of justice.

Obviously, I am writing what follows from a Christian point of view, and with current Christian concerns for dialogue, collaboration, and hope. The Christian sense of God is always "mediated" by the Judeo-Christian experience of God and the long biblical expression of that experience found in the writings of the prophets and sages, the apostles and evangelists. Still, one of the great blessings of the present era is the interreligious context in which much of the world lives. Christians can learn much from Buddhist styles of meditation and spiritual detachment, from the reverent discipline of Muslims in their prayer and fasting, from the Hindu sense of ultimate reality and selfhood—and more humbly, from the sacramental sense of nature in the Australian indigenous peoples.[26] Under the luminous sky of boundless mystery, we human beings are provoked into keeping our horizons open and responsive to the light, and to the continuing revelation of what is all-important in the conduct of life and in understanding the origin and end of all that is.

SPEAKING IN THE PRESENCE OF GOD

Although theology as it is understood today aims to articulate a reverent and intelligent discourse on the subject of God, it is a continually taught humility. It has to embrace what most defeats it, namely, the reality of God. The more theology tries to speak *of* God, the more it ends in speaking *about* God in some way. It is caught between knowing, and being too knowing, ever alert to the problem of saying too much about the God who is "No-thing," who is not like anything in the world. Consequently, Christian discourse on the subject of God is limitless in its upward, inward, outward, downward, and forward dimensions. Aquinas considered that theology, or "sacred doctrine," as he called it, should consider God, and all things in relation to God—everything as a "God aspect," *sub ratione Dei.* It remains that though in prayer and worship, we may speak *to* God, we can never talk directly *of* God, but only *about* God, about the infinite creative reality at the beginning and end of all that is.

Even the most precise articulations of the meaning of God must leave so much unsaid, and even unsayable, lying outside all clear frames of reference.

Paradoxically, as the sense of God grows, the question arises: Can human words realistically refer to God? The more our sense of the infinite mystery of God is intensified, the more saying anything meaningful on the subject of God is a problem. All our images and ideas are drawn from immersion in the world. Our experience of life, love, beauty, and power are necessarily shaped by the capacities of human minds, hearts, imagination, and senses. Though reverence before the inexpressible infinities of God is imperative, something can and must be said. Here, speaking about God learns from a language supported by a great tradition. This, in turn, has been formed by all those who have tried to speak *to* God in the first place, and, consequently, to speak *about* God to others, in all the variety of languages and cultures.

Beyond all that varied expression, there is the source of a deeper confidence found in biblical tradition. God has chosen to be revealed, to speak to mind and heart through the inspired word of Scripture, through the prophets, through Christ and the continuing witness of the Church, and through the faith of all believers. In all this, God is revealed in human words and images arising from experience in the world. More concretely still, Christian belief in the incarnation, the Word made flesh, underpins the possibility of speaking realistically of God in human terms. God is self-revealed in these very human terms—for the Word became flesh and dwelt among us (John 1:14).

We note first of all that theological discourse is always analogical.[27] It is not univocal, as is the case when one word or idea covers a limitless number of individual cases. Nor is it equivocal, as when one word has different meanings, as happens in most developed vocabularies (e.g., a pen as an instrument for writing—or an enclosure for animals). In contrast, analogy appreciates sameness and difference.[28] Without this analogical dimension, theology would be at the mercy of a rigid, monodimensional pattern of univocity. At best, this would end in an immobile mythological system. On the other hand, if words and ideas in relation to God and the world have nothing in common, then there would be no sense in pretending that they did, and theology should accept its defeat. In contrast, the way of analogy registers different realms of meaning and experience: There is an unobjectifiable excess of meaning that can never be reduced to more of the same.[29] In all this variety of discerning language, some ideas and words are particularly unlimited in their connotations: *good, true, beautiful,* and *personal* stand out. When it comes to speaking of God, there is a range of meanings arising out of experiences that don't, of themselves, imply any limitation. For example, *good* need imply no limit, even if one's manifold experience of goodness is always limited. The meaning of such words is firmly located on the ground floor of our experience, even if the stairs or elevator may go up to an endless number of floors, without offering any view of the ceiling or the top. Consequently, religious thinkers have typically felt free to attribute such open-ended qualities to God, even if the manner in which God is infinitely good, loving, wise, powerful, and beautiful is beyond the reach of human intelligence.

There is the continuous play of language in the biblical witness to God. Christians are most familiar with descriptions of God in terms of light, the fountain of life, the Good Shepherd, and so forth. And there is the imaginative exuberance of the Book of Revelation and its Old Testament influences (e.g., Ezekiel). Then, in another register of figurative and personal expression, the divine persons are invoked as "Father, Son and Holy Spirit." Though such figures of speech are not literarily true—God is not "father" or "son" in a human biological sense, nor "breath" in a physiological sense—such figurative ways of expressing God are obviously very important in the biblical narrative and liturgical expression. Figures of speech are more vivid than big ideas by themselves. Figurative language evokes in the depths of experience a sense of God that can never be fully objectified, nor abstracted into clear and distinct concepts.

Speaking about God implies a movement in three stages. First of all, we confidently affirm, with the whole thrust of existence, that "God is good," for instance. Then, there is an immediate awareness of the limitations of thinking and speaking in this manner: God is not "good," in the ordinary limited ways we experience what we call "good" in things or persons. And then, after that moment of healthy hesitation, the mind can spring forward into the open free air of what God must be: God is good in a boundless, inexpressible manner, beyond our capacities to understand or imagine. The final affirmation leaps out of the defeat imposed by the negative—even if it leaves us silent and unable to add anything more.

Second, analogy operates in a limitless field of disclosure and attraction. For the divine mystery, far from being an object of detached intellectual curiosity, is our destiny, the last end, the supreme Good whose attraction is felt through the whole of creation, and especially in God-ward orientation of the human heart.[30] To suppress this dimension would deprive theology of its basic future-oriented dynamism. Analogical knowing, therefore, anticipates a God-intended eschatological beatitude and is animated by the gifts inherent in the incarnation and the outpouring of the Spirit. In this respect, God is at once the subject of theological inquiry, the source of the data it considers, and the light and the love in which such data are interpreted.

Theological language has similarities with the language of poetry. Its expression is dependent on metaphor and all kinds of imaginative representation. It is therefore easy to strike a wrong note, either by overdoing the imaginative expression or by being content with abstractions, when addressing the topic of God. Still, without this risk and possibility of error, the horizon of creative expression shrinks. If there is little sense of the limitless mystery of life, light, love, creative power, and all-embracing presence, the air in the house of faith soon becomes stale, and the expressions of faith appear arid and oppressive. On the other hand, Christian faith confesses many mysteries in the incarnation, death, resurrection, and ascension of Christ. All this and more is celebrated and endlessly explored in the "we believe" of the Church—in many languages, cultures, and historical contexts. And behind all the particular expressions of faith, there lies the inexpressible and infinite mystery of God. The heights and depths of God are the communication behind and within the biblical witness. God is the original agent in the biblical narratives and in the mission of Jesus as presented in the Gospels. Without this sense of God, present, living, and acting, the Church's sacraments are mere rituals, and lack their transforming energy; and the Church becomes an empty shell, a spiritless organizational framework. If the life of faith no longer breathes a sense of God, the mystery within and beyond the vast and varied worlds of faith's expression, the articulation of faith easily veers toward the trivial. It becomes an atomistic collection of unrelated "things to believe in," possessing, at best, only mythological significance.

To say anything about God is, therefore, a daunting task. The unique problem is the incomparable otherness of God, and that is usually glossed over as obvious. That problem is so discouraging when the writer or speaker or reader or listener—or any or all of these—will admit quite happily that God's otherness is "obvious," and, therefore, we should get on with the task in hand, namely, to make this obvious otherness more familiar in order to minimize the mystery of God. And if there are still problems, further discussion can be pragmatically deferred to some other time when circumstances might favor a more satisfactory solution. And yet, without that sense of otherness, of the infinite otherness of God, our ideas float like gossamer in the wind and our words pile up like dried sludge. The stream no longer flows, the rush of experience and the wave of longing that once demanded expression cease, and the sediment builds up. Nothing is so dry as religious language that has lost its living sense of direction and has become too full of itself. When mind and heart are encumbered with a pile of stale and exhausted words, the only escape is silence...and a new beginning.

But even then, a sense of futility can paralyze fresh inquiry. To say anything new, or to say old things in a new way, may well seem pretentious and impossible. Nonetheless, what makes us press on is the conviction that only our best efforts are in any way worthy of the utter mystery of God. Even if we are never far from failure—the failure to understand and the failure to communicate what we are trying to express, to say nothing of the failure to live up to it—God was worth the effort!

A remedy for the fragility of the human position has often been sought in attempting to prove the existence of God. It has been often tried, and there is a long, rich, and even growing tradition in that regard.[31] Clearly, there are many approaches to the possibility of proving the existence of God. Questions have been asked and answers proposed with a massive repetition and regularity. I do not intend, therefore, to follow that noble and well-worn path. In the world of St. Thomas, his famous "five ways" begin and end in a metaphysically luminous universe. For the contemplative mind, these "ways" converge in the mystery of God, grounding the manifold structure and dynamism of the created universe. Within this world, we are oriented to the God who remains ever beyond it. Yet the medieval world is inhabited as the theater in which the unknowable God is intimately present and ever active. The reality of the world is experienced as quasi-sacramental. It is to be contemplated as a totality, intrinsically God-ward in its constitution. As a site of wonder, it impels the mind beyond itself, beyond commonsense visible appearances, into the "No-thing-ness" of what and who God is.

Wonder and gratitude lead to a critical acknowledgment that reality, be it personal, cosmic, or universal, cannot be radically intelligible without acknowledging the creative presence of God. Given the absence of God in modern materialist culture, proving that God exists will serve a need, even if it remains both an ambiguous and courageous project. After all, who is going be convinced by such a proof? Is God really provable or demonstrable by such a procedure? Indeed, can anything (or anyone) truly worthwhile be proved to exist? The problem with many kinds of proof is the notion of God that is implied. One assumption is that God is remote from human awareness and needs to be captured somehow in a proof or demonstration. Though that may be an initial assumption, it is hardly the conclusion, since the different approaches lead to the conviction that God, as the infinite, actual, original, and all-fulfilling reality, must be implicated in all that is, including our conscious existence.

Now, that brings us close to the particular starting point of this inquiry, namely, the assumption that God is present to human existence, indeed, in a self-communicating capacity. There is nothing religiously controversial in that. Paul proclaims (Eph 2:2–9) and John declares (1 John 4:19) that God has first loved us. And so, the question—the real question—arises, not of proving that God exists, but more of "proving" in some way that *we* exist in a God-related manner, open to the light and mystery of God. That would mean allowing the infinite, loving, and merciful One to appear, both on God's own terms and in such a way as to meet the deepest needs of the human mind and heart. If we begin with a preshrunk notion of an abstract absolute, with a conclusion that God is a mindless demiurge of some kind—a world-soul in a cosmic body, or a kind of universal process—how can such narrow perspectives throw light on God as the infinite, all-embracing, and self-communicating mystery?

ANOTHER WAY OF KNOWING

Each sphere of reality demands its own approach and its own method of exploration. For example, the method of an astrophysicist collecting data on a distant galaxy is startlingly different from that of an educational psychologist studying the dynamics of a classroom. The method must suit the reality, for you don't try to catch butterflies with a shotgun nor collect galaxies in a net.

In the modern university, it is usually presumed that philosophy and theology belong to different faculties or departments, as was remarked above. Though such divisions were foreign to Aquinas himself,[32] eventually the strain of integration would tell. Luther takes the difference to the extreme so that theology has no place for philosophy, and theology has no place in the university.[33] This had a parallel in Catholic thought with the return of nonacademic wisdom and spirituality in the person of the great mystics and with the influence of such figures as Francis de Sales, Pierre de Bérulle, and François Fénelon. The separation continues with Søren Kierkegaard and Karl Barth in their rejection of a Hegelian superrationality. Eventually, with the emergence of some powerful Christian thinkers such as John Henry Newman,[34] the artificiality of previous university-based separations became more evident. Further, spiritual theology—faith seeking its appropriate experience—continued to be marginal and lacked any consistently methodological integration into the whole theological enterprise until recent times. Indeed, the unity of theology was lost as soon as theology identified itself as a university discipline. Still, in the conflicts and rivalries that ensued, theology emerged in the university as the bad conscience of a rationalistic philosophy.[35] Nonetheless, a more integrated approach is developing with greater attention both to the overbrimming character of experience, and to world-shaping events that gave rise to faith.

The depth and reach of consciousness leads to certain restlessness in human existence. To search for the ultimate meaning of all meaning and to seek the value of everything we find worthwhile does not make for a restful existence. We are involved in something that is always *more*, as we live and die, as we know and love and act, immersed all the while in this uncanny universe and caught up in the emergence of a now global culture of humanity.[36] We can know what is going on only by being involved in it, and by participating in what is emerging. This demands a different kind of knowing, bringing with it a larger awareness. It is not a question of reading a map of some terrain, but moving through it and thereby having a first-person, participative familiarity with it. A suggestive instance of a participative mode of knowing is the blind person's use of the white cane—a metaphor favored both by the physicists and philosophers. For the visually handicapped, the cane is of immense benefit in tapping and feeling one's way along the path ahead, with all its twists and turns, its steps and bends. But the cane must be held firmly if it is to feed back a sense of the shape of things and be felt as an extension of hand and arm. If, however, one holds it too loosely, the long stick can be an impediment, more likely to trip up its user than be of any help in finding one's way around. At the other extreme, if I hold the cane too tightly it will be merely a rigid extension of my groping hand and body; it will not have sufficient "give" to feed back to my touch the turns and bends and drops and rises of the path ahead.

The courage and skill of the blind in their use of such a cane serve as a model for a larger, more participative kind of knowing. We are all in the dark when it comes to the fullness of reality. But wherever we start on our path of exploration, we can begin with "the white stick" of our search for meaning, truth, goodness, and beauty. Whether I am a scientist, an artist, a committed believer, or, in different proportions, a mixture of all these, I am never a pure spectator. I am plunged already into the whole of what is, participating in it, indwelling it, moving within it. And, in moving forward, we have enough to go on with, as we explore, learn, and collaborate with others along the way.

Now, all this is to illustrate how God is absent, and not "seen" as a particular being in the world, however "supreme." Rather, God is known in a personal mode of knowing, and through participation in the forward direction of life. The basic instance is that of being loved and loving. The more our existence is lived as a life of loving, the more we are conformed to the reality that God is. In short, we know God in our loving; and only through loving can anyone arrive at an inside knowledge of God, and be enabled to share in the love life that God is. The God we cannot see is known in love's movement toward those we can see (see 1 John 4:20). All this suggests a description of God as the unsurpassable fulfillment of the movement of life itself, so that the meaning of *God* comes home to us only "in action." The more we step out of ourselves in love for others, the more we awaken to beauty and the demands of truth and goodness, the more the word *God* takes on meaning. It is implied in the answer to a particular question, as to what and why we should love:

> Beloved, let us love one another, because love is from God; everyone who loves is born of God and knows God. Whoever does not love does not know God, for God is love. (1 John 4:7–8)

What God means and who God is cannot be looked up in a textbook or dictionary. On the other hand, God is not visible to the eye or comprehended by the mind. Indeed, "No one has ever seen God" (1 John 4:12). The mystery remains; words, ideas, theologies, and philosophies grope impotently, and fall flat and exhausted before what is unutterably beyond this world. But still, "if we love one another, God lives in us, and his love is perfected in us" (v. 12). Familiarity with God means making space for the other and consenting to the being of the other. It follows that God is the great space of communication and communion, the gracious space in which we coexist, in self-giving relationship to others.

John, the great elder of the early church, seems to suspect that we will tend to be rather nervous about all this love talk. All that is loveless, numbed, and defeated in us serves to remind us that an exalted spirituality might be all right for archangels but not for the ordinary human beings to whom God can seem far away. Nonetheless, John encourages his readers to start loving from where they are, in the presence of these particular others. That is to find ourselves taken quietly into an ever-growing mystery of eternal life: "as he is, so are we in this world. There is no fear in love, but perfect love casts out fear" (1 John 4:17–18). In that movement of love for the other, in praying for our neighbor, forgiving wrongs, helping the needy, receiving strangers, God is found and known in action: in moving on and out, in overcoming self-absorption, in matter-of-fact self-transcendence. A disturbing observation states that some people imagine they love God because they love no one. John would seem to agree: "Those who do not love a brother or sister whom they have seen, cannot love God whom they have not seen" (v. 20). The meaning of *God* is experienced only by participating in the love, life, and reality that God is. The believer, who in this case is the lover, comes to enjoy an inside knowledge of the reality of God. As the New Testament puts it, "God is love, and those who abide in love abide in God, and God abides in them" (1 John 4:16). Hence, the startling and always unsettling conclusion: only by loving others can we be "born of God and know God."

Despite the affirmative weight of such Johannine statements, there is that nonnegotiable limitation in this life: "No one has ever seen God" (1 John 4:12). On the other hand, a vital intimate relationship with God is possible: "if we love one another, God lives in us, and his love is perfected in us" (1 John 4:12). The implication is that, even though our minds are soon exhausted in their capacity to envisage the infinite, we come to the truest sense of God by way of action—by loving and moving out of ourselves in generosity, compassion, and forgiveness. That is to have a living sense of God and the inexhaustible love that is characteristic of the divine life.

In short, in this Johannine perspective, it is through loving that we know God; and we know God by participating in the love life that God is. This intimate form of knowing is a long way from merely proving God's existence and having lofty ideas about who or what God is. God is, therefore, not an abstraction, let alone a distraction, from real life. Rather, God is the energizing mystery at work in the depths of real life, especially when that life is lived out in loving. Conversely, life without God is to be out of touch with where life is leading. Although atheists and agnostics can show impressive selflessness in their concern for others, it is never clear what that kind of sincere love is based on, what it draws on, and what it leads to. Admittedly, no ideas, words, or images are ever adequate when speaking of God. In this respect, talking about God is like talking about love. Both topics can be talked to death, leaving only the sensation that too much has been said, and that the great mysteries of life and love should be treated with a certain reserve and discretion. On the other hand, there can be psychological obstacles. Any deep trauma may lead to the difficulty of believing in God, or even believing in love—or in accepting, for instance, that one is worthy of love, or that others deserve love. Doubts on that score reduce any life to a dismal history of personal defeat, distrust, and depression.

While this other way of knowing is both theoretically subversive and demanding, there is a larger methodological context to be considered. All worthwhile knowing is, in some way, personal and participative. A couple cannot look up the meaning of their marriage in a dictionary, for it is found only in the living and the loving. A work of art is not produced by simply following a book of instructions. Artists know what they have to offer only by doing it. The greater the reality, it would seem, the more our knowledge is tacit and the more we must feel our way forward. That means living on the inside of experience and being content with a participative knowledge that we can never stand back from.

This is not to deny objectivity in this manner of knowing, or leaving the way open to pure subjectivism. There is a kind of objectivity that is the product only of our deepest feeling, taste, experience, imagination, insight, and sense of reality. In the core of our being we are beholden to what really matters and drawn beyond ourselves to fulfillment in the Other. We arrive at objectivity only by exploiting all the resources of our conscious subjectivity. To take another biblical example: In contrast to 1 John, the Apostle Paul speaks more generally. Having noticed the inscription on the altar "To an unknown god" (Acts 17:23), he addresses the theoretically inclined Athenians. Referring probably to Epimenedes, a philosopher-poet of an earlier age, he acknowledges that God is revealed in nature and in history so that people everywhere

> would search for God, and perhaps grope for him and find him—though indeed he is not far from each one of us. For "in him we live and move and have our being"; as even some of your poets say,
>
> "For we too are his offspring" [the Stoic Aratus]. (Acts 17:27–29)

These words bear a rhetorical similarity to Paul's doxological reference to the one "God and Father of all, who is above all and through all and in all" (Eph 4:6; see also 1 Cor 8:6). Here, too, a kind of participative knowledge is implied. Faith knows the divine mystery only by participating in it and dwelling within it. Bernard Lonergan appeals to the universal occurrence of spiritual experience:

> It is as though a room was filled with music though one can have no sure knowledge of its source. There is in the world, as it were, a charged field of love and meaning; here and there it reaches a notable intensity: but it is ever unobtrusive, hidden, inviting us to join. And join we must if we are to perceive it, for our perceiving is through our loving.[37]

Despite everything that would reduce human life to a flat calculation of satisfactions, possessions, and power, despite all the forms of selfishness and isolation that contribute to the spiral of cultural decline and frustrate genuine progress, the presence of the inexpressible Spirit of God still inspires a more humane sense of things. We are moved to think beyond ourselves, to move beyond our domestic, social, national, and cultural defenses, to live the difference that is most needed.

When exploring the Mystery of God, any approach must include prayer and reverence. *God* may be a word on a page, and, indeed, an overused word in some cases, and certainly part of a profane vocabulary. Conventional irreverence is hardly blasphemy, for that would presuppose an explicit, personal sense of God. In most literally blasphemous talk, the transcendent realities verbally referred to are only faint connotations of religious meaning, and quite remote from the realities in which the speaker lives. The starting point—and the end point as well—of exploration must be more personal. It must engage, at some deep level, one's sense of life's direction and worth. Such a self-involvement offers a preliminary notion of "God" as the One to whom we pray. The personal "we" is important at this point, for it implies a certain other-directed solidarity, a sense of common purposes and destiny. The great family of humanity, one way or another, faces life and death, suffering, and hope for the future, in the overwhelming contingency of existence, with the religious conviction of God's presence as the infinite, all-gracious, creative mystery.

Questions regarding God, or who God is, and how God "means the world" to faith, cannot be answered by looking up information in a book. As just mentioned, something more personal is implied, a self-involvement and even self-surrender. The reality of God is not simply given for us to analyze and dissect and pass judgment on. After all, as all God seekers acknowledge, it is we human beings who are being examined in the light of God as to our receptivity to what God is, who God is, and what doing the will of God entails.

Jewish tradition refrained out of reverence from pronouncing the sacred name, *YHWH*. Other names and titles for God were employed, such as the *Lord*, the *Holy One*, *the Most High*, and so forth. While it is true that Christian faith in the incarnation introduces a new kind of familiarity with God into human history, there is the need for Christians to constantly refresh a sense of reverence and wonder in regard to the infinities of God's love, wisdom, and power. Without such awe, religious expression becomes increasingly banal.

Prayer finds its varied expressions in desire, hope, adoration, thanksgiving, and praise. It provides the right "laboratory conditions," so to speak, for knowing God. Humbly praying to God precludes making "God" in our own image, merely a projection of human consciousness. On the other hand, praying presumes a willingness to enter into the depths and heights of the human experience of God, past, present, and in the future, and to cooperate with what God is doing in the world.

The Bible presents privileged data from the past. In the experience of Abraham, of Moses, of the whole people of Israel, especially in the great prophets and sages, God was self-revealed as "the Lord," the Holy One to be adored and loved, trusted and obeyed. In the different experiences of John the Baptist, of Jesus himself, of Mary and the apostles, and in the different communities of the early Church, the One God is present in a climactically personal way—loving, merciful, self-giving.

In other words, there is a vast fund of privileged data in the Bible. But it would go unnoticed or unappreciated if it were not received and reflected on in the light of another special kind of data, namely, that of our own hearts and minds. Only by being in touch with this experience of searching and hoping and loving and praying, only by entering consciously into the uncanny mystery in which we live, that is, only by deeply enjoying and suffering the reality of our actual lives, can that past data speak to our present exploration of God as the light of life. The Psalms of the past and the prayers of the generations of believers who have gone before us must be heard in the heart awake to the wonder and fragility of existence.

FROM THE GIVENS TO THE GIVER

The privileged data of the Scriptures speaks to present experience, above all when set in the larger context of the spiritual and religious experience of all peoples and cultures. God's all-inclusive love (John 3:16; 1 Tim 2:4) is a biblical conviction. The hope of believers expands into a boundless horizon. It envisages a common God-given destiny within the one God-created universe.[38]

Although the appreciation of other religions, spiritual traditions, and cultures is always limited, every effort to reach out sends us back to the here and now of our own faith with a deeper, richer sense of what it means. "Their experience" in the past, as it is recorded in the Bible, is given to illuminate experience in the present. The experience of struggling, hoping, loving, living, and dying puts us in fruitful contact with all witnesses to God, as they experienced the Holy Mystery in different ways.

Such experiences can occur in what are commonly called "limit situations."[39] Any speech about God is earthed in fundamental human experiences—so fundamental in fact that without them we could not speak at all, let alone refer to the ultimate reality.[40] Hart's bracing exposition is based on a specific claim:

> My claim throughout these pages is that the grammar of our thinking about the transcendent is given to us in the immanent, in the most humbly ordinary and familiar experiences of reality; in the case of our experience of consciousness, however, the familiarity can easily overwhelm our sense of the essential mystery.[41]

In the presence of God, we human beings experience limitation. Not only do we confront out own mortality, but also all other limitations to our existence, whether in mind or in action, and in all the ways we might experience human fragility and confess that we are sinners before God. Great simple words, such as *love, joy, peace, beauty, insight*, try to convey a certain range of elemental experiences. At the other extreme, there are moments or states when the words like *guilt, powerlessness, suffering, despair*, and *absurdity* resonate as more honest expressions. These expressive words indicate the positive or negative situations in which, one way or another, we are taken to the limit. When that happens, we go, as it were, to the edge of our routine patterns of experience. Whether we like it or not, we are brought to the frontier of something else and something quite "other"—it is to touch the fringe of inexpressible mystery. Limit experiences are as large as life—such as falling in love, the experience of parenthood, loss and bereavement, the impact of beauty, the brokenness of guilt, and the joy of forgiveness. In such experiences, we touch on "another world," as might happen when, entranced by great art or struck by someone's goodness, beauty, or wisdom, we are pulled up short. Ordinary horizons suddenly expand to new dimensions. The routines of life, even of religious practice, suddenly explode in the presence of what cannot be contained—the disclosure of a nameless Something or Someone. Quietly or dramatically, for both the young and old, life draws us to such limits. Such experiences refresh what the word *God* can mean. Whether such occurrences are felt as unsettling edges of this world or as the frontier of another world, they are "God moments." They attune us to the biblical stories of hope, joy, repentance, and new life. They are windows both into what God has meant in the past, and what God can mean now. Such experiences shape our deepest selves. The current of life is continuously taking us beyond ourselves, to questions about what life means, where truth is to be found, and what is the truly good. In this sense, we are ecstatic selves, moving out, moving on, and moving toward what is present yet absent as it calls us on and attracts us further. It seems that to be human is to be essentially unsettled. The whole universe is our dwelling place, but instead of being a cozy habitat, we are not here as spectators or simply passengers. We are here as participants, drawn out of ourselves, part of the *whole,* and immersed in the *all.*[42] That is to live, in awe and hope, in relationship to what is immeasurably Other and yet inexpressibly close.

This kind of expression might sound rather philosophical. But it is the reality implied in what we mean by saying we have a "soul," that we are free, and that our existence is truly personal. More to the point, a muscle-bound rationalism finds difficulty in appreciating the improbable wonder of human existence. For our being is a continuous becoming. There is a dynamism implicit in the way we are. Our consciousness is always unfolding, stirred by questions, longing, and hopes. We can't stay locked up in ourselves, defiantly self-centered and closed against the other. A whole world of colors and sounds, tastes, smells, and textures keeps breaking in on its own terms. There is the insistent and often unsettling intrusion of others who name us, know us, and call us to account. Life won't let us just float along in a haze of images, feelings, impressions, and demands, in a buzz of opinions, bright ideas, and endless information. Eventually questions must stir: What is really true in all this? And then conscience stirs, and with it, come even sharper questions—if we are truly to share the world with others in some kind of decency and justice. We are more than spectators; we are to participate in what is going on and collaborate with others as trustworthy participants in human society. All this is involved in the restless adventure of being human. We are being pushed from within and pulled from beyond. We feel the sharp edge of questions such as these: Where am I going? What are we doing here? What should I give myself to? Who, then, am I, and with whom do I stand?

The question of God stirs in a deeply personal way. The very fact of asking that question anticipates something of an answer, a presentiment of what and who God is. We can feel that we are drawing near to a mysterious homecoming. Human consciousness experiences capacities to sense, to imagine, to question, to judge the truth of things, and to decide what is best. It also experiences what it is to arrive, peacefully and with a certain joy, at a point of fulfillment. However dimly or implicitly, the deepest self finds what it was looking for. It comes to a point of rest—and then, the beginning of a new kind of exploration. Such is the impulse that gives rise to the search for wisdom.

What can be called "open-mindedness" is a further and often unsettling requirement. More specifically, it is the hospitality of genuine intelligence collaborating with others in the exploration of truth. It becomes a little wearisome for anyone seriously involved in a philosophical, religious, or theological exploration of reality to be told—especially by those who have taken no interest in any collaborative search—that one's work is scientifically pointless, and that access to reality is limited to the physical, chemical, or biological sciences. Methods of scientific verification and control have been wonderfully successful when applied to the material phenomena observable through the five senses and the resulting play of imagination. But when we move to the exploration of another order of reality, the powers of seeing, hearing, touching, tasting, and smelling necessarily fall short. That is not to deny that even our highest thoughts are earthed in bodily experience and analogies deriving from sense experience. But when it comes to what might count as valid knowledge of God, or of such realities as spirit, love, person, and value and even of scientific method itself, an empirical method of a sense-bound type is frustrated. It is incapable of intellectual hospitality and collaboration. In contrast, given their respective explorations, the philosopher, the theologian, to say nothing of the contemplative or the artist, can have no problem recognizing the value of science. The material and physical-chemical or evolutionary aspects of reality in an emergent cosmos and the evolutionary dynamics of life on this planet can be, and are, rigorously investigated. There is no contradiction, however, between empirical methods designed to explore material realities, and the realms of reality accessible only to mind, consciousness, and a more holistic intelligence. The most constructive approach in the midst of manifold interests and achievements of the human mind is to maintain an open-minded and collaborative exploration of reality, including all the methods and perspectives that might disclose things as they are.[43] Such a stance is in contrast to the arrogance of declaring beforehand that only one's own particular materialistic, empirical method is to be tolerated. Such an approach cannot but appear narrow and self-defeating. It is a very limited scientific method that confines itself to a small band of data and its own defensive and narrow methodology.

Bearing in mind this larger hospitality of human intelligence, what follows in this reflection on God is more exposition than proof or explanation. Indeed, it might be that the best proof in the contemporary situation lies in a telling exposition in the face of the cultural trivializations of both words and ideas on the subject of God. A lot of talk about "God"—even from religious people—often sounds superficial, dry, and stale. At best it gives the impression that God is a big being of some kind—the biggest thing in a world of many things, "the supreme being," as the hallowed phrase has it. There is a problem here. It suggests that God at best is some kind of superior angel or spirit, occasionally intervening, and even interfering, in the natural evolutionary or humanly planned unfolding of things. As a result, "God" appears as a kind of personal idol, "my god" or "your god." From earliest biblical times, that was a familiar problem—confusing the infinite God, the Creator of the universe, with a local or tribal idol, either divinizing nature as *Baal*, or glorifying political power as *Moloch*—and even material possessions and comfort as *Mammon*. Such projections are a long way from affirming of the universal significance of the one true God. It seems that the spiritual path of every person and community is to get over and go beyond all individual or tribal "deities," if there is going to be any awareness of the infinite Creator.

"God seekers" in philosophy, theology, art, prayer, and meditation usually intend by *God* the absolute Other in relation to all created realities. God is expressible only in terms of boundless mystery, infinite intelligence, goodness and limitless creative power, omnipresence, and beauty. To use such language is not to indulge in some form of inflated rhetoric or pious incantation, especially for those to whom such a vocabulary is foreign. On the other hand, such words belong to the native language of anyone who wishes to speak seriously of God.

Admittedly, there is no question of capturing the infinities of God in precise formulations or a neat set of ideas. Nonetheless, such ideas and the words that express them do suggest a deep orientation of mind and heart. Questions—and all attempted answers—on the topic of God are indications of an unfolding spiritual adventure. What is at stake is finding oneself in the presence of the limitless and most intimate mystery, and responding to it, answering its persistent summons to love what and who one calls "God," with all one's heart, mind, soul, and strength. God is the primordial beginning and the ultimate end, the goal in every good intention, and the One to whom the heart homes for its peace and hope.

In this regard, a kind of reverent pragmatism is needed. Both mind and heart can be paralyzed in the search for an absolutely impregnable starting point in an exploration into God. In the meantime, life goes on. And in that movement, there is a sense that, by confessing the reality of God, there is enough light and strength to keep moving forward. It is an instance of Pascal allowing that the heart has reasons that reason itself does not know—and so to loosen up the muscle-bound rationalism that has so constricted the range and movement of intelligence.

Biblical faith, however, is not a result of human searching, but a response to God's free self-revelation. The experience of faith brings a sense of God's *Yes* to who and what we are. On the part of believers, it calls forth, in return, an unreserved *Yes* to who and what God is. God becomes, in the most intimate way, the *You* who knows, loves, heals, and forgives who *I* am, and who *we* are, in our deepest selves. That awareness is one aspect of what has been traditionally called "the state of grace." It can flood our whole being, making us radically aware of being loved, and called to share in love, in thought, word, and deed.

We might indeed be left without precise words or clear images to express what is going on, or even who this *You* really is. Words and images refer primarily to the limited, routine realities of ordinary experience. Still, in the presence of this *You*, the believer experiences a point of fulfillment. It is both a homecoming and a new point of departure. Language is stretched to accommodate a new frame of reference and to operate in an unbounded horizon. Our words are further challenged to express what can never be fully expressed in order to name more fittingly who and what is involved.

In traditional religious language, only God can "save our souls." That phrase can be translated into other idioms. For instance, as already suggested, we can speak of the conscious, unfolding self finding fulfillment and both a point of rest and new movement in the presence of the mystery. That kind of experience is one of "salvation," or being rescued from meaningless and hopeless existence. To know oneself and one's world as known and loved by God is to see everything differently.

CONCLUSION

If God is allowed to fill the horizon of life, conflicts and differences are relativized and partisan views or policies can no longer exert their idolatrous attraction. Every generation is confronted with a radical choice as to what deserves its attention, given the shortness of time and the limits of human capacities. The resources of the past have never been more available, but the demands of the present are ever more urgent. Reflection on the ways of God lead into the deep center of history as it unfolds in time and space, in culture and society. The course of history is not calmly streaming ever onward. It moves as a turbulent torrent with its whirlpools and hidden reefs, its incalculable events and movements. In the postmodern world, nothing is fixed and structured within an overarching philosophical, cultural, or even theological narrative. This massive relativity affects not only our forms of objectivity but also the subjectivity of one's lived identity. Everything can be called into question. The sense of identity that once derived from a particular secular or religious standpoint is compromised, and a widespread relativistic corruption of culture is feared. Consequently, everything must be regained anew within this hurried world of fragments and inconclusiveness. It is time for renewed affirmation of God—in the realization that we are not the origin, the center, or the goal of the universe—but that there is One who is.

There can be no harm in feeling the tension vividly expressed in the words of two great doctors in the Western Church. First, Aquinas: "God is honored in silence, not because we say or explore nothing about him, but because we understand ourselves to fail in comprehending him."[44] And more threatening for us theologians, Augustine: "Woe to those who are such great talkers if they are dumb when it comes to You."[45]

The question of God returns to prayer. The prayer of all religious peoples is classically expressed in the Great Upanishad, quoted by Pope Paul VI in his visit to India:

> From the unreal, lead me to the real;
> From darkness, lead me to light;
> From dying, lead me to immortality.

Chapter 2

THE BE-ING OF GOD

Limitless Mystery

The second chapter attempted to clear the ground for such a consideration of God that excludes both idolatrous and mythological fundamentalism. There are classic resources to be retrieved in Aquinas's notion of God as sheer, all-actual, Be-ing, but not as a "supreme being" among many "beings." Such a notion need not distract from the personal and concrete sense of personal faith and replace it with a vague colourless abstraction. The sheer, all-actual Be-ing of God forms the horizon in which all biblical, doctrinal, and experiential data on the character of God can be appreciated in their depth and singularity. Not to attempt this can lead to a flat fundamentalism. Such expressions of faith lack a sense of wonder and are incapable of speaking with conviction in the dialogical situation of faith today, especially concerning God as what Friedrich Nietzsche calls life's "transfiguration and eternal Yes."

This chapter has a certain ground-clearing aim. It is designed to suggest the horizon in which speaking about God can make sense. At the same time, it is an exercise in retrieval of the classic theological tradition as represented in Aquinas. There are difficulties: the celebrated American writer Flannery O'Connor used to read the *Summa Theologica* of Thomas Aquinas in bed before going to sleep in her home in Milledgeville, Georgia. Apparently, such an exercise was both instructive and sedative—perhaps a mixture, for she admitted that "Thomism usually comes in horrible wrappers."[1] In what follows we will be trying to make the "wrappers" less horrible while making the content more intelligible, and even less sedating. Accordingly, we will select some aspects of Aquinas's approach to God in order to indicate something of their perennial relevance to every question and every statement about God, even in this less metaphysical time so far removed from the medieval period.

DIVINE BE-ING

There have been obstacles to a critical appreciation of the classic Thomist notion of God. Michael J. Buckley's *At the Origins of Modern Atheism* contends that a decaying Scholastic philosophy was pressed into the service of a defensive theology, overanxious to be philosophically respectable.[2] From another perspective, John Milbank comes to similar conclusions in *Theology and Social Theory: Beyond Secular Reason*: for Milbank, understanding God in terms of undifferentiated being legitimates a narrow and secularistic rationality in its various guises.[3] By depicting the classic Thomist inheritance, however, in terms of a rationalist caricature, with little attempt to locate it historically and theologically, critics have had too easy a target. They are rightly concerned with the sorry results of reducing the experience of the living God to an immobile world of metaphysical concepts. On the other hand, Aquinas referred to "God" as *Ipsum Esse*, "To-Be, itself," thereby naming God as a verb rather than an abstract noun. In more modern parlance, God is affirmed and experienced more as an all-originating "event" than a particular entity, however supreme or large.[4]

Whether it begins from the "within" of the human mind, or from the "beyond" in terms of the continually unfolding universe, Aquinas's integration of philosophical and theological thought insists that God is disclosed, from within and from beyond, as limitless actuality, both transcendent and immanent. This is best signaled by referring to the divine reality as "Be-ing," to bring out the active verbal force of the idea, the *esse*, or the sheer "to be," of God.[5] God, therefore, is not *a* being, one among many beings, but what is given and communicated as the infinite limitless energy or act of "Be-ing," actively involved and present in everything. Such is the classic medieval affirmation of God as sheer *Is-ness*, as sheer unrestricted "to be," boundless "Be-ing" (*ipsum esse subsistens*).[6]

To judge that something *is*, and so to affirm the "is-ness" of anything, the human mind moves from the immediacy of sensation, through the representations of images, through the activity of its conceptions and ideas, to what is neither sensed, nor imaginable, nor even able of being conceptualized, but nonetheless is affirmed as true. To know something is not to see it as the eye sees color, but to be drawn into the wonder of a universe of being—a profoundly disorienting experience for those who think of knowing as having a good look!

There are objections: Does this notion of God as divine Be-ing distort a theology focused on God's love and self-communication with an exotic philosophical abstraction? And even philosophically speaking, when the "end of metaphysics" is widely declared as the end of an immobile taken-for-granted system comprehending everything, the notion of God as Be-ing cannot but appear as anachronistic—as a more dismal metaphysical abstraction. Though such objections can be answered, it must be admitted that there are dangers inherent in thinking of God in this way. A generalized notion of "being" tends to imply that God is "a supreme being" in a universe of other and lesser kinds of being. As a result, the infinite distance between God, the Creator, and limited kinds of being constituting creation, is downplayed. Even referring to God as the (or a) "supreme being" gives the impression that ideas of both God's Be-ing together with all other beings are comprehended in a general notion and located in an all-encompassing system of thought. In that case, God is regarded as an instance of "being in general," an eminent being in a universe of beings, and an object of thought like anything else. On the other hand, to think of God as infinite and all-actual Be-ing negates any tendency to reduce the divine reality either to a symbol of pure possibility, or as a big force or a factor within an evolving world. More positively, if God is sheer Be-ing in a uniquely all-exhaustive manner, then the very essence of God is "to be." God essentially *is*, in contrast to everything else that just happens to be. Everything that comes into existence as a particular and contingent being derives from the One who essentially and necessarily *is*. Infinite Be-ing is the originative source of all beings. It alone essentially is while nothing else has an essential claim on existence. Created beings cannot hold onto their being-ness without the risk of going out of being. To be is to be given being, the only source of which is infinite Be-ing. The universe in its entirety, and each particular, is a gift.

It is certainly possible to get lost in generalities and abstractions. The theological structure and content of the *Summa*, for instance, presuppose Thomas's life-long exposition of the *sacra pagina* of the Scriptures. For him, consequently, the notion of God as sheer Be-ing not only happily coincided with the biblical revelation of the divine name as "the One Who Is," but was demanded by it. In the relevant article,[7] Thomas asks whether "the One Who Is" is especially a proper name for God. Thomas cites as his authoritative source the passage from Exodus referring to the giving of the divine name: "You will say to them 'The One Who Is' has sent me" (cf. Exod 3:14). In reference to this biblical context of God's self-naming in relation to Moses's God-given mission, Thomas can argue that naming God as "Who Is" is appropriate, and in the highest degree. He gives three reasons. First, because such naming implies no limitation of form or mode of existence. Since the very essence of God is "to be," God is fittingly named as "the One Who Is," with no qualification or limitation. Second, there is the argument from the universality of its connotation. All other names are specific in that they suggest characterizations of divine Be-ing. But since we cannot understand what God is in this life, we have to make do with analogical approximations that leave the divine reality radically unknown and unsayable. Thus, "Who Is" is the most open-ended kind of designation, evoking, as St. John Damascene suggests, the manner in which God is as "a kind of boundless and unrestricted ocean of substance." Third, "Who Is" is most appropriate because it connotes the ever-actual, eternal Be-ing in which there is no past or future (he here refers to Augustine, *De Trinitate*, book 5). However, as regards the actual unique reality of God, Aquinas considers that the religious names, such as *God*, *YHWH*, *Lord*, and *Father*, that are found in the dialogical history of revelation and faith, are more appropriate. In this interweaving of philosophy and faith in the search for wisdom, the naming of God as sheer Be-ing does not replace the religious designation of God, but works to elucidate it, and to establish the open and unconditioned horizon in which the language of faith and prayer has meaning. In other words, the history of salvation unfolds in a universe grounded in God as its source and horizon. God's Be-ing connotes the boundless depth and breadth to anything that can be affirmed of God. Though God is first known in the effects of his actions, the divine agent transcends creation and is neither caught up in nor conditioned by any created economy of exchange or interaction. "The One Who Is" is utterly outside the created order. Aquinas writes,

> The "is-ness" [*esse*] of reality is the most perfect in comparison with all other considerations: for it is related to everything else as en-acting it. Nothing has any actuality unless, and in so far as, it is. Hence the act of be-ing is what en-acts what is real in its every aspect.[8]

It is true that both contemporary biblical scholarship and postmodern philosophy find the blending of the biblical and the philosophical suspect. To such critics, the "metaphysics of Exodus" (to quote Étienne Gilson) appears as a confusion of two different modes of discourse. Yet, one would expect the biblical authors to be rather nervous about speaking of God as "not being." While the Lord is not in earthquake, the wind, or the fire, but in the "sound of sheer silence" (1 Kgs 19:11–13), it would be hard to tell the authors of the Book of Consolation in Isaiah that God "is not," not to mention the more explicit philosophizing of the thirteenth chapter of the Wisdom of Solomon. No less a scholar than Eric Voegelin, in his monumental *Order and History*, has interpreted both the cultural movement of ancient Greece and the religious journey of Israel as a progressive conversion to the "transcendence of being," as he terms it. For him, these ancient symbols suggest a movement of *metaxy*, of the "in-between-ness" of symbol and being. His approach amounts to a kind of deconstruction of religious and philosophical symbols in the light of ever-transcendent being—what we have been calling Be-ing—thereby precluding any gnostic idolatry. He differs from the generality of biblical historians who cannot imagine how an early nomad people could come to such a transcendent sense of God. On this point, however, Voegelin agrees with Gilson: while there is no metaphysics *in* Exodus, there is a certain metaphysics *of* Exodus. Consequently, Voegelin allows that "the Christian interpretation is well founded on the text," in accord with the interpretations of Damascene and Aquinas alike.[9]

GOD AS NO-THING

Aquinas's strategy in the *Summa* is of special interest. By identifying God with sheer Be-ing, he "removes" God from the created world, and so precludes the tendency of considering the divine reality as one more particular object within it. Clearly, the medieval theologian is not refuting atheism in any modern sense—the Greek, Jewish, and Arab thinkers and commentators did not doubt the existence of God—but he does invite the believer to take up a position in the world. For instance, his sketch of the "five ways" shows how each way has its starting point in a particular feature of the universe that exists only in a limited, contingent, and interrelated manner.[10] The cosmos of all that is, including human existence and its intellectual activity, is a question looking for an answer. Consequently, St. Thomas invites those who follow him along these "ways" to move on toward a horizon of ultimate meaningfulness, opening up from experience of the actual universe. Human intelligence, in following the directionality of the universe of what is, consents, as it were, to the fundamental dynamism of existence itself. It leads to both the possibilities and impossibility of naming God—for God is like nothing in the world. There is a necessary negation in any knowledge of God. In presenting his five ways, Aquinas is more a continuator of the older monastic theology than a modern analytic philosopher. Each of his *viae* plots the ascent of the mind to God. Aquinas is not applying concepts or metaphysical labels to God, but he inviting his fellow *viatores* into the movement, the *via*, of beings to Be-ing itself.[11] He is certainly using concepts of causality, perfection, intelligence, and so forth; but his use of such categories is radically affected by his identification of God as sheer Be-ing. In this respect, the notion of God as Be-ing, as *Ipsum Esse*, functions as a kind of clearing space in which the mystery of God can be explored, affirmed, but never known. Hence, the Be-ing of God is not a concept, nor is a mystical intuition of Be-ing implied, nor any way beyond words and language to affirm a truth that cannot be contained by any human concept or adequately represented in the domain of discourse. But within the critical performance of language, *the One Who Is*, even if radically unknown, can still be really affirmed.[12] This "knowing unknowing" is made possible because of the "effects" of God's action—in creation, grace, and revelation.[13] In other words, the divine Giver is known only in the divine giving, even while transcending any adequate understanding of either the Giver, the kind of giving, and even of the gifts themselves.

There is another instructive text, especially as it deals directly with the more intimate form of knowing God through the divine self-revelation:

> Although through the revelation of grace we do not know the "what is" of God in this life, and so we are joined to him as it were to one unknown. Nonetheless we know him in a fuller fashion in as much as more numerous and more excellent effects are shown to us, and in so far as we attribute to God through divine revelation what human reason cannot attain, such as God is both one and three.[14]

Even though experiencing the indwelling of God in grace and receiving the divine self-revelation through the incarnation and the gift of the Spirit, theological wisdom must be content to remain in the dark. Faith lives from a union with the One whom it must confess as radically unknown.

Nor is the divine reality somehow subsumed under categories of being or understanding, even though conceptualizations such as absolute and relative, necessary and contingent are extensively employed in theological discourse.[15] The great Thomistic commentator Cardinal Thomas Cajetan (1469–1534) warned over four hundred years ago, as he reflected on Thomas's account of the divine transcendence, that

> we err if we approach God with the categories of absolute and relative as though we imagined such a distinction to be established in some way prior to the divine reality itself, and believed that one member of the distinction was subordinate to the other. For the divine reality is prior to being and its differences; it is above *being*, beyond *one*, and so on.[16]

The complex creativity of human language culminates at the point where no more can be said, other than that God *is* in a way that cannot be known. An ultimate silence and simplicity are characteristic of Aquinas's thought as a form of knowing-unknowing when it comes to God.[17] Indeed, the ultimate point in our human knowledge of God is reached when we know that we do not know God. That is to say, we know God to be in a way that exceeds everything we know of him.[18] Theology is, therefore, a *docta ignorantia*.[19] That is, it is not simple ignorance, but a tutored or learned "unknowing." In fact, Thomas was increasingly severe on what he took to be the excessive agnosticism of the great Jewish commentator Maimonides (1135–1204).[20] There is an essentially positive orientation in our knowledge of God as it intends the true and the real. Human intelligence is carried by the divine "effects" to their transcendent cause and source. The mind moves from the gifts to the Giver. Still, the way in which such judgments are true of God is certainly an absence at the heart of all theological discourse. All our efforts to name God "fail in representing him."[21] There is no question of visualizing the divine or of conceptualizing the manner in which God is God. The living God of theology and philosophy is never reducible to one more religious or philosophical object.

And yet, while the divine mode of Be-ing is utterly beyond theological comprehension, God is nonetheless present in every act of divine giving. Sheer Be-ing shares itself in the universe of beings. A movement of negation is clear. While God is present, there is no implication of the divine reality entering into any kind of composition with created reality. Nor is God a factor in a universal process or system. God is not the "world soul" related to the body of creation, as though the divine reality is a partial principle of a larger totality. Sheer Be-ing is not part of anything. It is pure self-possession.[22] Nor is the sheer actuality of such Be-ing a kind of potency, "prime matter" as the unfortunate David of Dinant had held, awaiting formal determination in other beings—an opinion condemned by Thomas with uncharacteristic severity! God as Be-ing is present not as admixed with being or beings, but, to adapt the Scottish theologian John Macquarrie's happy phrase, as "Being which lets beings be," without confusing the one with the other. Aquinas writes,

> As long as any reality has being, it is required that God be present to it in the way in which it exists. "To be" is what is most within and most deeply inscribed into any reality, because the act of existence actualises everything else. Hence it is necessary that God be in all things and in the most intimate manner.[23]

Through the further gift of grace, the divine presence at the heart of all creation blooms in human consciousness, and so unfolds at a new level. In mind and heart, the human being is now enabled to commune with God. In Thomas's terminology, God is not only the "cause of being"—"from the outside," as it were, but is also now an "intentional" presence, as known and loved in a new intimacy. In this divine indwelling, God, as known and loved through all the virtues and gifts of grace, is experienced to be "within" those who know and love him. This amounts to an intersubjective communication between the divine consciousness and the created human consciousness.[24]

To contemplate the world in the light of divine Be-ing is to appreciate it as a universe of gifts, of giving, and as originating in a Giver. All is given, and the being of each existent is a gift, coming from the free giving of the One who is Be-ing. For God essentially *is*, the source of all being. If the existence of finite being is a gift, it exists because of the ever-continuing act of Being's giving. A conclusion follows: the divine Be-ing of the Giver is more present to each existing thing than it is to itself. That is to say that God is more within us, interior to us, than we are within ourselves in accord with a great Augustinian insight. Such a recognition affects the very nature of thought and clothes it with a quality of gratitude: *thinking* becomes fundamentally *thanking*, as was mentioned in the preceding chapter. We exist in a gifted universe with the Giver universally confessed in accord with David Bentley Hart's precise summary:

> To speak of "God" properly, then—is to use the word consonant with the teachings of orthodox Judaism, Christianity, Islam, Sikhism, Hinduism, Baha'i and a great deal of antique paganism, and so forth—is to speak of the one infinite source of all that is: infinite, eternal, omniscient, omnipotent, omnipresent, uncreated, uncaused, perfectly transcendent of all things, and for that very reason absolutely immanent to all things. God so understood is not something posed over against the universe, in addition to it,...all things that exist receive their being continuously from him who is the infinite wellspring of all that is.[25]

This brief outline of the character of divine "Being" from a Thomist perspective necessarily includes the notion of God as supreme consciousness.[26] In technical terms, Be-ing is mindful and intentional in its knowing and willing. This is a theme common to the great religious and philosophical traditions, especially when describing the divine-human encounter. In the world of personal subjects, to be without being conscious—at least potentially so—is not being at all. Furthermore, all reference to God as wise, loving, merciful, provident, and so on essentially implies that God is pure untrammeled consciousness and self-possession. Divine Be-ing is present to itself in everything it is and does.

The mode of this self-presence is made explicit in the particular Christian theme of the Trinity, as we shall see more fully in a later chapter. Divine Be-ing is present to itself in perfect self-utterance and self-expression in the Word, and in unreserved self-donation to the other in the Spirit. In this, the Word of God's self-expression is not "any kind of word, but a word breathing love,"[27] both within the communion of divine life, and in communication with creation. Theology employs a variety of images and analogies to give some understanding of how and why this is so, even if the inner vitality of the Mystery exceeds human understanding and control. The light in which theology proceeds is "nothing other than a certain participated similitude in uncreated light,"[28] actively "manifesting" everything that falls under it:[29] like all truth, theological truth results from a movement of the Spirit.[30]

This is to appreciate that human consciousness, despite its limitations, is itself a participation in the divine consciousness. In that radiance, the divine intelligence knows all that God is, all that other selves are, and all that is, was, and will be in an eternal and luminous self-possession. There is no implication of God looking outward to gain knowledge of what exists as if it were apart from, outside, or beyond God's Be-ing. Rather, divine consciousness is pure inwardness and transparency, the root and goal, of all that is and will be. In the Thomist vision of reality, all the limited acts of human knowing and the loving involved in the pursuit of truth and desire for the good reflect the infinite act of God's consciousness, the pure Light that God is. We have been knowingly and lovingly created in order to relate, knowingly and lovingly, to God in return and to manifest the Creator in the midst of creation.

A CRITICALLY AFFIRMATIVE KNOWLEDGE

Throughout Aquinas's theological approach, there is evidence of a critical modesty. His theological system is driven by a rigorously questioning mode of exploring the data of faith, just as it constantly acknowledges that no one knows what God is in this life.[31] Even the believer is united to the divine "as if to one unknown."[32] Thomas, in fact, extends the unknowability of the divine object to include even the subjective state of the believing theologian regarding "the state of grace." He allows for three possibilities. One possibility is that some may know their state through a special revelation.[33] But this does not seem to be a common theological privilege. Neither is it possible to judge one's state by sharing in God's own evidence, for that is intrinsically beyond human vision.[34] All that is possible—even for the theologian—is to make a discerning judgment "by way of conjecture through some signs" (*coniecturaliter per aliqua signa*). The signs include delight in God, contempt for anything less than God, and a pure conscience. This suggests a joy in the theological task and a refusal to reduce the mystery of God to an intellectual or cultural idol. The intelligence of faith here relies on a certain experiential assurance, *per quandam experientiam dulcedinis*, a consciousness receptive and responsive to the divine gift, the divine giving, and the divine Giver.[35]

Although related to the world and intimately present to it, God is eminently absent as a known and classifiable object within it. Here, the notion of divine Be-ing has a theological function. It makes a clearing space in which the limitless actuality of God can be appreciated as the source and end of worldly existence. The transcendent realm can be approached only "by way of eminence, causality and negation."[36] Infinite Be-ing remains what it alone *is*, outside the whole created order, with everything deriving from and related to it. But God is not to be thought of as frustrating the human effort to know the divine essence, but as lovingly respecting the creaturely mode of our present existence.[37] In this regard, we stand securely on the floor or ground of our existence, but without any ceiling imposed on either our understanding or desire.

To a visual or ocular model of knowing, the affirmation of God's Be-ing must appear as an experience of absence rather than of presence, a journey into "no-thing," an occupation of nowhere. But theological judgment has its own objective realism. As said above, given the supracategorial realm of divine Be-ing, the biblical name of God in Exodus as *Qui est* (Exod 3:14) is the most proper to God.[38] God exceeds all form and conceptions of being, as the boundless oceanic fullness of Be-ing in which we are immersed: "[The One] Who Is" is, therefore, the most appropriate name of God in our efforts from below to affirm divine Be-ing.[39] But as regards the action of God in history—God's action "from above"—the personal and biblically named "God," *YHWH*, the Father of our Lord Jesus Christ, or the Holy Spirit, are more appropriate in the context of prayer and worship. In this interplay of philosophy and faith—from above and from below—affirming God as Be-ing does not replace the religious designation of God but works to elucidate it. Theological reflection is set within a universe radiant with Be-ing, while Be-ing itself defers God's self-revelation in the history of salvation to be the fulfillment of what faith affirms, of what hope patiently waits for, and of what charity even now most desires. Despite its aim to rise from the gifts to the Giver, theological discourse meets a blank silence. All our efforts to name God "fail in representing him."[40] There is no question of visualizing the divine or of conceptualizing the manner in which God is God. The divine Mystery is never contained or objectified. There is an endless deferral inscribed into theological search, awaiting that final communication that only God can give.[41]

In short, Aquinas's steady intention is to present the universe of Christian existence and experience specifically in the light of the self-revealing God (*sub ratione Dei*).[42] Because in this life we do not know the divine essence, we must make do with the data of what God has done—the "God-effect" in the realms of nature and grace.[43] A theological standpoint thus opens onto the horizon of infinite Be-ing. The ever-actual and inner vitality of the Mystery is envisaged as communicating itself to creation and indwelling human consciousness. It is thereby known and loved in all our knowing and loving. Be-ing, although it is communicative and indwelling, is disclosed as what intrinsically exceeds human understanding. As a "word about God,"[44] theology participates in eternal light of God's own self-utterance. The light in which theology proceeds is "nothing other than a certain participated similitude in uncreated light,"[45] "manifesting" everything that falls under it.[46]

To recapitulate: first, theological discourse is always analogical.[47] Without analogical skills, theology would be at the mercy of univocal construction, to end at best as an immobile mythological system. The way of analogy defers to the unobjectifiable excess of

Be-ing, the communicative source of all that is.[48] Second, theological analogy operates within a field of divine self-communication and disclosure. For the divine mystery intends our beatitude. Far from being an object of detached intellectual curiosity, God is our destiny and our last end. The attraction of the supreme Good is felt through the whole of creation, and is especially manifested in God-ward orientation of the human being.[49] Third, though our pilgrim path must wait on the ultimate light of God, and though God in this life is the "unknown one to whom we are united," there are also those "many and more excellent effects"[50] of special divine revelation. These effects are *data* in a special sense; for they are indwelling and transforming *dona*—that is, "gifts"—actualized in the grace of the divine missions of the Word and the Spirit.[51] Forgetfulness of the economy of grace and the divine missions would bleach Thomas's approach of its trinitarian color.[52] For the gift of grace works its own transformation, enabling the recipient to know and love God in a new intimacy.[53] Analogical knowing, therefore, anticipates a God-intended eschatological beatitude and is animated by the gifts inherent in the divine missions. Just as the divine Word is "not any kind of word, but a word breathing love,"[54] so the Spirit is not any kind of spirit, but the Love who proceeds from the Father and the Son.[55] A certain holographic intentionality is implied, as the various dimensions of data are considered. God is at once the subject of theological inquiry, the source of the data it considers, and the light and the love in which such data are interpreted.

What is evident to God in the simplicity of the one Word[56] is necessarily complex in our minds, embodied as they are in space and time. Our human condition demands the laborious complexity of concepts, judgments, and doctrines. These take shape through the collaborative learning of religious traditions, clearing obstacles, rejecting errors, and focusing on the mystery of God as the simple but essential object of faith. Yet this is not to miss seeing the forest because of the trees. For irradiating the complex creativity of theology at work is the God-given intentionality of faith that already attains the divine reality and participates in the divine life.[57]

A fundamental determinant of the theological horizon is the assumption that God is related to the world and intimately present to it. At the same time, God is eminently absent as a known and classifiable object within it. Consequently, we have been stressing that the notion of divine Be-ing has a theological function. It makes a clearing space in which all the data and gifts of nature and grace might be appreciated as deriving from their divine source. In his presentation of God and of all things in relation to God, St. Thomas set himself to address, first, the divine reality itself, and then the manner in which God is the fulfillment of the rational creature. God's pure otherness as infinite Be-ing dominates the horizon in which the spiritual nature of the human can unfold.[58] These two indefinables, namely, the Be-ing of God and our transcendent fulfillment in God, are linked concretely in Christ as the way, not only of our journey into God, but in the visible mission by which God has made his way to us. Thus, the incarnation of the Word, the primary effect of God's salvific communication. The Christ of the *Tertia Pars* is the *via* incarnate, transvaluing the more general and abstract essential attributes.[59]

Yet the intimacy of God's self-revelation in and to the created world is determined by the boundless horizon formed by God's transcendence from that world.[60] There is, as it were, an ineffable space of God's absence and otherness. The "re-motion," this sense of the otherness of the divine reality in relation to the created universe, prepares for another dimension of otherness, namely, that of the trinitarian interrelated otherness within God as expressed in the doctrine of the *distinction* of the persons.[61] In due course, the trinitarian differentiation of the notion of divine Be-ing will lead to a consideration of the manner in which all created being comes forth from God. Creation is marked with its trinitarian origin, especially in the knowing and loving of spiritual beings.[62]

From within this world, we are oriented beyond it, to God, even if in a veiled and confused manner (*sub quadam confusione*).[63] Awareness of the world of beings is an overture to the infinite ground of all that is. As mentioned above, Aquinas's *viae* are not refuting atheism in any modern sense.[64] There was no denial of the existence of God to be found among Greek, Jewish, and Arabian thinkers and commentators to whom he refers. Rather, his *viae*, or "demonstrations," serve as invitations for believers to position themselves, receptively and reflectively, within the universe. Human intelligence, in following the movement of universal existence, consents, as it were, to its fundamental dynamism. And this leads to both the possibility, and the ultimate impossibility, of naming the God who is like nothing in the world. In his concern to inspire the ascent of the mind to God, Aquinas is not applying general concepts of the existing world to God, but inviting his fellow travelers (*viatores*) into the movement, the *via*, of beings to Be-ing.[65] The world is inhabited as the theater in which the unknowable God is intimately present and ever-active. It follows that the reality of the world is quasi-sacramental. It is to be explored and contemplated, not only as a sphere of objectively visualized entities, but as a totality intrinsically God-ward in its constitution. As a site of wonder, it impels the mind beyond itself, beyond commonsense visible appearances, into the "no-thing-ness" of Be-ing. In the five ways of disclosure, the experience of the universe takes the mind beyond its perceptions, beyond the immediacy of sense data, beyond the power of the imagination or the fertility of conceptions, to the all-actuating presence of unknown Be-ing.

In this theological horizon, God and human intelligence are not so much confronting one another in opposition, but rather as related in a form of mutual disclosure: the world cannot be really known unrelated to God; and the divine source and agent of all that is cannot be disclosed unless through the effects of divine action within that world. In this primal connection, the self-revealing God is described already in relationship to the world.[66] The revealed name of God in Exodus 3:14, "I AM WHO I AM," while evoking the particular history of revelation, is located within a larger context—within the consciousness of what all name as "God."[67] As Thomas goes on to state, "The name, 'God,' is employed to signify the reality which is beyond everything, and which is the principle of all things, so that this is what those using the name 'God' mean."[68] Aquinas's notion of God is firmly located, not only with regard to the biblical and doctrinal data, but also in such a way as to include a much larger history of knowing and naming God. This is an evident outreach to other religious and philosophical traditions—of his time, and ours.

The movement of negative theology results, as St. Thomas himself admits, more in a consideration of how God is not. Divine Be-ing infinitely exceeds every mode of being within the immediate world of our existence. God transcends the finite realm, by being its immanent ground, ultimate intelligibility, and transcendent fulfillment. Aquinas deploys categories such as causality, perfection, and intelligence, but never in order to efface the background notion of God as sheer Be-ing. It functions as a kind of clearing space in which the mystery of God can be explored and affirmed, even though never to be fully known.

Still, given the essential radiance of God, theology is bat-like in its search:[69] the bat cannot bear sunlight, as it flits through its environment only with radar-like soundings of its dark world. Still, our state is not essentially nocturnal; for there is a natural desire to see God, and to come into the light. The clouded state of our intelligence[70] already participates in the divine light—"in your light we see light" (Ps 36:9). The culmination of God's self-revelation is the vision of God, face-to-face in "the light of glory" (in Latin, *lumen gloriae*).

But God is not to be thought of as frustrating the human effort to know him. Rather, God lovingly respects the creaturely mode of our present existence and the limitations to human knowledge that result.[71] In this regard, we stand securely on the floor or ground of our existence, but without any ceiling imposed on either our understanding or desire.

It is worth repeating that Aquinas's exposition of the topic "God" does not in fact begin, as is usually presumed, with the *de Deo Uno*, as though *de Deo trino* is then added after the more philosophical section so as to be an explicitly theological series of questions. Aquinas is always intent on the one God of Christian faith. To this end, he begins with questions concerning "the unity of God" and then moves to "the trinity of persons." He proceeds with a series of questions relating to the singular divine transcendence in relation to the created world. He uses such an order of disclosure to throw some light on the trinitarian mystery of God—from which the universe, along with our capacity to understand it, has emerged.[72] Second, Thomas's habitual employment of the Aristotelian four causes (efficient, material, formal, and final) have been criticized as inadequate. These causes, nonetheless, have a rough and ready application to the ordinary world of common sense as when the carpenter intends to make a table (final cause); he chooses wood as his medium (material cause) and shapes it in a certain proportion (formal cause), using both his skill and the requisite tools (efficient cause). Now, this repertoire of causality runs into difficulties in any consideration—then and now—of how "Be-ing lets beings be" (to quote John Macquarrie), or of how the divine Mystery communicates itself in Word and Spirit. Today, quantum physics will speak of the complex origination and interrelationship of what is, and the manner it comes into being, and the correlation of factors in various particular contexts. Thomas, despite his position on the reality of creation, intriguingly affirmed that God had "no real relation" to the world based on such patterns of causality.[73] God is outside any system, and divine causality is not annexed to any economy of cause and effect in the created world.[74]

Human beings are made in the divine image. But the divine image is not simply an external exemplar or model, for it structures the innermost dynamics of human existence. To be, to know, to love—each of these acts is a manifestation of a primal gift so that the human spirit images the divine reality. As Aquinas succinctly puts it, "We discern the likeness of the divine image in human nature in that it is receptively open to God [*capax Dei*]—namely, by attaining to him in knowing and loving."[75] More particularly, in our specifically theological knowledge of God, a dynamic conformity to the divine persons is implied in that they are "sent" to the soul in the gift of grace. The all-defining meaning of theology as "word about God" is not its own conceptualization or utterance, but the Word who indwells the mind through grace. It is, therefore, not "any kind of Word, but one which breathes love."[76] Aquinas goes on to say,

> The Son is sent not in any perfection of intellect, but in that instruction of our understanding by which it bursts forth in the affectivity of love....Such a perception implies a certain experiential knowledge which is properly called wisdom, as though it were a tasting kind of knowledge.[77]

Consequently, the mind's knowledge of God does not consist in the formation of a conceptual idol. The divine Word is given as an illumination that leads to love and an intimate experience of God. In Aquinas's perspective, being and acting in the divine image depends on an interior conformity to the trinitarian reality. Likewise, the phrases "a certain experimental knowledge" of "a tasting kind" suggest an experience of subjectivity and a mode of consciousness that could be more fully expressed only in more recent times.[78]

There is another problem. When creation, the universe of finite beings, is understood within the Thomist perspective as participating in the divine Be-ing, when human knowing and willing likewise participate in the divine consciousness, the fear of pantheism stirs. Imagination might suggest that everything is part of God. And as result a certain caution enters quite traditional ways of speaking about God's relation to the world. An impression can be given that the more we—or the whole of creation—participate in the Be-ing of God, the less we are who and what we are, and the less creation can be itself. It is as though the Be-ing of God so floods creation deriving from God that it ceases to have its own independent existence. On the other hand, not to insist on a participative sense of being in God—in whom "we live and move and have our being" (Acts 17:28)—will tend to isolate God from creation, and, for that matter, separate human existence from its divine source. A special term was coined in order to avoid any pantheistic connotation, namely, *panentheism*—God existing in all things, and all things existing in God.[79] This is a useful notion provided there is no suggestion that everything created *necessarily* exists in God, or that God does not create freely, or that God is a big container of beings, or an extra element in the make-up of each particular being. Leaving aside these problems of imagination, the value of the term *panentheism* consists in signaling that God and creation do not exist side by side, nor are the Creator and the created being confused or reduced to one reality. Panentheism signifies that creation, in its innermost being, is related to and derives from God. Note the connotation of the proposition *in*, as in the phrases, "beings participate *in* Be-ing," and "Be-ing is *in* all beings," as freely giving rise to the universe of beings. In this respect, the finite does not add to the infinite fullness of divine Be-ing, but merely expresses it in a finite mode.[80]

THE INEXPRESSIBLE EXCESS OF BE-ING

This brief presentation of some of the salient points of Aquinas's notion of God is prompted by the conviction that our idea of God is so often so small. Perhaps this is unavoidable—an intrinsic defeat to all efforts to express the boundless Be-ing of God. However, in many cases, there is almost a deliberate belittling when God is thought of as a *being* rather than appreciated as the unbounded act of Be-ing. With Aquinas's emphasis on God as essentially Be-ing, the manner in which God is "ultimate reality" can be more clearly affirmed. Compared to a whole world of real and particular beings, God is the most real, the "really real," the all-deciding reality. Though that is a most general observation, the phrase conveys something more specific. What is judged to be "real" is critically affirmed, and, therefore, opposed to the imaginary, the sentimental, and the whole world of subjective impressions and feelings. In contrast, the ultimate reality, the "really real," possesses a commanding objectivity irrespective of our tastes and surmises. In religious language, God is the light in which everything and everyone is judged. That does not imply that the ultimate reality is less attractive as the supreme Good and fullness of Beauty. Nor does it suggest that God is less transformative in our regard, the fulfillment of our quest for meaning, truth, goodness, and beauty. But God is not merely "my/our God," for ultimate reality infinitely transcends all subjective frameworks and projections. What and who God is beyond all the realities of the world of our experience and thought—"out of this world," even while "meaning the world" to the religious intelligence. In short, God cannot be classified within some larger class, and given a place in the world of things, material or spiritual. Though this ultimate reality cannot usually be referred to except in figurative terms drawn from the routine scope and range of our experience (e.g., God as light, rock, fountain, king, shepherd), the divine reality is not explicable by any other reality nor dependent on it. Compared to all else, God is infinitely, eternally, uniquely—"otherwise"!

The adjective *ultimate* suggests what this "otherwise" might mean. It connotes what is ultimate in terms of the goal of human existence and, indeed, in terms of our ultimate destiny. God is our "ultimate concern" and "last end," that to which all else is ordered, as both a means to and in anticipation of the eventual fulfillment. The notion of "the ultimate" connotes resonances of depth, of ultimate desire and concern in human beings, the deepest meaning in what stirs beneath the surface of our experience, even despite inevitable obsessions and distractions. Further, while "ultimate" suggests the final measure of what is most attractive and the deepest in our sense of reality,[81] it also implies what is first in the origin of all creation, giving rise to all that is, the kind of things that exist, and the kind of fulfillment they need.

This may sound all too heavily philosophical, and a long way from any familiar biblical idiom. On the other hand, there are other supportive voices in these "postmodern" times: anxious about the disillusionment and nihilism of the age, von Balthasar remarked, "The Christian is called to be the guardian of metaphysics in our time."[82] That is not to say that the singular personal mystery of God is to be replaced by metaphysical abstractions. The exploration of God neither begins from, nor leads to such abstract notions. After all, as has been abundantly implied, God is not the final factor in some great mathematical puzzle, or one great agent among many in the creation and evolution of the world. God is rather the mystery in which "we live and move and have our being" (Acts 17:28), thereby suggesting that the divine presence is the very atmosphere oxygenating interpersonal existence and communication. There is an essentially experiential component in our sense of God in that human consciousness under the sway of ultimate questions. The desires of the heart and the eyes of the mind reach toward a final realm of fulfillment, even though full comprehension and adequate expression are lacking. That, after all, is Pascal's point: the heart *does* have its reasons even if intelligence is either embarrassed or incapable when it comes to expressing them. It is important therefore to attend to the whole of human experience and the whole scope of consciousness.

Modern culture has become too tolerant of one-dimensional statements that bypass any notion of the Creator or creation. For example, there is the insistence that the universe is limited to the physical cosmos, and that the cosmos is only matter powered by the dynamics of evolution.[83] What is left out in both cases is the phenomenon of consciousness itself in which the universe, including the physical cosmos and its dynamics, *becomes known*. In other words, the universe is that which is knowable in the human mind and heart; and the cosmos, even in its physical, chemical, and evolutionary structure and composition, becomes aware of itself in human intelligence. To leave out the experience of the conscious self, wondering, questioning, and exploring the universe, prejudices the starting point. But whatever the starting point, be it in evolutionary naturalism or the experience of consciousness, both consciousness and evolution presume the gift of being!

On the other hand, every affirmation of God is loaded with an inexpressible excess. All that God is, all that I am and we are, at this moment, all that the universe itself it, is happening in the Now of each affirmation. Each instant is born out of the events of a particular past as it carries us forward into an incalculable future. In each Now, the dimensions of past, present, and future come together in an instant of consciousness, a psychological present moment. To this degree, the Now of our experience is touched with the eternal Now of God. A venerable philosophical phrase speaks of God as "Pure Act," *Actus Purus*. Such an expression seeks to name the inexpressibly actual, the limitless, absolute, unceasing active reality of God in its perfect self-possession and consciousness. Nothing further can be added to the actual reality of God, for there is in God nothing unfinished or restricted. From the actuality of the utter plenitude of God's eternal Now, there derives the Now of our own consciousness. It is this that is increasingly conformed to the eternal moment of God's Now and participates in it.

What is distinctively Christian finds its focus in a personal event. The all-embracing actuality of God is reconfigured in the unique event of the incarnation. The Word was made flesh; the divine has appeared in our midst, in solidarity with all human beings, in Christ's life, suffering, death, and resurrection. His transformed humanity already draws believers to itself in anticipation of a universal fulfillment. Thus, the Pure Act of God overflows into its seeming contradictory: it becomes flesh, in the time, space, hopes, and vulnerabilities of the human condition—and thereby set the natural limits of our humanity in a new horizon. Through the resurrection and ascension of Christ, we begin already to live in another dimension.[84]

The notion of God as pure consciousness and self-presence, and any suggestion of ourselves as participating in such consciousness, has to contend with a particular scientific mentality arguing that all reality is reducible to matter, and, indeed, to its lifeless components. It is likely that the materialist scientist will admit that there is indeed some glimmer of consciousness in the human brain, at least in the self-awareness of the scientist. That is regarded, however, as more or less a freakish experience in the universe as a whole. Consciousness is beside the point—when the point is that the universe is declared to be basically a force-structured mass of lifeless matter. A certain embarrassment results when such a view of things is brought into the open and shown to be blinkered and one-dimensional. When a flat, materialist vision of reality seeks to account for everything that makes up the world, a persistent blind spot is in evidence. It fails to recognize the obvious, namely, that knowing and exploring are conscious activities. In that consciousness, "everything" that is known becomes known by a knower. Admittedly, an unreflective extraversion can suppress the immediate experience of the knowing self. That narrow inattention not only arbitrarily reduces the scope of objective knowledge to the material. It also truncates any possibility of appreciating the self-in-action, in its essential activities of knowing and willing. Nonetheless, the restlessness of questions remains, as do the delight of discovery and the growing experience of wonder. Karl Rahner sharply observed,

> Is human existence absurd or does it have an ultimate meaning? If it is absurd, why do human beings have an

> unquenchable hunger for meaning? Is it not a consequence of God's existence? For if God doesn't exist, then the hunger for meaning is absurd.[85]

The present context of discussion is often polarized between proponents of theism and atheism. It is worth insisting that Aquinas is not a theist in today's sense. He is more the supreme realist,[86] affirming the reality of God from the depths and in the expanse of what truly is, inspiring wonder, and revealing itself in human history.

Chapter 3

THE GOD OF HUMAN CONSCIOUSNESS

In the previous chapter, we presented aspects of the great Scholastic and Thomistic achievement in expressing the reality of God in objectively ontological terms, above all by employing the resources of Aristotelian metaphysics. We now move to explore the same realities from the perspective of human consciousness, the better to interiorize our notion of God, and to develop a better possibility of dialogue with the scientific mentality of our time. Science has shown a particular magnificence in its concentration on the empirical data dealing with the material constitution of the universe. It has, however, tended to neglect the data of consciousness that enable the question of God, human consciousness, and science itself to be examined in a much more ample and integrated fashion.

THE PHENOMENON OF CONSCIOUSNESS

Given the knot of questions around current debates on the topics of "intelligent design," creation, evolution, and the convergence or divergence of scientific, philosophical, and theological perspectives on such questions,[1] it is especially necessary to note how our imaginative propensities and prejudices can lead critical intelligence astray. If, for instance, we try to imagine creation as a noun, we naturally tend to envisage this totality of something to which we, and our own creativity, are oddly extrinsic. We can have the impression that our thinking and feeling, praying, desiring, exploring, and making are just a faint mode of being, ghosting the reality of the evolutionary cosmos, but not really part of it. Creation, or the physical universe, is thus imagined as a rather objective state of affairs human beings must come to recognize, with or without the creative hand of God.[2]

The whole thing appears differently if human consciousness is appreciated as an intrinsic feature of human beings and as an aspect of creation itself. Consciousness is not an idea, but a primal experience.[3] It is disclosed as a continuing self-presence in our acts of sensing, imagining, questioning, understanding, judging, deciding, acting, loving, and contemplating. In this sense, it is the inward dimension by which reality reveals itself. According to an ancient insight, there is a certain identity between the mind knowing reality and reality known. We are not detached spectators looking at what is somehow already "out there." Rather, our consciousness is the site in which what is to be known is given to sense, imagination, and intelligence, provoking questions as to what is or what might be the case. Objectivity, even the highest scientific objective knowledge, can never be attained by pretending that there is not someone who does the knowing. Grammatically speaking, all "third person" statements, even in science, depend on a "first person," expressed in such statements as "I have found this to be so," "I cannot deny that this is the case without lying."

For those who might fear that such a suggestion is dangerously subjective, we readily admit that subjectivity is indeed dangerous if we should pretend that what is real and true is merely a projection of our own feelings, imaginations, or bright ideas—*subjectivism*, in fact. On the other hand, the only way to what is genuinely objective is through the conscious, critical activation of our capacities to sense, to imagine, and to understand and weigh the evidence. We can never be so objective, so "third person" in our extraversion as to leave out the subjective, the "first person," dimension in our knowing. Nor, at the other extreme, can we be so subjective as to refuse to acknowledge the demand to go beyond ourselves into the awesome otherness of all that is—the "third person" account, you might say, typically expressed in scientific writing as the "third person passive."[4] At every point, there is a wonderful conjunction of intelligence exploring reality, and reality communicating itself to intelligence in the one activity of knowing.

THE HUMAN MICROCOSM

Given the whole panoply of creation, the human being is conscious of itself in the universe as a microcosm. The human combines in itself material and spiritual dimensions of reality. This is a favorite theme of, say, Maximus Confessor, and looks back to Plato's *Timaeus* for its origins.[5] Today, we can take this idea further. As embodied in the material and physical cosmos, the human being is immersed in the whole dynamic interaction of matter and energy. The body is not simply contained by its skin. In the one web of evolutionary life, human beings are related to all other living beings on this planet. Moreover, there is the much greater cosmic connection. We are made of stardust. The physical and chemical constitution of our bodies and brains owe their origins to vast cosmic occurrences billions of years ago that formed the hydrogen and carbon that are the basis of all biological life.

The spiritual dimension of human existence is related to the "soul." In Aquinas's oft-repeated phrase, the human spirit is "in some measure all things," *quoddamodo omnia*.[6] This overture of the spirit to the whole universe arises out of the distinctive experience of human consciousness, as it transcends the range of material and purely physical reality. Human consciousness, for example, experiences itself as being able to reflect on itself reflecting. Nothing is in principle beyond the ambit of its explorations, be it spiritual, material, or the divine mystery itself. The spiritual phenomenon of consciousness is, therefore, of cosmic and universal significance. However inchoately, in the human mind, the cosmos awakens to itself as an expanse of wonder and as an uncanny gift. The overture of the human to the universe and its mystery caused Goethe to observe, "Man is the first conversation that nature holds with God."[7] Long before him, Maximus Confessor considered that

> the human person...is the laboratory in which everything is concentrated and itself naturally mediates between the extremities of each division, having been drawn into everything in a good and fitting way through becoming.[8]

Human being exists within a dynamic field of interconnections and interrelationships. It is potentially open to everything within the universe. Its spiritual scope reaches beyond even this, to the abiding source and goal of all existence.

SOUL

Now we come to what today are more controverted matters. Can the material cosmos alone explain the spiritual overture of the human person to the whole? Clearly, our bodily constitution is the outcome of cosmic physical, chemical, and genetic forces of unimaginable complexity. They work to structure and energize the life of our bodies and wondrous workings of our brains, the most complex system in the natural world. Each of the brain's hundred billion neurons is connected with hundreds or thousands of others, resulting in a possible one hundred trillion synaptic connections. But matter alone cannot explain the genesis of the human spirit. What we call the "soul" pertains to what is deepest in the universe as God's personal creation. However mysteriously and however intimately connected with evolutionary dynamics, only God can create the spiritual.[9] On the one hand, the human spirit is embodied in the totality of the created universe. On the other, the soul is immediately created by God so that the human can be drawn into a dialogical relationship with its Creator. In this spiritual dimension of human existence, we are "faced" with God, at every stage of existence, whether in the present space-time structure of biological life, or after death. In this regard, the soul is a principle of continuity in the identity and history of the human being: whatever the human state—living, dying, dead—or in some state beyond (such as purgatory, hell, heaven, or full bodily resurrection), it is the one and the same person created by and for God. The whole mystery of salvation is oriented to bring to completion the living dialogue with God that is the basic feature of our being. Though we co-exist or "in-exist" within material creation, we are more. We "ex-ist," that is, we "stand out" from material creation in an immediate relationship to God. This is what distinguishes the human creature from all else in the material universe. To be human is to be beholden to the "No-thing" that is outside all creation, even while being its source. It is to be faced with the "No One" that is like no other. For the spirit inhabits a limitless "Nowhere" beyond all boundaries and locations. It touches on the "No Time," the eternal, which gives meaning and direction to all our days. It a living relationship to the utterly transcendent, and unimaginably immanent, "Other," the source of all being.

Consciousness of this transcendent relationship discloses the spiritual depth and Other-ward orientation of our being. It inspires the language of self-transcendence. Human consciousness is ever on the move, unfolding in wonder, love, and exploration. It grows in responsibility. It expands through art and contemplation. It is hidden in the daily round of the lives of innumerable good and decent people. It animates the great religious traditions and spiritualities that have formed human history. The movement of this spiritual consciousness is a deep undertow in our embodied existence. Various theologies suggest that consciousness is released to its full range in the experience of death. In our passing from this world, our radical God-orientation is revealed for what it is. Even in "the souls of the damned," however we might conceive of that possibility, the radical God-wardness remains.

Holding to the immediate creation of the soul by God is not a regression to pre-Christian view of things. It is rather a matter of appreciating the depth dimension of creation itself. Embodied in the physical and biological world, the human being is alone summoned, "called forth" into existence by God's immediate creation of each human soul. In each instance, creation is opened to its original and final mystery. Such a perspective leads to a deeper appreciation of the meaning of eternal life. It is not as though God looks down from heaven and decides to save souls. The deepest truth is that everything emanates from the love of God: the world is good, and related to God in a particular way through the human spirit. In the words of Aquinas, "the love of God is [ever] infusing and creating the goodness of reality" (*amor Dei infundens et creans bonitatem in rebus*).[10] Scientists are searching for a "Theory of Everything" (TOE) to explain the immense interactive field of the emergent cosmos. But in the universal domain of God's creation, only the original love of God is the ultimate explanation. It is a love desirous of communicating itself to a creation made capable of receiving it. God creates matter to earth and ground the spiritual, and creates the spirit or soul to render that created universe capable of receiving its crowning gift. Through the dialogical openness inscribed into human existence, the human being emerges as the creature capable of receiving God's ultimate communication.[11]

John Polkinghorne is a theologian eminent in bringing scientific expertise into dialogue with the theological tradition. In his treatment of the soul, he picks up the Thomist point that the soul is the form of the body. In a more contemporary idiom, he modestly, but astutely, suggests that the soul can be understood as the information-bearing pattern perduring through the space-time-energy manifold of the metabolic history of the body.[12] When this link is definitively severed in death, the soul-pattern endures, not as a reality in itself, but only in the memory of God.[13] But such a view seems to lack theological realism. It is not as though God has to remember what he has definitively created in order to reconstitute it in a new form. Divine faithfulness, therefore, does not consist in having a good memory of the personal pattern each one once was, but in actualizing the potential of the already existent spiritual reality that each one is. For the spiritual form of the human person is a God-willed and God-wrought dimension of creation itself. It was always more than a tenuous information-bearing pattern, limited to a particular embodied unit of being. As form, it is intrinsically related to matter, with its specific and individual limitations. But as spirit, it is also intrinsically open to the infinite, so constituted as to express itself in a dialogical relationship with God. Certainly, it informs matter now and in some future mode of embodiment. But, even though incarnate in matter, the soul is the subsisting God-created capacity for dialogue with the Creator. In its God-relatedness, this soul is not reducible to an information-bearing pattern that ceases in death. It is rather a continuing openness, in every phase of human existence, to the infinite mystery. Fundamentally, it is through the soul that creation is made receptive to God, *capax Dei*.

On the other hand, reducing the God-created and God-oriented openness of the human spirit to the capacities of matter has consequences. It can take the form of a crude materialist form of reduction. For example, some might argue that the human being is nothing but a concentration of chemicals, or a particular genetic instance in the wider web of evolving life. The experience of the spiritual dimension would be simply an epiphenomenon of our purely physical-chemical constitution. Soul is merely an ethereal aura explicable in terms of brain waves or particular cerebral states. But there is also a more benign sense of materialist reduction. It is motivated by a concern to give a more holistic sense of the emergence of human consciousness. What is termed "spirit" or "soul" emerges from God's working through the complex biological and evolutionary influences at work in the occurrence of life on this planet. God, in this case, uses finite material agencies to produce the soul and its transcendent capacities. The more traditional conception of the soul being immediately created can be abandoned in the interests of a more holistic sense of divine activity. God "creates" or forms the soul through the mediation of finite, material agencies.[14] Such discussions are usually focused on the extraordinary neural complexity of the human brain, a wonder of nature to an astonishing degree.[15]

OVERLOOKED DATA

Both cases of reduction of the spiritual to the material prove unsatisfactory. If science is limited to what can be seen, weighed, measured, and in some degree controlled, no amount of observation, measurement, and intervention is going to demonstrate a spiritual component—except in the intelligence of those who perform such activities. It would be like saying there are no birds to fly because they are not found on the ocean floor. For spirit and consciousness are of a different order of reality compared to the material. This other dimension is experienced, perhaps in a disconcerting fashion, in the imperative registered in the mind and the heart of even the most materialist-minded scientist. The demands of honesty, truthfulness, thoroughness, and responsibility in the conduct of research are unavoidable. In other words, the drive to understand, the demands of truth and the workings of conscience generally, are not irrelevant data: they form the mind of the scientist at work. This kind of data also demands an explanation, and no amount of computerized calculation and sense-based empirical method offers it.

There can be no argument against the creative Spirit of God working through the mediation of innumerable, finite physical and genetic influences to summon the embodied human person into existence. In that perspective, the critically established findings of the cosmological and evolutionary sciences are entirely acceptable.[16] Unfortunately, Darwinian evolution has been made a feature of a mechanistic narrative rather than contributing to a more refined and subtle understanding of creation and providence. Still, the point remains. While interweaving cosmic and biological factors "cause" the human body, only God creates the soul. The spiritual form, or soul, of the human person, cannot be educed from matter. Nor can matter, in whatever form, however manifold and complex its causality, create spirit. Only the creative Source of both matter and spirit can summon the embodied spiritual person into existence. In this regard, the reality of spirit is not a form of tenuous matter. It belongs to a different order of reality, activity, and relationship. Because of its limitless overture to all truth, goodness, and being, the spiritual soul can be summoned into existence only by the One who is the Truth grounding all truth, the Good from which all goodness flows, the limitless act of "Be-ing" that is the source of all finite being.

We have delayed on this point because any position on the God-created reality of the spirit and soul has important consequences. For instance, the notion of the soul/spirit as immediately created by God is of great relevance to the dialogue with people of faiths and spiritualities different from Christianity. Meeting with the other becomes a moment in the shared experience of being created by and for the infinite mystery that can never be fully named or known. And yet, the spiritual reality of the soul, especially when understood in its intrinsic relationship to matter, opens the way to a richer communication on what hope for the fullness of life might envisage. The idea of the God-created soul suggests the coexistence of all, not only in the wonder of the physical cosmos, but in the transcendent reality of a divine creation. It is not clear how a reductively materialist account of spirit can be related, say, to Buddhist enlightenment, which is beyond all fixation in finite or limited desire. Nor is such a materialist account immediately hospitable to the Hindu notion of self-realization in the infinite bliss of the Brahman, beyond all the appearances of the empirical ego. Likewise, Islam, with its unconditional submission of the self to the will of Allah, testifies to a self-surrender that cannot be conveyed in materialist terms.

This is to say that the multidimensional universe of God's creation is not limited to scientifically observable material universe, for there is the dimension of spirit. This other dimension, however, is not accessible through data of the senses, but relies on another kind of data, that of consciousness. This consciousness expands as we wonder about why there is anything at all, in our unrestricted drive to explore and understand, and in the manner we live under the sway of truth. It is intensified in the manner in which consciousness becomes conscience and feels the burdens of moral responsibility. It finds a special peace, and even joy, in prayer, thanksgiving, and adoration.

CONSCIOUSNESS AND THE BRAIN

The rapidly developing brain science of our day reveals many wonders. Though the human brain is a neuro-physical organ of incredible complexity necessary for our embodiment in the life of this planet, it is not a personal subject. Physically speaking, the brain is an observable organ of a certain size and weight located in the human head. Scientifically speaking, it is a theoretical construct, approachable through different models of experimentation and research. Paradoxically, the brain as such is never directly experienced in consciousness, even when the astonishing reality of its neural networks is being increasingly explored. What is immediately evident to consciousness is the variety of intentional acts (observing, recording, interpreting, imaginative modeling, weighing the evidence, etc.) employed in exploring the reality of the brain. In short, the mystery of the consciousness is more than the brain. Since it would take us too far afield to refer further to mind-brain-body interconnections, we can simply record our agreement with the remark of Sir John Eccles, Nobel Laureate:

> Let us be quite clear that for each of us the primary reality is our consciousness—everything else is derivative and has a second order reality. We have tremendous intellectual tasks in our efforts to understand baffling problems that lie right at the center of our being.[17]

In the compact exploration of "the primary reality of consciousness," explorations can occur in the ascending vector, "from below-upward." Science observes, records, generalizes, and extrapolates from an empirical range of data. In the case in question, the human brain is located within the web of physical, chemical, biological, and genetic factors that govern our embodied existence. Yet, in a critically scientific exploration, there is also the descending vector, "from above downward." In that case, we seek for an explanation of the human spirit and its origins in the transcendent creative causality of God. The soul, however, is the form of the material body, and the body is the cosmic expression of the soul. The brain serves the activity of the spirit, and the spirit calls forth, in a sense, the structure and functioning of the brain. Spirit and matter are interrelated. Matter serves the spirit and finds its highest complexity in union with it. But the spirit needs matter to express itself in a world. The creative Spirit of God, reaching deeper than anything we consider "from below," and operating higher than anything we consider "from above," summons the whole human person into existence.

If, however, the soul is interpreted as a function of matter, then the realm of spirit is closed off from reflection. A comprehensive view is skewed from the beginning. It is constricted to the physical cosmos as we know it in the space-time of the present. If our vision is limited to the material cosmos, then God has either to perform the function of the soul, or to act as some universal principle of potentiality, not unlike an Aristotelian version of prime matter. In contrast, the God of creation is the continuing sustaining source of all that is. The Spirit of God actively works in all causes and conditions of the material and spiritual universe. If the goal of the universe is union with God, the divine mystery must act to create the human soul. If our God-given destiny is to share in the divine life, then the human person must have the spiritual capacity to receive this gift.

Further, not to admit the existence of spiritual reality of the human soul is to live in a peculiarly isolated existence. If human beings are purely material, purely body, then only God is spirit. If, however, the Holy Spirit creates spirit as well as matter, then the way is open to retrieve many aspects of the biblical tradition that have been neglected. For the biblical tradition, and the liturgical consciousness it inspires, assumes that the human is not the only form of spiritual existence. The creativity of the Creator is not exhausted with the human. The universe includes other forms of intelligence, unlimited by matter, namely, the angels. There are, in that understanding of the created universe, innumerable, immaterial spiritual beings, each one of which is a separate species, as Aquinas reasons—since each angelic form is unrestricted and unlimited by matter.[18] In that regard, the angels manifest the superabundant creativity of God and the vast cosmic communion of life in the Spirit.[19] Humanity joins with them in manifesting the infinities of God's creative love. When the sense of creation does not include this other personal dimension of existence, it is impoverished, just as any view of evolutionary biology limited to humans or koalas would be deficient.[20]

Given the size and wonderful productivity of the cosmos, we have often been led to ask, Do we have a big enough notion of God? But once we come to some sense of the infinite creativity of God manifested in the realm of the angels, another question arises. If a whole dimension of created reality is dismissed or repressed—

leaving only the human in possession—we have to ask, Do we have a big enough sense of universe? Not to ask such a question is to leave human self-centeredness in possession, and to be closed to dimensions of the universe manifesting the unimaginable reaches of divine creativity.[21] No finite mind comprehends the whole. Our capacities are always limited, and our knowledge can never be so absolute that no further questions remain.[22] Hence, only through collaboration with countless others. Only when "first" and "third person" meet in "second" person communication—when *I* and *It* are housed in the shared consciousness of the *We*—is the compound activity of knowing complete. Each dimension of experience indicates the necessity of collaboration and the radical open-endedness necessary in the expansion of all knowledge. Knowledge advances, collaboration increases, and genuine progress takes place.

It would be an odd situation, then, to screen out the picture of what is most obvious, namely, the consciousness in which the picture appears in the first place. The phenomenon of consciousness cannot be relegated to the possibility of some future discovery of the interaction between the brain's neurons. Brain science is not conducted by unconscious scientists, for consciousness is taken for granted in scientific investigation as the most obvious datum; and without it, no investigation could proceed or attract attention. Indeed, from a materialist perspective, the denial of the existence of God has a strange parallel in the denial of the existence of the self, together with the phenomenon and range of consciousness![23] After all, the affirmation of the reality of the objective order is the outcome of human creativity in all its modes. It is true that the scientific knowledge of the universe is more than an ensemble of human acts of understanding, and more than the creativity of human minds. But without such acts and such creativity the universe would not be known or further explored.

SELF-TRANSCENDENCE AND OBJECTIVITY

Objectivity can appear as a mythic ideal if one imagines a pure, abstract, objective viewpoint unadulterated by the human subject and abstracted from human consciousness. Critical objectivity is something quite different. On the one hand, any human consciousness that is closed against the demands of objectivity would necessarily collapse into solipsism. The world, however, insistently draws us out of ourselves, and it is only by allowing consciousness to be taken beyond the narrow confines of a habitat that the self can expand to its proper proportions. Aristotle and Aquinas agree that the human soul is in some measure open to everything (in Latin, *anima est quodammodo omnia*). In fact, Aquinas, following Aristotle on this point, finds the objective consideration of nature is a healthy corrective to a diseased or distorted subjectivity. In the "book of creation," he notes that there are so many creatures "that deliver the truth without falsehood. Wherefore Aristotle, when asked whence it was that he had his admirable learning, replied, 'From things which do not know how to lie.'"[24]

But today's challenge is to reappraise the seemingly simple requirement of being objective, so that an integration of the subjective dynamics of the mind with the self-transcending process of being objective can take place. It is not enough to downplay the subjective as the area where, in the judgment of Aristotle, lying is possible, through deceit, bias, or foolishness. It is necessary, therefore, to notice that any objective statement about what is the case is, in fact, the complex outcome of the mind consciously being itself, and going beyond itself in self-transcendence. Intelligence needs to focus on what is given, the *data*, to question what this might mean, to weigh the evidence for this or that possibility, and finally to arrive at a responsible judgment, however qualified it might be. Lonergan's axiom applies: "genuine objectivity is the fruit of authentic subjectivity."[25] Subjectivity is authentic when the subject concerned is present to itself precisely as responding to all the demands of reality. Affirming the truth in any instance presupposes attention to all pertinent data, and, in the process, refining one's sensibilities and vitalizing one's imagination. Then questions arise regarding the possible answers in specific areas of meaning, so on that a reflective intelligence must ponder the emerging evidence if it is to ground a genuinely disinterested judgment. Only by respecting such a process and allowing for each of its components can I take my place as a trustworthy agent in the vast collaborative exercise of illuminating the manifold mystery of existence—and of forming a more human world.

In genuine scientific objectivity, all such activities must be present. But, to repeat, the typically overlooked area of data is not that of the senses—concerning what is heard, seen, handled, tasted, smelled, weighed, and so on—but the data of consciousness itself. This includes especially the consciousness of scientists themselves since they do not go about their work operating as automata, nor are they unconscious of their acts of understanding. Aquinas considered that the human mind knows itself in action: "the human soul understands itself by its understanding, which is its proper act, perfectly demonstrating its power and nature."[26] Eight centuries later, a scientist makes a similar observation:

> We must try once again to experience the human soul as soul, and not just a buzz of bioelectricity; the human will as will, and not just a surge of hormones; the human heart not as a fibrous sticky pump, but as the metaphoric organ of understanding.[27]

There is deep spiritual significance in recovering a sense of the "soul" in the classic philosophic sense. It is the metaphysical expression of human subjectivity in philosophical and religious language.

All this is to say that the question of God can never be satisfactorily raised if science methodically excludes scientists themselves from its considerations. They are not mindless automata, for they have a first-hand experience of their own conscious acts of intelligence and responsible decision. Out of that experience, an intimation of the meaning of God can arise.[28] It will not be an idea of God as a patriarchal projection, nor as a temporary stop gap, nor as a particular cosmic force, nor as primeval matter, nor as a symbol of universal order. Rather, God is the limitless ecstatic intelligence and love that gives rise to the universe, and in which the human mind and heart participate in the knowing and loving of the responsible self. The human mind participates in the light and the love that

God is, as it progressively elucidates what is the case, and grows in responsibility out of concern for what should be.

We can experience God, therefore, in a far more intimate fashion than in the classical form of "demonstrating" or "proving" the divine existence. In this regard, the basic argument in such proofs pivoted on the intelligent conviction that no existent reality, nor all such realities taken together, could be the explanation of why anything or everything actually exists. The objective inexplicability of the actual reality of the world is taken as the starting point for proving the existence of the Creator—the first cause, final end, supreme perfection, and so forth. But there is a limitation in this approach. It does not pose the question of the Creator God intimately enough, for it allows the impression of human existence and consciousness as being that of a spectator. Certainly, the world of reality is considered by the human mind, but as some kind of neutral observer or spectator, watching, as it were, from another realm, and somehow outside the whole emergent process.

In contrast to imagining the universe as a brute objective fact inspected by a neutral spectator, our conscious experiences of observing, imagining, understanding, and valuing are dimensions of the actual universe that includes our conscious selves. Their activities of sensing, imagining, understanding, and judging are the aspects of creation with which we are most familiar, and that make the question of creation freshly and piercingly intimate. What creation is and what the character of the Creator is[29] are questions posed from within our lived existence. The very activity of knowing, and the very fact that everything is in principle intelligible, raise the question of whether there is a boundlessly creative intelligence behind it all, as the ultimate explanation of all our explanations. What is more, the character of the universe is felt in the unqualified attractiveness of the values of truth, goodness, justice, and compassion. By including in our explorations the experience of wondering, knowing, and responsible selves that we are, we arrive at a sense of being beholden to an Other, the source, enablement, and fulfillment of the deepest orientation of our being. We find ourselves, not at the controlling center of the universe, but as participating in its limitless mystery.

To view the universe in a mood of disillusionment and sadness makes it into a sorry world. Fortunately, there is another perspective: photographed from outer space, Earth is revealed as the beautiful blue planet. It breathes an atmosphere in which life in such a variety of forms has flourished. In the expanding immensity of space, Earth glows, for us a tiny homeland in an unimaginably vast universe emerging from a cosmic history of nearly fifteen billion years.

Today we are at a frontier of wonder when it comes to the uncanny character of our planetary existence. To the Psalmist of old, "The heavens are telling the glory of God; and the firmament proclaims his handiwork" (Ps 19:1). Solomon supposed that his contemporaries were "little to be blamed" for revering cosmic powers such as "fire or wind...or the circle of the stars, or turbulent water, or the luminaries of heaven" (Wis 13:2–6). But thunderstorms, the sunlight, moonlight, and starlight, along with the steady glow of the planets, the shimmering Milky Way, are only a tiny fraction of the realities that intrigue the modern mind. For instance, today the glory of the heavens includes newly discovered planets and their satellites. It is estimated that there are one hundred billion stars of the Milky Way in a universe of an estimated hundred billion galaxies. Observations extend to ultraenergetic quasars, to explosive enormous supernovas, even to the space-time rifts of "black holes" and an incalculable amount of "dark matter." Light blazing through space at 300,000 kilometers per second takes 100,000 years just to span our particular galaxy. Our nearest star, Alpha Centauri, is still four light years away. From the quark, with its six variations, to the quasar, it is a universe of incredible proportions.

Today the immeasurably great and the immeasurably small dimensions of physical matter have also to include hitherto unimaginable expanses of time, and within that time, the evolutionary dynamics that have produced the living world. Human consciousness, trembling before the uncanny extent of the more then fourteen-billion-year history of this universe, comes to realize that these thousands of millions of years are, quite literally, the human past. All its seemingly chancy gropings have led to this moment of consciousness in which the uncanny wonder of the universe comes home to us. In the first few seconds of these billions of years of cosmic time, there appeared all the fundamental particles and constants without which life on this seemingly insignificant little planet would have been impossible. The velocity of light, the charge on the electron, the mass of the proton, the constant emissions of energy, are exactly the conditions for life to emerge. A slight difference then would have meant no life now.

With the passage of time and expansion of space and the creativity of human intelligence, human history has now at its disposal enormous energies such as electricity, atomic and solar energy, fossil fuels, and the controlled energy of tides and wind. These were largely hidden to civilizations in the past. Human existence with its computerized calculations and productive capacities is charged with possibilities of making and shaping—or destroying—the world in unimaginably new ways.

More hopefully, our bodies, minds, and hearts can contribute to an awakening cosmic mystery. Paul in his letter to the Romans had a sense of the whole of creation as groaning in one great act of giving birth (Rom 8:22). He saw us human beings as groaning too, for the fulfillment that is not yet. More mysteriously, he understood the creative Spirit of God groaning within us, so as to inspire hopes worthy of the mystery at work (Rom 8:18–28). Against this cosmic background, the prophet's words spring into new life:

> The one who prepared the earth for all time
>   filled it with four-footed creatures;
> the one who sends forth the light, and it goes;
>   he called it, and it obeyed him, trembling;
> the stars shone in their watches, and were glad;
>   he called them, and they said, "Here we are!"
> They shone with gladness for him who made them.
> This is our God;
>   no other can be compared to him. (Bar 3:32–35)

To be caught up in a mysterious cosmos so immense, so finely balanced in all its proportions, raises a question for believers in God. Is our idea of God big enough, wonderful enough, to be worthy of the mystery described by Paul as that in which "we live and move and have our being" (Acts 17:28)?

In the Judeo-Christian tradition, art is barely comprehensible save as a kind of ancillary creation within divine creation. For instance, it is not so much here that a theology of creation is related in one way or another to the poetic imagination, but that poetry is a kind of theological act. The words of Sir Arthur Eddington in his *The Nature of the Physical World* point to a larger view that deserves its own exploration:

> We all know that there are regions of the human spirit untrammelled by the world of physics. In the mystic sense of the creation around us, in the expression of art, in yearning toward God, the soul grows upward and finds the fulfilment of something implanted in its nature. The sanction for this development is within us, a striving born with consciousness of an Inner Light proceeding from a greater power than ours. Science can scarcely question this sanction, for the pursuit of science springs from a striving which the mind is impelled to follow, a questioning that will not be suppressed.[30]

If the consciousness of the human subject is bypassed or suppressed, it is, in effect, banished from the known universe. The wonder of knowing the world and participating in its unfolding is not accessible. As a result, to speak of God in terms of an all-luminous conscious act of self-possession, and to refer to human minds as sharing in that consciousness, must appear irrelevant. The assumption takes hold that an unconscious universe is unconsciously produced and peopled with irrelevantly conscious subjects. To allow oneself to be numbered among this unconscious population is to feel oneself a stranger in the universe—haunting rather than inhabiting it—and unable to allow the universe to become luminous to itself in the human mind, heart, and imagination.

The topic of creation is, then, an area where deep methodological questions reside concerning the collaborative character of human knowledge as it touches on a hitherto "absent frontier." Is there a way of respecting the whole range of the human exploration of meaning? There is no point in talking about creation and the Creator of all (including the human mind and heart) if some of the data are declared inadmissible, above all, when the *datum*, the "given," of our own conscious selves if ignored. After all, we are each alive, conscious, pushed, pulled, and immersed in a world of daily meaning, communication, and responsibility. In that world, love brings forth what is best in our lives, just as beauty in art or nature continually refreshes our perceptions of the uncanny gift of existence.

Though no one denies the value of scientific research, there is no need to accept that reality in all its forms and dimensions is knowable only through exclusively scientific methods as these are currently understood and practiced. Scientific exploration must be located in a larger field of human experience and exploration. Indeed, a theology of creation provides a spacious background in which all diverse human creativities can improvise their variations on the theme of truth and goodness as contributing to the great symphony of reality. The scientist and philosopher Michael Polanyi points to the manifold and dynamic structure of human knowing. He suggests possibilities of generous collaboration among science, philosophy, and theology—even if that remains a remote ideal:

> Admittedly, religious conversion commits our whole person and changes our whole being in a way that an expansion of our natural knowledge does not do. But once the dynamics of knowing are recognised as the dominant principle of knowledge, the difference appears only as one of degree. It establishes a continuous ascent from our less personal knowing of inanimate matter to our convivial knowing of living beings and beyond this to knowing our responsible fellow men. Such, I believe, is the true transition from the sciences to the humanities, and also from our knowing the laws of nature to our knowing the person of God.[31]

To admit, therefore, different degrees or levels of increasingly convivial and personal knowing is to experience the question of God inscribed into the self-transcending dynamics of human existence. It helps frame questions as to the creativity inherent in human culture, cosmic emergence, and biological evolution. For instance, in the human world, what has enabled the chaos of atoms and molecules, of life forms and consciousness, of relationships and processes, to enter into our awareness at this present moment?[32]

GOD EVER CREATING

Creation is a verb. It is not immediately understood as the product, but as the action of the Creator. For theological or philosophical reasons, we might propose that creation is an original and continuing divine activity. It may be imagined, therefore, as a rather superior kind of doing something. The essential jolt to this imaginative fallacy is traditionally supplied by the addition of a mysterious little phrase: God creates "out of nothing," *ex nihilo sui et subjecti*. The divine creative act presupposes nothing already in existence—no raw material, no chain of events, no previous dispositions.[33] God is not conditioned by anything outside God. There is nothing already *there*, already in existence, existing before or beyond God's creative act. The imagination, however devout, tends to represent God as the biggest actor in a world of doers and movers. It tends to place God, perhaps like a big angel or at least as a particular agent, within a cosmos of causes, principles, and particular energies.

In contrast, God's creating is not as one category of causing or doing or deciding, but is a transcendent, unimaginable mode of causing everything to be and to act. Consequently, the Creator acts in the acting of everything, and causes in the causality of every agent.[34] Such a notion of creation strains the imagination. We need to recognize that we are dealing with radical mystery, unlike anything in the world of doing and causing. God is, indeed, the ungraspable ground and energy of all being and acting. To appreciate that requires a deeper reflection on the notion of God.

It is tempting to try and discuss creation without using the time-(dis?)honored word, *God*. Indeed, the biblical and philosophical traditions that have formed Christian understanding of creation know other terms. For example, we have the Word, Light, Spirit, Source, Life, Love, Be-ing (note, a *verb*, as in the Thomistic, *Ipsum Esse*—literally, "Sheer *To-Be*"), limitless Act (i.e., the *Actus Purus* of Western philosophic tradition), ultimate reality, the font of being, the final good, the first cause, and many others. Often discussion is blocked by the emotional fixations, imaginative distortions, and conceptual straightjackets with which a variety of cultural conflicts have imbued this one word, *God*. Nonetheless, we must persevere with it. After all, it does not let us escape from the unredeemed elements in our history. Nonetheless, other terms are available. In dealing with the mystery that transcends human language, we need, as far as possible, to keep in play the whole vocabulary, while maintaining the reverent restraint so characteristic of the Jewish tradition in which the personal name of God, *YHWH*, was seldom pronounced.

The real problem, however, is not with words, be they marks on a page or vibrations of sound. It resides, rather, in how these terms are used, and in what they are supposed to mean. For the believer, the first and fundamental notion of God is found in an orientation to that limitless, living fullness of being and goodness that, in the deepest sense of the traditional term, alone can "save our souls." In more contemporary language, this intimation of God is as the ultimate Other who is the point of homecoming for the human journey. The meaning of God is, as it were, progressively anticipated in the human search, an attraction toward the ultimate and absolute meaning of truth, beauty, goodness, love, and mercy, as we human beings reach beyond ourselves, outward and upward, to what the world cannot give. The experience of faith is concentrated at that point when the history of human search is met with a divine self-disclosure. To believe in this way is to recognize that God is not indifferent to our seeking, but is in fact its source—as is revealed in the words of the prophets, in the wisdom of the holy ones, in word of Sacred Scriptures, in the coming of Christ. The meaning of *God* is forged within the furnace of history as idolatrous projections are undermined, and the demons that infest individuals or societies are exorcised.[35] But more than anything else, the meaning of *God* comes as a gift, indeed as a self-giving on the part of the Creator. It is marked with a particular excess when the divine Word became flesh and dwelt among us in such a way as to enter into our suffering humanity. Though God may "mean the world" to the believer, words necessarily fail in the effort to express such an event, for all human words are subject to an unending process of translation. Faith might use sensory language to name, in some analogical manner, how it sees or hears or touches or tastes the reality of God. In self-surrender and adoration, however, faith might cultivate a vivid sense of the unknown, ever attractive mystery. In prayer, God is the silence in which all words fall away, the darkness where our brightest ideas fade in the radiance of the Light, and the all-welcoming Love in which our restless hearts come home. If words can be spoken, God is first of all the invocable, all-relational *You*, before the third-person objectifications of the divine in terms of *It* or *He* come into play.

Not to recognize the anticipatory, ongoing character of the meaning of *God* makes dialogue with the reverently agnostic all but impossible, be they scientists or meditative searchers. The result is all too often a collision of congealed concepts and a struggle between disciplines defending their respective borders. In such a rival situation, the scientifically enunciated version of reality is deemed to be sophisticated, while the religious account is considered naive. This, I believe, is the problem that continually crops up in the confrontation between the materialist creed of reductive scientism and the religious creeds of unthinking faith. At the very least, believers must bear in mind the healthy biblical agnosticism that admits that God is not yet seen face-to-face, and that God "no one has ever seen" (John 1:18). Even though God is the object of our love and faith and hope, the mystery is disclosed only in a progressive darkness.[36] With the shattering of our idols, be they erected by feelings, the need for security, or intellectual systems of thought, faith inspires a naked surrender to the original and ultimate mystery so as neither to grasp or contain it.

There is another pertinent point. Believers speak of creation because, however obscurely, they have come to have some notion of the One who alone can create. Admittedly, in the religious case, there is a certain undifferentiated affirmation of Creator and creation before philosophical, historical, or scientific questions are asked. As contexts develop, the creation question is framed to meet the demands of different mentalities evident in all the varieties of philosophy and psychology, scientific method or aesthetic sensibilities, evolutionary biology, and quantum physics. If faith is to seek further understanding, it has to move through many contexts and encounter many such different mentalities if, in the end, it is to grow to its full intellectual, ethical, and spiritual potential.

Those who have attained a highly theoretical or scientific mentality approach the question of the explanation of the universe in a form quite different from those who have, say, a specifically spiritual or religious standpoint. These latter tend to pose the question in terms of a prior faith in order to seek further understanding of how God is, acts, and is revealed in the manifold of a created universe. Scientists, as scientists, however, pursue their explorations by way of experiment, extrapolation, and hypothesis, by concentrating on a particular and tightly controlled band of data in, say, physics or biology. Science focuses on the most probable explanation of the data under consideration, in the expectation of arriving at a more comprehensive explanation. The experience of searching is so vivid to the scientific mentality that scientists might find themselves suggesting that religious believers must wait on their determinations before any belief in creation or the Creator can be judged legitimate. By implication, only when all the evidence is in, can the God of some philosophical, theological, or aesthetic tradition be reasonably affirmed.

The features of an inevitable and confusing clash of views are clear. Those who freely adore the ultimate mystery disclosed to their faith as the source and goal of all, are dismissed as "simple believers," conventionally religious because they know no better. On the other hand, believers who might legitimately rejoice in an intimacy with the divine Ground of creation can often lag behind, especially in scientific matters. Through lack of leisure, or training or commitment, to say nothing of suspicion, fear, or laziness, they can be unfamiliar with the explorative value of thought, be it in science or theology. To them, a religious sense of creation is in danger of being replaced by some purely human method, from whose esoteric procedures they are barred. They might feel that the universal reach of faith is being made to yield a sophisticated elite presiding over the secrets of the universe. Believers can feel pressured, therefore, to become less believing in God, and to give more credence to the current assertions of science.

A dialogical, collaborative attitude on the part of all is clearly necessary. After all, over a century ago, the 1913 edition of the *Catholic Encyclopedia* serenely observed,

> The gist of the theory of evolution as a scientific hypothesis...is in perfect agreement with the Christian conception of the universe; for Scripture does not tell us in what form the present species of plants and of animals were originally created by God.[37]

We can be grateful for the philosophical component in Catholic tradition. Protestant Christians, entirely admirable in the commitment of faith, cannot avoid a certain sense of crisis when faith suddenly begins to give rise to metaphysical and epistemological questions. We must wonder at the extent to which the neglect of the following biblical remark on different kinds of wisdom has left religious thought somewhat impoverished and awkward when it comes to face the great evolutionary and cosmic questions of our own day. The biblical sage reflects on different kinds of wisdom. For some, the "scientists" of the day

> were unable from the good things that are seen to know the one who exists,
> nor did they recognize the artisan while paying heed to his works;
> but they supposed that either fire or wind or swift air
> or the circle of the stars, or turbulent water,
> or the luminaries of heaven were gods that rule the world.
> If through delight in the beauty of these things people assumed them to be gods,
> let them know how much better than these things is their Lord,
> for the author of beauty created them.

> And if people were amazed at their power and working,
> let them perceive from them
> how much more powerful is the one who formed them.
> For from the greatness and beauty of created things
> comes a corresponding perception of their Creator.
> Yet these people are little to be blamed,
> for perhaps they go astray
> while seeking God and desiring to find him.
> For while they live among his works, they keep searching,
> and they trust in what they see, because the things that are
> seen are beautiful.
> Yet again, not even they are to be excused;
> for if they had the power to know so much
> that they could investigate the world,
> how did they fail to find sooner the Lord of these things?
> (Wis 13:1–9)

Today "the good things that are seen" have been immeasurably extended. The magnitude of the energies and the infinitesimal intricacies of pattern and design are so fascinating, and so subversive of former visions of reality, that scientific language verges on the religious and the poetic in its effort to express the numinous value of the cosmos it celebrates. For on a purely scientific level a new enchantment with the beauty and wonder of the cosmos is apparent. Little wonder that there are those who feel they have discovered "the gods that rule the world." In comparison, the God of traditional faith seems little more than a naive projection.

Whatever the case, we find ourselves in an exuberant Babel of languages. Different mindsets and different methods seek to name the ultimate. Those concerned for a more holistic or integrated approach try to overcome the crude disjunction of scientific and religious perspectives. Still, the biblical sage graciously admits that those who confuse the wonders of creation with the wonder of the Creator are "little to be blamed." Genuine exploration keeps moving on. The real wonder of the world inspires confidence in the beauty, complexity, and sheer uncanniness of it all, experienced as an invitation to keep searching into the ultimate explanation of all explanations.

And yet there remains the possibility of stopping short: "how did they fail to find sooner the Lord of these things?" Further questioning can be silenced with all the versions, both ancient and modern, of the late Carl Sagan's creedal proclamation: "The cosmos—as known by science—is all there is, all there was, and all there will be."[38] Likewise, the bleaker confession of the geneticist, Jacques Monod, commented, "The ancient covenant is in pieces: man at last knows that he is alone in the unfeeling immensity of the universe out of which he emerged only by chance."[39] Yet, for others, the promise of further searching is evident. The eminent physicist, Werner Heisenberg, wrote,

> Although I am convinced that scientific truth is unassailable in its own field, I never found it possible to dismiss the content of religious thinking....Thus, in the course of my life, I have been repeatedly compelled to ponder on the relationship of these two regions of thought.[40]

A NEW COLLABORATION

It would be less strange to the biblical sage than to the modern materialist thinker to witness the recent tendency of scientists to rehabilitate the question of God within the realm of science in order to explain the uncanny design of the universe. Paul Davies, for example, is a leading popularizer of this shift:[41] He writes, "It may seem bizarre, but, in my opinion, science offers a surer path to God than religion."[42] The "bizarre" character of such an assertion is more perceptible to the modern scientist than to the most venerable philosophical tradition of the West. As Etienne Gilson remarks, himself quoting the scientist Louis de Broglie,

> "The great marvel in the progress of science is that it reveals to us a certain concordance between our thought and things, a certain possibility of grasping, by means of the resources of our intelligence and the rules of our

reason, the profound relations existing among phenomena....One cannot but be astounded enough at the fact that some science is possible." If one thinks that philosophers have been amazed at this since the time of Plato at least, that is to say, more than twenty centuries, these words take on unexpected meaning and relief. They mark the moment when science itself recognises the mystery which lies over its existence. The fact is even more worthy of mention in that L. de Broglie's remark joins that of Einstein, "the most unintelligible thing on the subject of the world is that it is intelligible."[43]

Davies's "bizarre" sense of the disclosive possibilities of science comes as the result of his unwitting discovery of a whole philosophical tradition stemming from Plato (the *Timaeus*), and Aristotle (his *Physics* and *Metaphysics*). And, though medieval theological tradition would admit a whole range of complex distinctions between knowing God by reason and assenting to the divine mysteries in faith, its peculiar brand of hardy intellectualism would not be amazed by what Professor Davies had to say. There were a variety of medieval efforts to "demonstrate the existence of God" from the fact, the structure, the movement of the world of our experience. In that tradition, every created being exhibited a "vestige" of the divine.[44] More surprising to the post-Newtonian science of today, the scientific approach to God accords with the conviction of Newton himself in the twenty-eighth query at the end of the *Opticks*: "The main Business of natural Philosophy is to argue from Phaenomena without feigning Hypotheses, and to deduce Causes from Effects, till we come to the very first Cause, which certainly is not Mechanical."[45]

Admittedly, there is a certain limitation in searching into "the mind of God" (as Paul Davies and others had done) with no consideration of the relevance of love, death, values, ethics, art, grace, or the possibilities of a self-revelation on the part of the Creator. Then, too, there is the problem of evil. The mind of God cannot be explored with complete profit if the mind of the explorer is mathematically inured against the evil and violence—as either suffered or caused—that afflict the human condition. A purely scientific or mathematical exploration can look like a sophisticated way of escaping from the most radical issues in our lived existence. The more dramatically people are exposed to the tragedy and wonder of life, the more they are tempted to dismiss exclusively mathematical explorations of God as the productions of autistic savants.

But it need not be so. The very fact that so much of the cosmos is found to be profoundly intelligible and so elegantly beautiful, luminous with that *splendor entis*, that "radiance of being" of which Aquinas speaks, invites the mind into its ultimate adventure: an exploration of the original mystery of it all. But there is a gently insistent question: "If they had the power to know so much...how did they fail to find sooner the Lord of all things?" Judith Wright, from her experience of the world of nature, points forward:

> My search is further.
> There's still to name and know
> beyond the flowers I gather,
> the one that does not wither –
> the truth from which they grow.[46]

These lines evoke a beautiful expression of medieval wisdom:

> Creatures, as far as in them lies, do not turn us away from God but lead to God. If they do turn us away..., that is due to those who, through their own fault, use them in ways that are contrary to reason.[47]

At this point, let us sample something of the classic medieval account of the meaning of creation. In many ways, it is a surprising resource. In *Summa Contra Gentiles*,[48] Aquinas asks whether the consideration of creatures is useful for the enlightenment of faith. His third reason is most fully expressed:

> The consideration of creation sparks in the human soul a love for the divine goodness. Whatever goodness and perfection is spread out in different creatures, it is a

> totality brought wholly together in the One who is in the source of all goodness....If therefore the goodness, the beauty and the delicacy [literally, *suavitas*] of creatures so lures the human soul, the source-good of God himself, diligently compared to the streams of goodness in the variety of creatures, inflames and attracts totally to itself our human souls.

To search the world of creation is to find that no creature is independent in its existence—a "stand-alone" explanation of itself—and that no element of our world is "the first cause" of everything. Yet there is a precious particularity in the need to value the variety of created realities within the englobing mystery of existence, and to receive it as a gift. According to this medieval vision, the variety of creation radiates from the one inexhaustible divine origin:

> For what exists in the cause in utter simplicity, is realised in the effect in a composite and pluriform manner....It is fitting, then, that there be a multiplicity and variety in created things so that God's image be found in them perfectly in accord with their mode of being.[49]

The being and variety of creation are aspects of the totality of the Creator's gift. We must emphasize that God's love is not first attracted toward something already existing. Rather, everything, inasmuch as it exists, is loved into existence by the divine freedom. Creation, in that perspective, is enacted as a communication of the divine joy in the existence of what is other. It is sheer gift: "Good is diffusive of itself" (*Bonum est diffusivum sui*). The universe, therefore, is to be contemplated as a divinely chosen differentiated totality. It is not a kind of necessary emanation from, or completion of, a remote deity. In all its variety and connectedness, and, we might add, in its evolutionary potential, the created universe is a communication from the heart of God.

The stable world of particular natures linked in a great chain of being, as envisaged in the classic medieval vision, differs from the evolutionary universe of today. In contemporary thinking, the whole is a process before it is an ordered collection of particular natures. But here, I think, two remarks might be made. First, we can share in Aquinas's serene delight in the specific value of each element of creation as loved into being. Each being serves to manifest the divine goodness in a particular way. To that degree, such a vision mitigates the cosmic sadness pervading an uncritical evolutionary myth that reads like an obituary for the casualties of evolution. The fittest survived; the weakest did not; and even what survives is subjected to the blind, harsh law that values only the future. In contrast, the medieval vision, even while it leaves unknown the mysterious ways of providence, finds an existential value in things simply because they exist—or once existed in a certain way at a certain time. It is a reminder to those who would hurry to frame the laws of evolution to take two considerations into account. First, each individual entity is a world of mystery in the sheer fact of its existence. Before it can be considered a link in the chain of evolution, or as an aspect of the larger emerging complexity, it is, or was, *there*! The evolutionary potential—or lack of it—of the *Marella splendens*, or of any of eighty thousand extraordinarily complex creatures unearthed in the Burgess Shale in Western Canada, does not evacuate the fundamental wonder of its existence in the play and contingency of what once happened.[50] The unique existence of the individual entity is so often "the missing link" in evolutionary thinking. Second, the seemingly purposeless variety of what once existed or is existing in its unique manner should make us wary of any premature closure on the whole story of what is going on. The human mind is not a detached spectator, but is part of the emerging process. Our reconstructions and extrapolations, whatever the progress of science, access only fragments of the meaning of the whole process. The Thomist emphasis on the necessary plurality of creation and on the value of each existent not only contests the simplicity of evolutionary myths but serves to keep evolutionary theory attentive to a truly inclusive wholeness. The system must remain open. The full story awaits, in patience and tentative exploration, the full understanding of creation that resides only in the Creator.

While so much has changed as knowledge has expanded, we mention again that in the biblical vision of creation, other and higher forms of life were presumed. Their presence is now largely mediated to us only through icons and religious art, and in the various liturgical prefaces in which the assembly is invited to join with "angels and archangels, cherubim and seraphim" in a cosmic hymn of praise. At least to evoke that largely forgotten biblical dimension of the cosmos suggests a more wonderful view of the living universe than that of a flat materialist anthropocentrism. The cosmic feelings and symbols of solidarity with all that is both below and above our form of life cannot but promote a greater awe and fresh questioning in the presence of so much that is still unknown. While the realm of created suprahuman intelligence is largely ignored even in current theological preoccupations, it still has a suggestive power. It functions at least as a symbol of dimensions of reality that have yet to be considered in our efforts to understand the commonwealth of life and the community of consciousness in the universe of our present perceptions.

The classical way of affirming the reality of creation led to a more or less contemplative disclosure of the necessary existence of the Creator. That comparatively simple way of philosophical contemplation yields today to controlled experiment and brilliant mathematical hypotheses deduction. The enormous intricacy of the "how" of the emergent process of the physical world seeks intelligibility in "Theories of Everything." These are elaborated as all-embracing mathematical schemes amalgamating all the fundamental forces and particles of physics together with the structure of space and time. Compared to such, the philosophical tradition looks vague and amateurish—until one realizes that many scientists are themselves loath to allow their own disciplines to pretend to a universal competence. Others, on the contrary, enclose the intelligibility of the universe in some great container of mere facticity. The universe simply happens to be what it is; and that is that, requiring no deeper explanation. To appeal to an ultimate, let alone divine principle of explanation, looks suspiciously like a new version of "the God of the gaps." It is crucial then to return to the point: God is not the missing factor in a mathematical or physical account of the way things are, but the all-engendering mystery inherent of all that is and the Light in which the human mind participates in order to make the universe luminous to itself.

As the Irish Dominican priest Herbert McCabe perceptively observed, past efforts to prove the existence of God were an implicit affirmation of the validity of scientific research.[51] There are interesting parallels in the experience of art.[52] The God question is a way of insisting that there can never be a finished explanation of everything. We exist, as it were, in an open system within a limitless expanse of mystery. Our explorations, be they intellectual, moral, or artistic, occur within the universe, to converge in different ways on the original and ultimate question implicit in the dynamism of knowing everything and anything. However relative or provisional, the inexhaustible excess of meaning implied in all meaning, and the search for the sufficient reason of all our relative sufficient reasons, preclude any scientific or philosophical totalitarianism.

An affirmation of God is born out of the radical questionability of the world. It is not a matter of coming to know more about the universe, except in the sense of recognizing its emergence from an incomprehensible fullness of Be-ing, life, and goodness.[53] God does not exist, therefore, within the world as a part, or an aspect, of what is. The universe exists in the boundless ocean of divine communicative Be-ing. The universe of limited beings derives from essential Being, while each being possesses its own act of being, and thus stands forth from nothingness. To affirm that the cosmos or nature is God's creation is to set the whole of our actual and potential experience of the world in a field of mystery, of supermeaning, of gift, transcendent freedom, and purpose. This perspective makes space for the presence of the Creator, the all-embracing, all-originating mystery. God is "removed" from any intraworldly system or function because the limitless Be-ing of God, its sheer "To-Be," is not a specific instance of some generic form of being.[54] This insight allows the reality of creation to be what it is, with its own laws, processes, and independent being. When there is no confusion of the Creator with creation, creation is given to us to explore, even while the mind and heart that do the exploring are themselves dimensions of that one creation.

God, from this point of view, is as Macquarrie writes, "Be-ing that lets beings be." God is more intimately present to each and every existent reality than it is to itself. Aquinas explains,

> God is present in all things, but not as part of their nature, nor as a modification of their being, but in the way something which acts is in contact with what it acts upon....Since God is by nature sheer Be-ing, it must be he who causes being in creatures as his characteristic effect...God has this effect on created realities not only when they first begin to be, but as long as they are kept in being, as light is caused in the air by the sun as long as the air remains illuminated. So, for as long as anything is, God must be present to it in the way that it has being. But "to-be" [*esse*] is that which is the most intimate to each thing, and what most profoundly inheres in all things: everything else about any reality is potential compared to "to be." So God must be in everything, and in the most interior way.[55]

When the being of the creature is understood in the process of becoming, we have the modern form of the doctrine of continuous creation. In the words of the theologian Denis Edwards,

> Theology affirms that what enables the creature to be what it is, and enables it to become more than it is in itself, is the power of active self-transcendence, which is the pressure of the divine being acting upon creation from within....Evolutionary change is empowered by the dynamic presence of the absolute being of God. Evolutionary change occurs because of the presence of transforming love, which continually draws creation to a surprising and radically new future from within.[56]

Edwards is here invoking the evolutionary perspective of Karl Rahner. Though it might seem foreign to the classical medieval tradition, it can be understood, not so much opposed to the classic tradition, but as completing it. We need not pretend that the Scholastics had any familiarity with the contemporary evolutionary model of reality. Still, there is a precious insight to be found in Thomist thinking, namely, that created autonomy does not set the creature against the Creator, but is a deeper manifestation of the creative presence of God. The more autonomous and self-transcendent a created reality, the more intimate the presence of the Creator to it. In other words, the Creator truly gives being, and the completion of that gift is its power to act. If the modern evolutionary optic sees a self-transcending surplus or excess in the emergent process of the world, that does not diminish the creative presence of God, but manifests it more fully. As Aquinas pithily notes, "To detract from the perfection of the creature is to detract from the perfection of the divine power."[57]

Atheistic positions are seldom a rejection of God in the terms we have been employing here. The special antipathy that the nonbeliever feels is focused on premature and often naive religious or philosophical descriptions of God. If these suggest a smug religious answer suppressing intelligent questioning, the antipathy is intensified. When the devout mind naively proclaims God simply as a big (male) person, or as a disappointed manager of human affairs, or as the cosmic architect, or as the clockmaker who has slightly overwound his artifacts, or as the superforce in the cosmic process, things appear as all too simple.

In the current evolutionary context, how should we think of God? One eminent philosopher makes a theologically instructive remark:

> To speculate creatively and imaginatively as to what the "personality" or "character" must be like of a Creator in whose image this astonishing universe of ours is made, with its prodigal abundance of energy, its mind-boggling complexity yet simplicity, its fecundity of creative spontaneity, its ever surprising fluid interweaving of order and chance, law and apparent chaos, and so forth. Must not the personality of such a Creator be charged not only with unfathomable wisdom, power and exuberant generosity, but also with dazzling "imaginative" creativity—might we say a daring Cosmic Gambler who delights in working out his providence by a creative synthesis of both law and order, on the one hand, and chance, risk,

> spontaneity, on the other—a "coincidence of opposites" as St. Bonaventure put it long ago?[58]

How might a more realistic and reverent dialogue between representatives of different disciplines be conducted? The following words are something of a Christian protocol for entering and promoting such dialogue, which allows that science can purify religion from error and superstition, while religion can purify science from idolatry and false absolutes. Each can draw the other into a wider world, a world in which both can flourish:

> The vitality and significance of theology for humanity will in a profound way be reflected in its ability to incorporate these findings....The matter is urgent. Contemporary developments in science challenge theology far more deeply than did the introduction of Aristotle into Western Europe in the thirteenth century....Christians will inevitably assimilate the prevailing ideas about the world, and today these are deeply shaped by science. The only question is whether they will do this critically or unreflectively, with depth and nuance or with a shallowness that debases the Gospel and leaves us ashamed before history.[59]

Philosophy, accordingly, has an essential mediating role in any dialogue on the basic questions we have been touching on. Philosophers, at least those familiar with the classic tradition, will recall the originally Aristotelian notion of "prime matter," that universal passive potency enabling a variety of forms to be "educed," which allows for the possibilities of change in any given entity.[60] "Prime matter" is, of course, not "matter" at all, for any matter we know is already informed and specified in some way. But this fundamental potentiality, even if it can only be understood in a negative fashion once it exists as "informed" in some way, is a principle of the contingent universe. It is possible that Einstein hit on something of this kind with his famous formula of $E=mc^2$, so that "matter" is, as it were, the "form" of a fundamental universal potency, "energy," to which it can return and be reshaped in other ways. It could be that Aristotle and Einstein have more in common than we usually think. By daring to explore their agreement and divergence, a comprehensive philosophy of science may well take a huge step in clarifying the emergent properties and evolutionary dynamics of our world.

In the meantime, there are challenging philosophic questions concerning the causality involved in the emergence of the higher from the lower. Take the evolution of different entities in the nonliving universe. It might be that all that is needed is the range of potentiality inherent in the original cosmic event, while this is gradually revealed in its full active potency. Things get trickier when we turn to the emergence of subhuman life. How does inanimate physical-chemical matter leap into sentience or sensitive consciousness? Does not this entail a further increment of potentiality somehow given from outside the physical-chemical system? Then the evolution of the human, above all the human brain with its trillion neuronal connections, is a wonderful problem in itself. But the sticking issue is the origin of the human soul, which both Aristotle and Aquinas regarded as "somehow all things": *anima est quodammodo omnia*. It brings another dimension into the universe—the universe conscious of itself, exploring itself in the human mind, and for that matter, celebrating itself in the human heart and imagination, so that, to quote Goethe again, the human is the first conversation that nature holds with God, its Creator. Philosophical and theological questions take us to the limits. But to the philosophers we must turn for some radical answers. Apart from the recurrent ideological resistance to the creative causality of God, especially on the part of biologists, appealing to the power of the mysterious "whole" to bring everything about seems evasive. Is it simply a way to forbid us thinking beings to think and to look for sufficient reasons? Still, I am not suggesting a return to a deistic notion in which the first cause sets up the universe to unfold as it will. Nor am I suggesting that sense of intelligent design in which God is pretty much like a big angel, intervening now and then and pushing things along in a certain direction when they are in danger of losing their way. However we account for the wonder and complexity of the universe, the way forward must conceive of the Creator's causality as transcending all modes of finite causation, respecting the seemingly chaotic randomness of the whole process, yet providentially working in them all to achieve an end that is evident only to infinite Intelligence.

Theology waits on the revelation of truth, and so needs to learn. Theological reflection relies on its faith-based data concerning what the ultimate purpose of creation might be. The horizon of Christian theology is determined by the love of God incarnate in Christ, crucified and risen, and the Spirit laboring through the whole groaning universe (Rom 8:18) to lead us to life eternal.[61] But to be a theologian is not to come to the end of questions, especially when faced with cosmic and evolutionary questions. These not only challenge faith to give an account of itself, but also to learn something more, and more worthy, from whatever source, of how God acts and what God is like. Then again, neither does the classic Darwinian scheme fit the Newtonian ideal when so much of the data enabling rigorous scientific prediction and explanation is lacking. Knock-down verification through experiment is not possible! Predictability is an issue: we do not have particle accelerators the size of the universe, nor the capacity to collect a few million planets like earth and observe their behavior over a few billion years. Nor, indeed, can God be called upon to perform an experiment for us. Further, there is a debate within science itself. If Newtonian regularity is the ideal, then some versions of more sophisticated "intelligent design" can never be science in this Newtonian sense even when faced with the amazing emergence of the cosmic conditions that make life and even human life possible on this planet. Then again, neither does the classic Darwinian scheme fit the Newtonian ideal when so much of the data enabling rigorous scientific prediction and explanation is lacking. What then is true science when faced with the contingencies of cosmic and biological emergence? At every point in such a debate, whether admitted or not, the participants are forced into profound philosophical questions if they are to get beyond impressions to exploration—and a new understanding.[62]

Undoubtedly, post-Darwinian science represents a paradigm shift in its focus on the dynamics of evolution. Traditional science and philosophy were habituated to thinking of things and their natural development along the lines of universally applicable laws of cause and effect. But that approach is now faced with another kind of data that can be approached only through statistical probabilities of random emergence. The old world of metaphysical or scientific "necessity" now yields to a world of contingencies and more complex types of causality. This is characterized by levels of interactive upward and downward influences within the whole and its parts. A dynamic field of interaction includes subatomic particles, atoms, molecules, enzymes, genes, cells, organisms, individuals, phyla, the biosphere and the emergent cosmos itself, and the "strange attractors" that entice each process to develop in a particular way. The old simplicity is lost. Faced with this apparent chaos of influences, attractions, and interactions, scientific theory attempts to recognize the complexities involved—as does any philosophical version of emergent probability (such as Bernard Lonergan's) in an attempt to make some sense of the multileveled interacting schemes involved. Philosophers, being themselves conscious and intelligent human beings, are themselves part of cosmic, biological, and human patterns of emergence that include hierarchies of innumerable systems. The higher integrations that have occurred look beyond mere survival to something more: what that is, how and why it is, become appropriate questions to ask, even as the contingency of the cosmos and biological life is revealed as stupefyingly "iffy" and contingent.[63] Fundamentalist ideologies of one kind or another—scientific or religious—try to blunt the edge of this new sense of contingency and randomness by insisting on comparatively simple small-scale cause-effect explanations. Such an outlook suggests a sense of a divinely imposed order and direction—lest the cosmic process lose its way.

However, the mystery of divine causality within the emergence of reality and the evolution of living things is increasingly strange in regard to a slow, graduated pattern of biological emergence. A multiplicity of perspectives is necessary if any holistic understanding is to be possible. This is a great opportunity for philosophy to come into its own regarding the explanatory power of science, especially when issues of morality arise—both for scientists themselves and for the world at large. Philosophy must have some responsibility in distinguishing among data, models, and scientific paradigms, and the epistemology involved in relation to metaphysics, objectivity, probability, truth, and so forth.

Questions remain. Given the scientific data on the evolutionary emergence of more complex and higher life forms from simpler and lower beings, how can this be metaphysically intelligible without violating the causal axiom that states that no effect can be greater than its cause? What is the sufficient reason for this progressive emergence? Is the intervention of some higher cause needed, from outside the previously given system? And if such is needed, from what source does it come?

For all the technological achievements of our age, the human imagination today inevitably tends to be structured along mechanistic lines, as though everything were in one way or another a big machine.[64] Science has its glories, but to limit the exploration of reality to the exploration of the material entities only, and only by means of empirical scientific methods, results in the intelligence operating in a shrinking universe. The universe is rendered inhospitable to the presence of consciousness, mind, values, person, art, and faith. The presumption is that what cannot be explored by scientific methods does not exist. Or, in another way of putting it, reality is limited to the limits of the usual array of scientific empirical methods.[65] An originally limited methodology comes to believe that it has exhausted all reality. There lies the peculiar quality of modern materialistic atheism—an all-but mystical reduction of all reality to available empirical data.[66] A narrowly scientific methodology had the sorry effect of leaving out the experience and activity of the scientists themselves. The refined precision of the empirical method, when unwilling to face the metaphysical commitments and questions implicit in its own procedure sees its intelligence atrophy within a wonder-free, flatly mechanistic view of reality. Humility begins with the admission that science cannot provide complete knowledge of anything—even if human consciousness unfolds in a universe of increasingly wonder and limitless questioning.

Chapter 4

TRINITARIAN CONNECTIONS

Inside Knowledge

The two previous chapters treated the "Be-ing" of God and the God-ward consciousness intrinsic to human beings. As we now move into a trinitarian consideration of both God's Be-ing and of divine and human consciousness, this chapter opens the way to a deeper exploration into God in an explicitly trinitarian perspective. From a more general standpoint, the theologian D. B. Hart has structured his profound treatment of our experience of God around the classic Hindu notion of God in terms of being, consciousness, and bliss—*sat, chit, ananda*.[1] Not only does such a tripartite attribution have profound metaphysical consequences, but to some degree it invites a phenomenological approach to the experience of a triadic, even if not trinitarian, mystery of God.[2] That would be a good beginning for a specifically trinitarian theology of God.[3]

AN INTRATRINITARIAN STANDPOINT

The classical doctrinal mode confesses God as Trinity in a communion of the three divine persons: Father, Son, and Spirit. Any effort to relate the Christian experience of God to a contemporary worldview cannot bypass the centrality of the Trinity. In the vision of faith, to be created is to be invited into the divine love life: God communicates in the incarnation of the Word and through the outpouring of the Spirit—and, indeed, in the final face-to-face revelation of the Father.

There is no suggestion, therefore, that being united to the One God means intimacy with infinite solitude. The One God does not live in self-contained isolation, but in the vitality of communion of interpersonal love and self-giving. The life of God, Father, Son, and Holy Spirit, is that of communication and endless self-giving to the other. God is one, but a unity-in-communion. Furthermore, the divine communion enfolds believers into itself—that they may dwell in God and find their unity within the divine life. The words of Jesus in the Gospel of John are a focal reference: "The glory that you have given me I have given them, so that they may be one, as we are one, I in them and you in me, that they may become completely one" (John 17:22–23). The surprising thing, textually and rhetorically, is the pervasive presence of triadic formulations in the New Testament writings. Even the earliest letter, 1 Thessalonians (written about AD 58?), speaks in a straightforward uncomplicated manner about the threefold character of God (1 Thess 1:1–5). It is assumed that everyone will understand what is meant in such expressions. While there is no need to be uncritically maximalist in this regard, the seemingly spontaneous use of a triadic rhetoric celebrating the New Testament experience of God's presence and action is striking. It certainly requires an explanation, especially given the long struggle for adequate doctrinal formulation that would occupy the Church in the four centuries to come. A triadic manner of speaking imposes itself, for example, in Paul's discussion of the law (Gal 3:11–14) and Christian freedom (Gal 4:4–6), just as it pervades his expressions of thanksgiving (2 Thess 2:13; Col 1:3–8). It is noticeable also in the way he expresses his prayers (Rom 15:30; Phil 3:3–6; Eph 3:14–16). Moreover, the unity and giftedness of the Christian community are presented with explicit reference to the divine three (1 Cor 12:4–8). A number of creedal and liturgical formulations are even more explicit. At the conclusion of Matthew's Gospel, the risen Lord commissions the disciples to go forth and baptize the nations "in the name of the Father and of the Son and of the Holy Spirit" (Matt 28:19). The most likely explanation of a deliberately ordered triadic pattern is a settled liturgical usage, the most well-known being 2 Corinthians 13:14.

Inchoately trinitarian elements in the early rhetoric of Christian faith can be further specified. They are evident in the two forms we name here as iconic and schematic, even if they are often interwoven (Acts 1:4–8; 2:23, 28; 9:17; 10:38; 11:15–17 in reference to the following).

Iconic forms occur where New Testament language works to construct an image of the divine mystery involved in the work of salvation:

- These are detectable principally in the Synoptics, such as the various depictions of the baptism of Jesus: the Spirit descends in the form of a dove, the heavens are opened, the divine voice proclaims Jesus as the beloved Son (Matt 3:16–18; Mark 1:9–11; Luke 3:21–23; and also John 1:32–34).
- Then, the Infancy Narrative (especially Luke's) gives something like a holographic impression of God's saving presence: the Holy Spirit is the divine power at work, Jesus is uniquely the Son of the Most High (Luke 1:32–35).
- Transfiguration passages speak of the cloud of glory (the *Shekkinah* of the Spirit?), the voice from heaven, the proclamation of Jesus as the Beloved Son (Matt 17:1–8; Mark 9:2–8; Luke 9:28–36).

- Jesus rejoices in the Spirit, to express the intimacy of his communion with the Father and his role in inviting others into it (Luke 10:21–22).
- In his ascension (Luke 24:50–53; Acts 1:6–12), Jesus as the risen Lord ascends to the divine realm, from which he will send the Spirit, as "my Father promised" (Luke 24:49).

Schematic instances accent less a symbolic content, but more the conceptual presentation of the fullness of salvation in Christ. Some Pauline passages approach a systematic presentation of the divine mystery—though without any awareness of the problematical nature of what is presented. Note the manner in which major sections of Romans (e.g., chapter 8), Galatians (e.g., chapter 3), 1 Corinthians (e.g., chapter 12), and Ephesians (e.g., chapter 1) are constructed: there is a strong emphasis on three aspects of the mystery of salvation:

1. The initiative of the Father.
2. Union with Christ.
3. Living in the unity and power of the Spirit.

One example of this kind of schematic structure is the following:

> There is one body and one Spirit, just as you were called to the one hope of your calling, one Lord, one faith, one baptism, one God and Father of all, who is above all and through all and in all. (Eph 4:4–6)

As we consider John's Gospel, it would seem that the evangelist is not only giving a coordinated account of the fullness of grace and truth now present to the world in Jesus Christ (John 1:14), but evidently attempting something more systematic. He is presenting the divine Three in the one mystery of God. No doubt, he is influenced by the problems that inevitably arose from the preceding triadic proclamation of the grace of salvation. It is not anachronistic, therefore, to suppose that John is already beginning to face a doctrinal challenge. If salvation begins with the Father who so loved the world (John 3:16), if the Son he gives for the world's salvation is to be confessed as "My Lord and my God" (John 20:28), if Jesus departed to send the other Paraclete from the Father (John 15:26), then the question could not be long in coming: How are these divine "three" related to one another?[4]

A significant inflection of Johannine rhetoric is its expression of the communion existing between the Father and the Son. To this degree, it points to a dialogue or conversation going on between them. The Word made flesh has a dialogical existence: his origin is from the Father, his identity is to be the Father's Son, just as his mission is to the Father's will. Existing from and for the Father, he is sent from the Father, receives everything from him, yet is one with him. Still, "the Father is greater than I" (John 14:28), for he is the origin and goal of all that Jesus is. No one goes to the Father but by him, but no one can come to Jesus unless drawn by the Father (John 6:44). The speech of the Son and the silence of the Father, who speaks only in this Word, express the character of the transcendent mystery into which all believers are drawn. The prayer of Jesus in John 17 is the climax of this kind of rhetoric: "...that they may all be one. As you, Father, are in me and I am in you, may they also be in us" (John 17:21).

On the one hand, compared to the interaction of Father and Son, the presence in the Spirit is not as directly expressed in John's Gospel. On the other hand, full attentiveness to the Word depends on the presence of the Spirit. For this "other Paraclete," "the Spirit of Truth," whom the risen Jesus sends, "will teach you everything, and remind you of all that I have said to you" (John 14:26). The Gospel can speak of the Father and the Son because the Spirit gives, and continues to give, his testimony (John 15:26). The Paraclete guides successive generations of believers into all truth (John 16:13). The Spirit is, therefore, a pervasive and implicit presence in John's Gospel, inspiring the understanding of Christ and guiding its development. A problem seems to have clearly occurred to the Evangelist: How was the presence of the Spirit related to the dialogical relationship existing between the Father and the Son? How did the Spirit figure in the communication taking place between the Father and the Son?

> I still have many things to say to you, but you cannot bear them now. When the Spirit of truth comes, he will guide you into all the truth; for he will not speak on his own, but will speak whatever he hears, and he will declare to you the things that are to come. He will glorify me, because he will take what is mine and declare it to you. All that the Father has is mine. For this reason I said that he will take what is mine and declare it to you. (John 16:12–16)

In this presentation, the Spirit of Truth is the one who hears and receives what is going on between the Father and the Son, that totality of communication that comes from the Father to the Son, and from the Son to the Father. The Spirit is "of truth" in that he makes this communication open to believers and draws them into it. The least that can be said is that John is aware of the problem in the rhetoric of faith. He begins to face it by presenting the mystery of the whole in the form of a logic serving to structure a way of thinking about the divine Three. Such logic draws its force from a sense of the divine as a field of loving communication characterized by an attitude of self-surrender to, and for the sake of, the other. The Son lives for the Father. The Father gives everything to the Son. Father and Son give everything over to the activity of the Spirit. The Spirit speaks not on his own authority, but from what he has heard from the Son, and, by implication, from the Father—in order to glorify them both.

THE GOD OF COMMUNION

The above remarks are a brief indication of the beginning of trinitarian theology and of the logic shaping its development. In the Johannine perspective, the divine Three are being presented in a unity that is at once a communion of life and a community of interrelated persons. Subsequent doctrinal formulation and systematic theology will necessarily address such issues.

At every stage, the New Testament offers an enriched cognitive sense of the meaning of God. In all that happens, the one God of Israel is at work, but with a singularity concentrated in a unique form of communication lived out between the Son and the Father. This is in contrast to any kind of monodimensional orthodoxy that would presuppose that God is not only one, but also that this God is ultimately alone, the absolute solitary. In contrast, the self-revelation of God, Christian faith insists, leads to the understanding of Jesus, as Word and Son, as utterly and originally "Father-ward," in eternity and in time (see John 1:1, 14, 18; 5:19, 30, 43). Likewise, the Father's "Son-ward" communication is stated in various ways: "The Father loves the Son and shows him all he himself is doing" (John 5:20). This "showing" includes the "work" of raising the dead and giving life "to whomever he wishes" (John 5:21, 26). Still, it is not only a matter of the Father's *showing*, but *giving* to the Son, the gifts of "all judgment" (John 5:22), of having "life in himself" (John 5:26), of the "authority to execute judgment" (John 5:27), and of "the works" that are his to accomplish (John 5:36). Further, the Father both sends and bears witness to the Son (John 5:37). What emerges is a differentiated unity enlivened by mutual relationships and intersubjective communication. Though the axis of the interrelationship is here presented along the lines of the Father above and the Son below, the Prologue (John 1:1–2) has already expressed the supratemporal dimension of divine communion that will be presented more fully in John 17.

By attending to the data of this distinctive experience, later theology and Church teaching will be led to affirm a singular mystery of divine self-communication. Thereby is implied a transparent reciprocity of relationships between the Father and the Son. The Son is constituted, as it were, in his identity and mission through his relationship to the Father. For his part, the Father is constituted in his paternal self-giving in relationship to the Son. In every aspect of the being and action of the Word, there is the "verb" of the Father's timeless self-utterance and engendering. The "subsistent relationship" of the Father is revealed in his ceaseless generation of the Son, even while the identity and mission of the Son is intelligible only in his continuing coming forth from the Father, in order to reveal him as the source of life and light.[5]

Two problematic expressions deeply affect any interpretation of the Johannine experience of God. The first is a straight declaration on the part of Jesus: "The Father and I are one" (John 10:30). The second gives expression to the hope that, through his performance of his Father's works (John 10:37), "you may know and understand that the Father is in me and I am in the Father" (John 10:38). Neither of these statements collapses the Son's relationship with the Father into undifferentiated metaphysical identity. Nor do they reduce the action of the Father to one of simple collaboration with what Jesus is doing. The Father is "in" the Son not as contained by him nor as confined to his scope of action. Rather, what is at stake is the Father's generative initiative in all that affects the life and mission of Jesus: "My Father...is greater than all" (John 10:29). Immense and complex theologies have struggled to appreciate each element of these statements. Themes such as the unity of the Son with the Father, their reciprocal coinherence (*perichoresis*), and the sense in which the Father can be understood as "greater" than the Son in a manner that excludes both the Arian and Sabellian extremes, will allow theology no rest.[6] The exploration of such high doctrinal issues begins from, and forever returns to, the compact experience that is constitutive of a Johannine sense of the gift of eternal life emanating from the Father.

If Socrates had counseled that "the unexamined life is not worth living,"[7] life, in the terms of the Gospel, is both examined and summoned to its highest reach, namely, communion with the Father and the Son: "that they may be one, as we are one, I in them and you in me, that they may become completely one" (John 17:22).

The coming of the Spirit is a further gift of an overwhelming positive significance in relation to the disciples, to Jesus himself, and to the Father. First of all, the Spirit of truth will guide the disciples into "all the truth" (John 16:13). Second, as the Spirit of *truth*, he will glorify Jesus, taking what is his to declare it to the disciples (John 16:13). Third, in declaring the truth of Jesus, the Spirit will be declaring "all that the Father has" is to be found in Jesus (John 16:15). In the light of these relationships, the Spirit is, so to speak, a luminous field of presence in the history of faith, through which believers can penetrate ever more deeply into what has been going on between the Father and the Son. Postbiblical doctrinal developments will speak of the Spirit as a "subsisting relationship" between the Father and the Son.[8] Already at this stage of faith's expression, the Spirit is identified as "in-between-ness" that makes possible the believers' entry into communion with God and into the fully bounty of the divine gifts. He is the God-given presence of the "revealed-ness" of what the Father has communicated to the Son and, through him, to the disciples.

And yet the full significance of the hour of Jesus will take its own time: "I still have many things to say to you, but you cannot bear them now" (John 16:12). Though the whole truth of Jesus's words will be the truth that heals, frees, and gives life, the disciples at this time find themselves on the dark side of the cross. In sorrow and fear they have a foreboding anticipation of their Master's violent exit from the scene. The full truth of the revelation to be accomplished in his death and resurrection is beyond what they can either imagine or expect. God's self-revelation takes time, and all the events of the hour must run their course. Even if the disciples were to receive verbal instructions from the lips of the Master, the "many things" yet to come cannot be fully communicated (John 16:13c). The Word made flesh will be fully incarnate among them only when, in the flesh of his existence, he will be glorified in the event of the cross. The realization of this event looks to the coming of the Spirit if it is to be grasped in its abiding significance.

As given into the limited horizon of the disciples, the Spirit will abide in them and be among them (John 14:18). As the field in which the full meaning of what is taking place will be progressively unfolded, the Spirit will guide the disciples into "all the truth" (John 16:13a). The Paraclete not only acts against the darkness, but also for the light, bringing home to the community of faith the fullness of the gift of truth that Jesus embodies (John 1:14–18; 14:6). He will guide the followers of Jesus into the way of living truth opened up through his passing over to the Father (John 14:6). Hence, the Spirit will not speak independently, but will communicate only what he himself hears (John 16:13). The Spirit has come, not to replace the message and mission of Jesus, but to make it a living reality in the history that is to unfold. In this sense, the Spirit is the light in which the opened heaven will be seen in all its truth (John 1:51).

Nonetheless, neither Jesus,[9] nor the Paraclete, is the originator of revelation. Both are sent by the Father (John 14:16, 26; 15:26), each serving the one revelatory communication of the Father—the Son, in the course of his coming from God and going to God (John 13:3); the Spirit, by coming after the departure of Jesus to bring out the saving fact that "the Father had given all things into his hands" (John 13:3). The Spirit will remain with the disciples as the Father's permanent gift, in the "forever" (John 14:16) that is in contrast to the "little time" (John 16:16–19) of Jesus's physical presence to them. Because of the coming of the Spirit, time is no longer a pointless succession of instants; nor is it a continuing cycle endlessly repeating itself; nor is it a memory of a privileged past. Time is experienced as moving to a divine fulfillment, for the Spirit comes to declare what is to come (John 16:13). There is a dynamism inscribed in time that looks to the fullness of divine revelation. Jesus and the Father will come to make their home with those who, despite the conflicts that history will produce, have made the persistent, yet peaceful, journey of faith (John 14:23). With the gift of the Spirit released through the death and glorification of Jesus (John 7:39), the worshiping community will move to meet the Father "in spirit and truth" (John 4:23–24).

Guiding the disciples in all truth, the Spirit of truth "unpacks" the full meaning of the Word incarnate in the historical conversation of faith. The Spirit will glorify Jesus, to communicate all that he has and is to present and future believers (John 16:14). As sent by the Father, the Spirit is impetus to a continuing mission of witness to the world (John 15:8). The Spirit of truth witnesses to the most original truth—that of Jesus's oneness with the Father; the Son is sent into the world from the heart of this unity.[10] The Spirit, however, proceeds from the Father and is sent by Jesus (John 16:7; see also 15:26). As their joint gift of the Father and the Son, he is the first witness to the unity that reigns between them, the divine and personal communicator of that all-enfolding unity to the world. The Father is not hidden, as one unknown, behind the mask of the Son. Rather, under the guidance of the Spirit, the community of faith finds in Jesus the true face of the Father turned lovingly toward it.

THE ENFOLDING TRINITY

Unfortunately, doctrinal controversies have often reduced this most illuminating and life-giving of Christian mysteries practically to the point of absurdity—at least in the minds of most Christians. What should have been a celebration of God as the absolute Being-in-Love in all things, the divine community enfolding all conscious creation into its own love life, has been reduced to an exercise in supercelestial mathematics in which one could neither be multiplied, nor divided, by three. In recent years, however, trinitarian theology has been undergoing a considerable renewal,[11] so that a distinctively Christian vision and moral practice is informed by a trinitarian faith, and the theological perspective is sharpened.

First of all, God, as the one ultimate reality, is revealed as relational. In John's Gospel, for instance, the transparent reciprocity of relationships between the Father and the Son realign our understanding of the immanent reality of God (*in se*) and the economic relatedness of God to the world (*pro nobis*). The Son is constituted, as it were, in his identity and mission through his relationship to the Father. For his part, the Father is constituted in his paternal self-giving in relationship to the Son. In every aspect of the being and action of the Word, there is the "verb" of the Father's timeless self-utterance and engendering, as mentioned above. The "subsistent relationship" of the Father is revealed in his ceaseless generation of the Son, even while the identity and mission of the Son is intelligible only in his continuing coming forth from the Father, in order to reveal the primordial source of life and light.[12]

The experience of God radically destabilizes ordinary identities and relationships. God can no longer be "kept in his place," for the Father has sent his Son into the world. For its part, the world itself has lost its self-made boundaries with what the Gospel of John calls the "opened" heaven (John 1:51). Nor can Jesus be kept in his place, as he leaves this world for the Father. Even death ceases to be in place for him as an opaque impenetrable limit to human life. His dying is integral to the radiance of the love of God revealed in the self-giving of the Son. As for his disciples, though they will suffer the grief of their master's absence, his love "to the end" demands of them an excess of mutual love that will leave them far more disturbed than any grief over his departure can cause. The reality of Jesus's absence leaves a space where no believer can ever live again in self-contained isolation: "Just as I have loved you, you also should love one another" (John 13:34).

This interpersonal reciprocity and the mutuality of relationships described in John's Gospel led in the centuries to come to the full-blown Athanasian trinitarianism of the post-Nicene doctrine.[13] A seismic displacement of meaning occurred: the culminating gift of truth (John 1:14) has broken open the range of human experience to the dimensions of the "opened" heaven (John 1:51). The truth of God's love occurs as an upheaval in the previously imagined world. The varied responses, of incomprehension, acceptance, or scandalized rejection, make the words of the poet Paul Celan especially apposite: "A Rumbling: truth / itself has appeared / among humankind / in the very thick of their / flurrying metaphors."[14]

What kind of reality is Christian faith trying to objectify out of its experience of God? How does such experience and meaning affect the Christian's experience of reality? The imagination of trinitarian faith envisages ultimate reality as intrinsically relational. Doctrinal theology, in order to avoid implying that the divine persons are three different substances, goes on to speak of the divine persons as "subsisting relationships." That is to say, that the divine three are understood only in relation to one another, as *for* and *in* the other. Thus, the absolute oneness of God is concretely realized in a pure self-communication to the other. God is God by being a communion of mutual self-giving. The Be-ing of God is, therefore, a communion of self-giving and other-directed love.

God as Father expresses his fullness in the Word, and rejoices in its infinite excess in the Spirit. In that self-utterance and self-gift, all that God is, all that the universe is or will be, is contained. The universe, emerging in the long ages of time, is ever being called into existence by the gift of God. Consequently, the eternal Now of trinitarian life is the matrix of time, not its contradiction.[15] That relational vitality within God, which theology calls the "divine processions" of the Word and the Spirit, creates the universe in its dynamic image. From the divine processions within God flows the "process" of the universe.[16] This is to say that the divine processions are imaged forth in the unfolding of the cosmic process. The universe finds its ultimate coherence as the *uni-verse* inasmuch as the Trinity draws it to participate in its own field of relationships. It unfolds in the light of the Word, and is energized by the power of the Spirit, just as it lives in every moment in thankfulness to the originating love of the Father. From its experience of this relational field of divine presence, Christian faith comes to confess the Trinity as the transcendent presence immanent in all existence. All instances of being, becoming, and life have their beginning, form, and goal in the "love life" of God, "so that God may be all in all" (1 Cor 15:28). The evocative language of Nicholas of Cusa returns such intense theological expressions to the world of mystical imagination: "The Godhead is the enfolding and unfolding of everything that is. The Godhead is in all things in such a way that all things are in God."[17]

The utterance of the Word "in the beginning" (John 1:1) is the primordial self-expression of the Father. Through this communication, God is self-differentiated, the "I" and the "Thou," the "I" and the "We," the self and the Other. The universe, created in the Word (in Greek, *Logos*) is a world of endlessly differentiated "words" (*logoi*), or meanings. As Aquinas reminds us, "created things cannot attain to the perfect image of God in a single form." It was fitting "that there be a multiplicity and variety in created things so that God's image be found in them perfectly in accord with their mode of being."[18]

In the order of the Creed, the third divine person is breathed forth by Father and Son. The Love that differentiated itself as Father and expressed itself in the Son and Word becomes, in the circulation of trinitarian life, the shared ecstasy of other-directed loving. The relational dynamics of creation can therefore be understood as a participation in the unifying ecstasy of the Spirit. The Breath of God moves the differentiated, distinct, and independent realities of creation into self-transcending communion of the self with the Other. In this perspective, the cosmos lives and breathes the mystery of the original, expressive, and unitive Being-in-Love at the heart of its existence.[19] If the original and ultimate reality is inherently relational, if ultimate unity is self-giving communion, trinitarian faith is a healthy disturbance of all closed little worlds of isolated independence.

Defensive alienation from the other, resistance to peace and reconciliation, all deliberate disharmony or exploitation in regard to the rest of creation set us outside the trinitarian flow of life.

Such a trinitarian conception of ultimate reality stands in contrast to a mechanistic worldview, however dominant and long entrenched. A mechanistically modeled science has little patience with any theology, let alone any theology needlessly complicated with trinitarian references to processions, relationships, and the plurality of the divine persons. Nonetheless, current views of the processive and relational character of the cosmos might well find some aspects of trinitarian theology quite intriguing. Contemporary paradigms of science and aspects of trinitarian thinking show signs of convergence. After all, for two thousand years, trinitarian theology has come to regard ultimate reality as a realm of processive, interpersonal, relational life. It turns on understanding God as concretely one only in a manifold of relationships. As a more holistic science becomes aware of this trinitarian perspective, dialogue is enabled, and a collaborative exploration of what constitutes ultimate reality is set in motion.

Traditional trinitarian theology after Aquinas passes from the consideration of the processions and relationships of the divine persons *ad intra* (i.e., in the eternal "within" of God) to their presence and relationships *ad extra*, in the God-created universe. The self-communication of the Trinity to the created world is treated under the heading of the biblical category of "mission" or "sending"—the way, for instance, God "sends" the Son and Spirit into the world.[20] The processions of Word and Spirit within God are, as it were, prolonged into the world of time. Given the present evolutionary horizon, much can be gained by retrieving some aspects of the classic trinitarian tradition.[21] In this brief remark, we are taking some liberty with traditional terminology in the hope of making it more meaningful in the present context. For example, Aquinas asks, How can a divine person be "sent"? The problem here is to imply neither inequality in the coequal Trinity, nor a primitive form of spatial movement from one place to another—as though God were not everywhere in the first place. In answer to this question, Aquinas makes two points: First, the divine person is sent inasmuch as the eternal procession of the Son/Spirit is prolonged into time and history. In this, the divine consciousness takes in the world of time and its emerging world. Because the mission is an extension into time of the eternal procession, it means that the divine persons begin to exist in the world in a new way:

> Thus, the Son is said to have been sent by the Father into the world, even though he was already in the world, but now he begins to be in the world in a visible, incarnate way manner. The Word was made flesh.[22]

We can therefore understand the divine missions as the self-immersion of the Trinity in the created universe. The risk and the fragility, along with the beauty and dynamics of a temporal world, have been given a place in God's trinitarian consciousness. In this way, the world is an aspect of God's own experience. From this point of view, the missions of Word and Spirit are the Trinity's opening out to the world and to history in order to enfold creation into its communal life.

But there is a second point. Aquinas allows for two dimensions of these missions, the "invisible" and the "visible." This traditional distinction, more fully understood, can prevent Christianity from being locked into a narrowness that is ill-prepared for the cosmic scope of its present challenge and responsibilities of interfaith dialogue. So, first, a word on the *invisible missions*. We begin with the recognition that God is present to everything and everyone in an absolutely fundamental manner, as sheer Be-ing, *Ipsum Esse*, the source of all being. It follows that, as the source of all being, God is present in the innermost depths of all reality. But from the depths of the ocean of Be-ing in which all exist, there comes a wave of divine freedom, of self-communicating love. God is not content, as it were, simply to be the nameless universal mystery at the heart of reality. Beyond giving ourselves to ourselves, the Trinity wishes to give itself to us, so that we can enter a new realm of selfhood and communion. This is the area of grace. By receiving this new gift we are not only God's creatures but also become God's intimates. Thus, the

Trinity is present in creation in self-giving love. God acts through all creation in the nakedness, creativity, and unifying power of love.

This trinitarian self-communication brings about a transformation of human consciousness—traditionally called "sanctifying grace." It brings about a special intimacy with the divine mystery.[23] The human self is "conformed to God." Through the experience of loving and being loved, the human person conformed is to the Spirit of love. Likewise, through the gift of faith and wisdom, believers share in the wisdom of the Word: "because by such knowing and loving, created consciousness [in Latin, *rationalis creatura*] lives actively in contact with God. The special mode of the interaction involved means not only that God is intimately present to human consciousness, but also dwells within us as in his temple."[24] All time or space opens out within this horizon of God's loving presence, for the Word and Spirit are said to be "invisibly" sent to indwell human consciousness. However unnamed, unexpressed, the depths of human consciousness are awakened to a new level of life and communion with God. The human being, however implicitly, begins to participate in the very consciousness of God's own knowledge and love. Wherever there is evidence of a consciousness lovingly alive, in reconciling wisdom and self-transcending love, it is evidence of the indwelling of God. And that is to be in the "state of grace." The Word of God is not some abstract form of information, but is given so as to reach the heart: "for the Word is not any kind of word, but the Word breathing love."[25]

On the one hand, this metaphor of "mission" might give the impression of the divine Word and Spirit being sent from some kind of outer space where God dwells. On the other hand, once the spatial limits of the metaphor are recognized, the reality of the divine missions is more like a blooming or an emergence of the mystery out of the depths of existence where God is ever present. What could have appeared to be a universe of simple fact, however uncanny, now appears as a radiant field of divine consciousness and communication. God dwells in us and we dwell in God in the circulation of divine life and love.

But there is more. The divine missions are not only "invisible" as the Word and Spirit illuminate and enkindle human consciousness within the indefinable horizon of life. They are also *visible*. The divine Word, who had been invisibly present in grace, becomes incarnate. The Spirit, too, who had invisibly dwelt in the hearts of all good people, is manifested as a movement in history. The gift of the Spirit transforms lives and forms communities of faith, hope, and love in an energy animating all witness and sacraments of Church. This visible dimension arises from the reality of God's self-giving as it is attuned to the embodied reality of our human being. God's self-communication takes shape in the time and space of this particular world. God is not to be found only in a transcendent realm, but more so in the flesh-and-blood of our world. Aquinas remarks,

> Now it is connatural for a human being to be guided by the visible to the invisible. Through the evidence of creatures, God has in some way manifested himself and the eternal processions of the persons. Likewise, it is right that the invisible missions of the divine persons be made manifest through visible creation. Now this occurs in one way with the Son, and in another way with the Holy Spirit:...the Son is visibly sent as the author of holiness; but the Spirit as the witness to that holiness.[26]

The embodied world of our existence is the natural milieu for human communication. Trinitarian communication respects this given "ecology" of human existence in order to draw human beings into the divine life of communion. The created world, in all its differentiation, structures, relationships, and dynamics already manifests the relational and communicative reality of God. A trinitarian dynamism is originally inscribed into every element of the created world. The trinitarian orientation of creation is intensified. The visible mission of the Word incarnate in Jesus Christ expresses in the world of human communication the transcendent mystery of God at work. And the Spirit, symbolized in the water, the wind, the air, the flame of our natural experience, opens into the field of ultimate connections.

In such a perspective, the Church is an extension of the visible missions. It can be identified as that part of the world that is expressly alive to the universal mystery of love at work. Accordingly, the community of Christian faith deals in words, signs, symbols, and sacraments in order to live and manifest the trinitarian mystery. The Church belongs to the ecology of divine presence and communication, even if it neither represents nor limits the total scope of God's grace at work in all creation.

The invisible and visible missions arise from the trinitarian vitality of God. Today these missions demand a re-expression in an evolutionary perspective. Both the Trinity communicating itself to the world and the world itself need to be understood in a vital and dynamic manner. In that regard, the invisible missions are *invisible* precisely because they energize the indefinable totality of the universe. Animated by such energies, the emergent universe can be contemplated in the light of one vast act of divine self-communication. In that horizon, the self-giving God becomes the soul, the heart, the mind of the world's emergence: "There is...one God and Father of all, who is above all and through all and in all" (Eph 4:4–6). Conversely, the *visibility* of the missions discloses the universe in terms of God's embodiment. The mystery of Love incarnates the Word in the body of creation as its form, structure, and goal. Love, too, enters the world as the Spirit acts in all the self-transcending dynamics that characterize our human and cosmic development. And, as the Father is intimated as the source of both Word and Spirit, the world of time moves toward its absolute future in God.

In this way, the trinitarian God is "enworlded." The divine communal life is the relational ground of a cosmos of growing connections and relationships. The mind of the Word incarnate finds expression in the desire: "As you, Father, are in me and I am in you, may they also be in us....so that they may be one, as we are one" (John 17:21–22). Then, there is the promise: "When the Spirit of truth comes, he will guide you into all truth...and he will declare to you the things that are to come" (John 16:13).

Realism insistently demands an acknowledgment of the tragic world of conflicts in which we live. Whatever our eschatological hope, this is no whole world of harmonious connections or gently conducted dialogue. We must realistically bear in mind that visibility of trinitarian grace in such a world must, first of all, be a force for healing and reconciling, before it is simply transforming. The energy of God's gifts—indeed of divine self-giving—is marked with the intensity of self-sacrifice. The missions of the Son and the Spirit are directed to human beings locked in an apparently insuperable problem of evil. The problem and its solution reach a limit when the incarnation of the Word results in the crucifixion of the Father's beloved Son. However, the Father himself is revealed as having no self-disclosure in this world other than through the crucified One. Similarly, the Spirit of love and peace is sent into the world of self-enclosure and exclusion of the other. In that world of resistance, the Holy Spirit witnesses to no power and no truth other than that of the selfless love manifested in the cross. Through the visible missions, God's visibility in the world comes up against our problem of evil. In that conflict, the self-giving love of God is exposed to the alienation, failure, and fragmentation of our world, but in a way that proves ever greater than the power of darkness. Its promise of transformation presumes that it is, first of all, a healing for the self-destructiveness manifest in our history.[27]

This, then, is an outline of the way in which the traditional schema of processions, divine relations, invisible and visible missions can be reworked in reference to the emergent global world. God's communication is not reserved for pure spirits, but meets the vast history of human existence in its temporal, historical embodiment.[28]

A CONTINUING EXPLORATION

There is nothing new in exploring the reality of God by way of analogy with created realities, nor in interpreting the world of created reality in the light of God. Augustine's "vestige" and "image" doctrine is a good instance.[29] In Catholic tradition, it developed into the typically Franciscan cosmic sense of all reality sacramentally manifesting God. For example, over seven hundred years ago, Robert Grosseteste, the first chancellor of the University of Oxford, contemplated a speck of dust, to find in its existence, form, and goodness a manifestation of the three divine persons.[30] Now, a speck of dust caught in the light beaming in through a medieval scholar's window is rather different from other specks we know today. For example, the Earth is a mere speck in a universe of some hundred billion galaxies. Indeed, the Big Bang represents the unfolding of the cosmos through 14.7 billion years from the infinitesimal super-compressed "speck" of its beginnings. Theology, therefore, in continuity with its past, can contemplate the originality, the dynamic form, the wonder and beauty of cosmic reality. In so doing, a reflective faith is coming to a fuller insight into the deeper implications of its central mystery.[31]

Likewise, St. Bonaventure, in his ladder of contemplation, could consider creation as implying a trinitarian presence on three ascending rungs of intensity. First, there are "footprints" (*vestigia*) of the Creator found in the prepersonal. Second, there is the divine "image" in the spiritual creature with its powers of intelligence and love. Third, there is the divine similitude or "likeness" brought about as the created spirit is transformed through grace:

> The creation of the world as a book in which the creative Trinity shines forth. It is read according to the three levels of expression, the ways of vestige, image and likeness. By these, as up a ladder's steps, the human intellect has the power to climb by stages to the supreme principle which is God.[32]

The implied metaphor of a stable ladder leading upward tends now to be replaced by the arrow of time moving forward in an evolutionary direction. The "footprints," or traces of God, now have to be tracked in the history of the billions of years of the world's emergence. And then the image of God is disclosed in terms of human consciousness emerging in such an evolutionary world so that world becomes known and appreciated as the gift of the Creator. The higher "likeness" of God, in its turn, is revealed in the transformation of consciousness as it indwells, and is inhabited by, the primordial mystery of creative Love.

For his part, Aquinas sums up the themes of the great Greek

theologians, especially Athanasius and Gregory of Nyssa, when he treats of the presence of the Trinity in the act of creation:

> The divine persons are causes of the creation of things in the order of their procession, since God acts from his knowledge and will as a craftsman acts in regard to what he produces. The craftsman acts through a word conceived in his mind and through love in his will in reference to what is to be made. Hence the Father creates through his Word which is the Son, and through his love which is the Spirit.[33]

In such a vision, the trinitarian mystery is implicit in what it means to be a creature. Moreover, the trinitarian processions of Word and Spirit are at the foundations of the cosmic process. Indeed, Aquinas goes on to say,

> The knowledge of the divine persons is necessary for us for two reasons: in the first place, to have a right sense of the creation of things. Because we say that God created all things by his Word, the error is excluded of holding that God produced things out of the necessity of his nature. Because we hold that there is a procession of love within him, it is clear that God did not produce creatures out of some extrinsic need, but on account of love for his goodness....In the second place, and this is more important, [the Trinity is disclosed] that we might have a proper sense of the salvation of the human race, which is brought about by the incarnation of the Son and through the gift of the Holy Spirit.[34]

First, that "right sense of creation" implies that creation is not a divine necessity. It is an act of love, a communication from the heart of God. Second, the "salvation of the human race" results from God's self-gift to human beings within the historical and evolutionary dynamics of their world. In continuity with its traditional resources, trinitarian theology is free to exploit anew resources of language and experience to explicate the trinitarian form of creation. It must explore the variety of ways in which the presence of the trinitarian God can be discerned within a relational and evolutionary perspective.

In this regard, trinitarian theology traditionally employed an evocative technique known as "appropriation." The essential divine attributes common to each of the divine persons (love, wisdom, union, power) are "appropriated" to the three in such a way as to bring out the distinctive character of each one. This theological technique works to personalize trinitarian faith in a certain sense by making the less known manifest through the more known.[35] That is not to imply that we already have an adequate knowledge of the divine attributes in question, nor that they can be considered abstracted from an explicitly trinitarian setting.[36] This is evident in the most developed form of appropriation, shaped by what is generally referred to as the "psychological analogy." This kind of analogy relies heavily on Augustine's *de Trinitate*, especially as developed by Aquinas in the thirteenth century. By examining what is involved in the human activities of knowing and willing, the psychological analogy offers some understanding of trinitarian consciousness in its relationships and activities. The result is a fruitful understanding of the biblical and doctrinal data. Moreover, it suggests an experiential intimacy with the trinitarian mystery so that it can be subjectively "appropriated" within the form and dynamism of our own intentional existence.

It is a psychological analogy that enriches the cognitive content of trinitarian theology. Believers are invited to reflect on their conscious experience of their cognitive and affective activities. And this can be applied within a much larger field of meaningful attributions in terms of historical developments and interfaith dialogue. This technique of appropriations is designed "to manifest the persons." Each is present and acting in the human heart and in history as a whole, and so contributes to "a manifestation of the truth."[37] The psychological analogy indicates a way of speaking of each of the divine persons in their distinctive characteristics, while connoting the essential attributes common to the three.[38] In all this, theology is forced to admit that the experience of faith is always more than even the best kind of analogical thinking. Within the trinitarian mystery there is an incalculable excess of meaning and interpersonal communication that necessarily transcends the partial understanding that any analogy can offer. If we follow Aquinas's ordered presentation of the mystery of God, we must first acknowledge the limitless space of the divine transcendence—the divine Be-ing and its attributes. We can then move forward through the psychological analogy to consider the trinitarian processions and the relationships. But in a third phase, there is a doubling back in order to include the whole of richness of tradition in its scriptural, mystical, and liturgical dimensions. The complete, but ever developing, field of faith's experience guides the activity of appropriation. Nonetheless, the divine reality always transcends—and expands—human conscious experience. For example, trinitarian theology has in recent times included specific attention of divine revelation related to the cross and resurrection.[39] That, in turn, has provoked an examination of how the psychological analogy works within the narrative drama of trinitarian revelation, calling into play further symbolic, aesthetic, affective, and psychological dimensions of human experience as subject to the transformative action of grace.[40] The possibility of a new range of appropriations emerges. The psychological image, rather than being replaced, is notably enhanced. In any theological scheme, the divine persons are never comprehended in rigid categories, but are more vividly disclosed through the play of appropriations based in the scriptural narrative. In this regard, the divine self-revelation is always more than the sum total of theological techniques.[41] Nor should it be forgotten that the gifts of the Spirit, especially wisdom, understanding, and knowledge, add an instinctive and suprarational quality to faith's experience of the trinitarian self-communication.[42]

In short, the practice of appropriation reminds theology not to lose contact with its scriptural data, liturgical practice, and mystical experience. The aim of appropriation, therefore, is to stimulate the most meaningful expression of the trinitarian shape of Christian experience. As a result, theology has growing resources in order to disclose the distinctive character of each of the divine persons. The

Trinity is appreciated more fully as the central truth to be explored, as the mystery to be invoked and adored.

Particular considerations of the unity of God and of the common divine attributes are thus given a trinitarian focus. For example, power, wisdom, and goodness are referred to Father, Son, and Spirit, respectively. Likewise, unity, equality, and harmony are notions applied in order to disclose each of the divine persons in their trinitarian order, and further triads of, say, efficient, exemplary, and final causality, and so on, are similarly employed. With such a plethora of terms, trinitarian thought tries to give some expression to the encompassing mystery of God "ever beyond us" as Father, the all-inclusive Source and Goal; of God now "with us," as Word and Son incarnate; of God ever "within and between us," the Holy Spirit, the inexhaustible gift of God poured out on the world. Appropriation, a particular personal way of speaking of the divine persons, goes beyond the constraints of any one theological system or synthesis, to anchor faith more creatively in prayer, liturgy, and meditation on the Scriptures.

Such traditional expressions anticipate a new set of trinitarian connections, drawn from "the book of creation" but now read through modern eyes. Many writers speak of the direction of evolution in terms of increasing "differentiation, subjectivity and communion."[43] The initial cosmic event unfolds into a marvelous variety of particles, forces, elements, life-forms, cultures. With that differentiation, there occurs an increase of interiority and consciousness. Living, self-organizing unities emerge in a growing complexity, through the nervous system to the human brain. In the human phenomenon, consciousness emerges as intelligence and freedom. Evolution becomes conscious of itself. The universe is self-aware. And in that self-awareness, the mystery of our common origins and shared destiny comes to expression. Beatrice Bruteau remarks the "cosmos has all the marks of the Trinity" in its unity, internal differentiation, and in the dynamics of its expansion and interrelatedness.[44]

An awareness of the trinitarian dimension of human existence profoundly affects the lived sense of human selfhood. Christian theology speaks of the divine indwelling, God dwelling in us and our dwelling in God. To search into who we are is to find ourselves in the presence of God, the "Self," as it were, in all our selves. The three classic biblical expressions of such intimacy with the divine mystery are familiar. We are temples of the Holy Spirit, members of the Body of Christ, sons and daughters of the Father. Through this indwelling and union with the divine persons, faith possesses an inside or participative knowledge of the mystery of the Trinity. It shares in the Love Life that God is:

> Beloved, let us love one another, because love is from God; everyone who loves is born of God and knows God....For God is love....No one has ever seen God; if we love one another, God lives in us, and his love is perfected in us (1 John 4:7–12).

To experience God in such a way is to find oneself as a relational identity, a self-to-be-realized in relationship to the other. Adoration of God and union with the divine persons orient the believer into a world of relationships and communion—of global, ecological, and cosmic dimensions. In that sense, the Trinity implies an agenda for conversion and transformation, for ourselves, our communities, and our global coexistence. In a world of both complex differentiation and growing interconnectedness, Christian faith can find a new health and a new wholeness in contemplating the universe in the light of its fundamental mystery—the Trinity gathering creation to itself. In the Trinity, the universe comes home, and all the struggling emergence of time finds its absolute future. Through such trinitarian reflections our exploration into God comes to rely on God's own "inside knowledge" as it is revealed to faith.

Chapter 5

CREATOR AND FATHER ALMIGHTY

This chapter follows on the previous ones on the Be-ing, consciousness, and Trinity of God, especially by treating three topics that often prove to be an obstacle to any projected "exploration into God." The topics concerned are conveniently summarized in the article of the creed, "I believe in God, the Father Almighty, Creator of heaven and earth." Hence our concentration in what follows on the meaning of "Father" and the "Almighty" and the universal extent of God's creative act.

A THEOLOGICAL HORIZON

But first a general comment. In our exploration into the reality of God, we are concerned with the divine mystery and its relationship to the world. We may well give the impression that God is mysterious, and that the world, by contrast, is a clearly understood entity. That is to assume that we know already what the world is. It makes a difference, however, if the world is understood in relation to God, its Creator. The question returns: What, then, is the world? In a theological sense, the world is not known until the world as God's creation, as the object of God's love and mercy, is made manifest.

The philosopher Jeff Bloechl observes that "the life of faith moves perpetually between distance and nearness, and thinking that attends to such a life must reckon with both of them."[1] In this respect, the notion of secular is as old as the distinction between the Creator and creatures. Furthermore, relating to God in mind and heart is itself a distinct way of being in the world. Indeed, liturgically and sacramentally, the consciousness is formed of being in the world understood as charged with the grace and redemptive love of God in Christ. This leads a view of the world in a certain affective tone and mood—quite different from that of scientific objectivity, and at variance with a blinkered reductive scientism.

As a classic expression of Christian faith, the Nicene Creed's "I believe in one God, the Father almighty, maker of heaven and earth, of all things visible and invisible" provokes continuing reflection. This first article of the creed introduces the one, all-creating mystery of God in, through, and for whom all exist (Acts 17:28). The boundless mystery of God is connoted as the atmosphere and milieu of all existence, so that God can be invoked as the beginning and end of all that is.

The distinctive way in which "the Father almighty" is the primordial "maker" of everything is usually expressed in the term of God's role as "Creator." The divine mode of making, doing, and acting in creating is expressed in a great variety of images in the Scriptures Christians share with Israel (see Gen 1—3; Sir 16:26—17:19; Wis 7:22–25). In that biblical understanding, God's making extends to all that is—in all the tenses of the verb *to be*, and all the modes of actual and possible being—in all that is, was, and will be; in all its being and becoming. That must include everything connoted in phrases such as *I am*, *you are*, *we are*, *they are*, and *it is*, in all the differences and relationships and actions implied in *all* this. God's way of "making" is, therefore, not like any other kind of action or creativity contained within the bounds of "heaven and earth." That is to underline, therefore, the uniqueness of God's creative activity. The "Almighty Father" does not act as one agent among a myriad others in determining the shape of the world. God is not busy in the great unfolding process of the universe as a particular agent collaborating with the rest of known, or as yet unknown, agents and energies that make things the way they are. God's making is different. The divine agent is present at the roots of all existence and in every creature's capacity to act. The creative activity of God is, therefore, not set simply alongside the rest, as one factor, however important, in the varied influences that determine the shape of the real. For God acts out of a sheer and unconditioned originality. As the source of all being, the Creator God is the ground of why there is something rather than nothing, and of why every being continues to exist in the way it is, from one moment to the next. God, in this biblical and creedal understanding, is the all-embracing cause of all being and becoming. From such a sense of creation flow the wonderful insights that are the common possession of the biblical tradition.

In the first place, as Creator, the One God is more intimately present to creation than the creature is to itself. The more the creature comes to be, the higher the degree of its life and love and creativity, the more God is involved and present, and the more does that created reality participate in the creativity of the divine. Our capacity as persons to be and to act is the outcome of what God has done and is doing. God is ever engaged in creating what and who we are, as participants in the wonder of existence. Divine Be-ing is the limitless matrix "in [whom] we live and move and have our being" (Acts 17:28), present and active in all creation as "one God and Father of all, who is above all and through all and in all" (Eph 4:6).

Second, in creating the universe, God acts freely. What is created is not a necessary or automatic overflow from some great reservoir of being. This is to say, that God's creative freedom is unconditioned, and depends on nothing external to itself. The acknowledgment of God's freedom in creating leads to the realization of creation as loved into being in the deepest possible sense. The creative freedom of God means that at the source of all creation, there is the exuberance of infinite love. That is to say that the universe, and everyone and everything in it, is primarily a gift. Since creation need not have happened, the universe of all that is, in its very fabric and every fiber, is given into existence. It is therefore loved into being and occurs as a gift.[2]

Third, the divine creative act presupposes nothing. As sheer gift, the universe is made "out of nothing"—a more negative way of saying that it is loved into being. For God has acted so that something other than God should exist to share in the divine joy in being, and to receive the gift and the giving that God is. And all this is for the sake of that perfect fulfillment to occur when "God may be all in all" (1 Cor 15:28). Inevitably, imagination envisages some kind of raw material on which God acts or which is presupposed to the divine act of creation. Beyond the limits of imagination, however, is the moment of wonder. Any "raw material," any presupposed cosmic energies or life forces, are themselves created. In short, the divine freedom presupposes nothing except divine creativity and generosity.

More deeply still, there is no goodness prior to God's action, or apart from the goodness of God. There is nothing outside God that somehow entices the Creator into the act of creating. God's own overflowing goodness is the only reason why there is anything at all: "the love of God infuses and creates the goodness in reality" (*amor Dei infundens et creans bonitatem in rebus*), as St. Thomas Aquinas notes.[3] The universe as a whole and in each of its particulars, in all its structures and processes, is loved into being, and so manifests the unconditioned goodness of God. Infinite Good spreads itself, shares itself, and gives itself so that all that is good might exist and be enjoyed.

THE DIVINE ARTIST

If creation is not like any other kind of making or doing, how can we speak of it within our world of limited making and doing? Language must here be analogical (as explained in chapter 2). We can dimly describe the divine creative act only in terms of the human experience of making and producing. For example, in a moment of inspiration, the artist is possessed of profound, original creativity. That moment of inspiration animates all the distinct actions and elements involved in the production of any work of art. All the varied elements and phases, be they notes and scales, words, paint strokes, or shapes and movements, are born out of an imaginative conception of the whole. The creative moment, as distinct from the demanding effort to "realize" it in some concrete form in a certain medium, is experienced as in some way wonderfully "given." It springs forth within the fertility of the artistic imagination, already anticipating the whole of what is to be produced or performed. Of course, the transforming moment of real art is prepared for by the long formation of the artist in a chosen medium. Even Mozart had to practice his scales, learn from others, and become familiar with the capacities and limitations of the various instruments at his disposal. But within those limits, his originality was seemingly limitless, and the world continues to enjoy his amazing art. Along with all artists in their respective media, he gave expression to what was original within him, and in what was other than him in the notes, the scales, the harmonies, and the instruments employed. The ecstatic self-expression of artists affect this human world by lifting it out of its routines of shape, sound, color, image, and movement to a point of surprise and wonder. The aftereffect of art is that the world can never be the same again.

Artistic creativity, therefore, can be taken as a dim metaphor for divine creation. God's creative action springs forth, as it were, from the divine imagination, in utter originality. No medium is presupposed, nor is there any other to appreciate it—except insofar as it too is created. In this respect, God is pure originality, pure self-expression. The creative act brings forth what is other than God so that this other—and others, ourselves included!—is not only the expression of the divine goodness and beauty, but also that it might share, in its own scope for self-expression, in the creative love of God.

Though the word *incarnation* is usually reserved to the Word made flesh in Jesus Christ, we can understand it in a more extended sense in the context of creation, and so regard the world, and the universe itself, as the incarnation of the love and imagination of God. This cosmic incarnation finds its culminating moment in the personal self-expression that occurs when the Word personally becomes flesh. In Jesus Christ, the original meaning and promise of creation takes explicit shape.

There is another analogical way of understanding what creation means. The original human community was made in God's self-image: "Let us make humankind in our image, according to our likeness...male and female he created them" (Gen 1:26–27). Living images of their Creator, human beings, in the generative capacities of body and spirit, go on to "make" one another in love and communication.[4] Through the creativity of nature and culture, in the family, and in society, the human person is formed in a way that far transcends any ordinary instrumental meaning of making. This communal, mutual creativity, through all the exchanges of human relationships, actively shares in the divine creativity imaged in our coexistence. In this experience of "making," and of procreating the other, we grow to a deeper sense of how God creates us and the universe in which we exist.

In this perspective, we are finally led to the distinctively Christian and most intimate understanding of creation as it is envisaged in the creed. All divine making flows from the trinitarian life of God. In that primordial mystery, divine life is eternally unfolding through an ever-original self-expression, namely, in the Father "speaking" the Word and begetting of the Son. This self-expression can never be separated from God's ecstatic self-giving, for the Spirit is breathed forth as the love motivating and informing all the gifts of God. In this regard, creation is an extension into time of the eternal circulation of divine life. What God creates bears traces (in Latin, *vestigia*) of its trinitarian origin: in the sheer wonder of existing, as coming forth from nothing, creation radiates a sense of the limitless Be-ing of the One Who Is, the eternal source and origin, confessed as "the Father."[5] In its particularity and varied forms, as *this* rather than *that*, in *this* actual universe, the universe participates in the divine self-expression characteristic of the Word. Each reality can be named in its own individuality, illumined as a ray of divine light and appreciated as the manifestation of infinite wisdom. Then, when creation is received as an interconnected and interrelated whole, moving into greater communion and deeper life, the universe images forth the presence of the Spirit, the love inspires all loves and all gifts. Creation in its deepest reality is, therefore, an icon of the Trinity. The trinitarian source of creation finally crystalizes when, through the power of the Spirit, the Word becomes flesh. Faith can glimpse how the perfect form and deepest meaning of creation is climactically embodied in Jesus Christ, "the image of the invisible God, the firstborn of all creation" (Col 1:15).

ALL IN HEAVEN AND EARTH

To confess God as "maker of heaven and earth" amounts to a declaration that there is, in effect, nothing outside the scope of the divine creating. The creativity of God embraces the whole of creation despite the temptation to divide it into two separate domains—the heavenly and the earthly. The scope of God's creative activity, therefore, is not limited to purely spiritual creation, as though it were involved exclusively with the production of souls and spiritual realities. God also creates the material world and all the physical energies presupposed in the structure and processes of the world as it is—the inanimate, the biological, and all the prepersonal structures, forms, and dynamics that, one way or another, support human existence—including the sexual, which tends to be unevenly accommodated in our spiritual traditions.

It is important to underscore the involvement of God in material creation for two reasons. First, modern scientific exploration of the physical origins of the universe leads us to awe at the quite uncanny emergence and astonishingly interconnected totality of the physical world. That overall sense of things cannot be dismissed as of no religious value. Admittedly, religion has been traditionally more at home with spiritual realities, with "heaven" and "the invisible." For its part, modern scientific culture has become marvelously familiar with "earth," "the visible," and the material. Despite the tension resulting from such different emphases and perspectives, faith in creation insists that the two realms are related in the one reality of God's creative self-expression.

Furthermore, stalking religious consciousness down the ages has been a noxious alternative—of belief in a material, or even evil principle somehow coexistent with, and even resistant to, God's creative power. Such a belief holds to a dark side of creation. Under the influence of such a dualistic view, the religious mind becomes intolerant of the bodily and the material. Dualistic spirituality favored an escape from the physical, in the conviction that the visible and the material belonged to an inferior and spurious mode of existence. In Christian history, there has been on different occasions an unhealthy emphasis on a "spirituality" nourished exclusively on the "invisible," as if we human beings were pure spirits haunting the earth instead of inhabiting it. The early Manichean heresy gave doctrinal expression to the tendency to dematerialize the integral goodness of creation. Preceding such a position, however benignly, there was an antimatter, antibody influence stemming from classical Platonism. As a result, mutilated versions of Christianity down the ages have been both deeply suspicious of the body and sexuality, and hostile toward scientific activity because of its involvement with physical reality.

In contrast, the movement of God's creation is toward incarnation. The invisible is embodied in the visible, while the divine mystery is present in the physical and material. God's creative love encompasses both heaven and earth, to bring the two together in the one blessed creation. The polarities present in our one human existence do not result in competing dualisms. There need be no rivalry between these two dimensions of created existence. Genuine spirituality does not demean the material and the physical, the bodily and the sexual, or the scientific exploration of matter. Likewise, true worldliness does not mean a lessening of contact with the transcendent, the divine, the spiritual, or the heavenly. The larger ecology of creation allows for different, interrelated realms and principles. Neither the spiritual nor the material can be ignored, unless to the detriment of both. For instance, a holistic sense of creation demands that faith make room for the proper independence of the secular, and the true value of the world in itself. Our hope for the life of the world to come cannot demean the worth of our present life in this world. On the other hand, life in the secular world will lack its full meaning if it represses the domain of the spiritual. Cut off from ultimate hope, it will be going nowhere: God is, therefore, confessed as "the maker of heaven *and* earth."

Out of a sense of the wholeness of God's creation, believers must accept the whole gift and bear the whole weight of that creation. As complex beings, we praise the Creator in and through that complexity. Whatever the diversity in our callings, lifestyles, and philosophies, faith in God the Creator excludes any monodimensional vision of existence. It likewise counters the dualism that compartmentalizes our experience of the world so that the underlying unity of creation is missed. Indeed, belief in God as maker of heaven and earth keeps us in a healthy awareness of the complexity of the creation in which we live, and the continuing need to make room for the whole. However complex the world is, faith in the Creator enables us to understand it as a "universe." That means both respecting and going beyond the purely physical cosmos of modern science. While faith need have no problems with the brilliance of modern "grand unified theories," or a "Theory of Everything," it must insist that however brilliant such mental constructs might be for correlating the four forces affecting all material things, there is still the larger consideration of the transcendent origin, form, and goal of the totality of material and spiritual existence. Only as created by God is reality in all its aspects, phases, levels, structures, and dimensions finally appreciated as a *uni-verse*, the one reality of creation. The doctrine of creation supports the most comprehensively holistic appreciation of reality, and keeps the *-holic* in the *catholic*—the universal dimension of Christian faith.

Belief in creation attunes faith to recognize the universe as a great symphonic event. Nothing in all its manifold dimensions of order and spontaneity, of nature and history, is outside the scope of God's creative activity. God's making includes the past, present, future, and all the dynamics of cosmic emergence, biological evolution, spiritual freedom, intellectual achievement, artistic expression, and ethical action. God creates not merely "things," but all the variety and levels of conscious existence, in which the great symphony of creation springs into awareness. Since God is the source of all that is, everything and everyone is interrelated in the one universal event of creation. Each element and energy participates in its own particular way in the one universal event of what God has made, and is making.

The universe is the totality of what is, of all that is already known, or is yet to be discovered. Faith in the Creator occurs within the universe that has brought us forth, in the many billion years of cosmic history. The creed is sung on the air of one of the planets of one of the hundred billion stars of one of the hundred billion galaxies of the known cosmos. No doubt there are forces and energies, dimensions and life forms that remain to be discovered—or rediscovered. Here I note the excess of reality that the liturgy celebrates in its exuberant listing of ranks and hosts of angels. If we adore the Creator and if we wonder at the dimensions of the universe, we must be slow to believe that human intelligence has exhausted God's creative power, and that the human is the only spiritual presence in the whole of God's creation. But wherever we turn, from quarks to quasars, from protons to supernovas, from the Big Bang to black holes, from the human brain to dark matter, from the beginnings of life to the defiant death of the martyr, from the brilliance of scientific exploration to the grandeur of simple moral goodness, from the human soul to the seraphim and archangels, there is one source from which everything derives.

ONGOING CREATION

God keeps acting. Creation continues. Divine creativity is not limited to the past. Unless the Creator continues to create, the universe would fall back into nothingness. Today, however, the continuing creative activity of God can be understood in greater depth. God's continuing creation not only prevents the universe from falling back into nothing, but enables it to increase its being in progressive levels of becoming. God creates the world, not as a fundamentally finished reality, but as an expanding event. An all-engendering love is still at work, creating the universe in its capacity to become more, and to unfold to its ultimate dimensions. We can picture God creating the world less from "on high" or "from above," and more as the infinite energy acting "from within," enabling it to emerge into new intensities of consciousness and communion. As the Spirit of God acts within all being and becoming, in all matter and life, it has brought forth human consciousness. In the human mind and heart, the world has become conscious of itself as an event of divine creation. In the contemplation and prayer, creation becomes intimate with its source, to wait on the final self-revelation of the reality from which everything has come forth.

In its coming forth from God, however, created reality remains genuinely other than God. It is given to exist in its own real, finite right. It has its own freedom, spontaneity, and principles of action and interaction. The Creator God, therefore, lets creation be itself. Being created does not mean that God crowds reality with a kind of overwhelming presence that never allows the creature to be genuinely other before God. Rather, created existence is a kind of dependent independence—*dependent* since God is always the ultimate ground of its being; *independent* since it truly does exist, with its own nature and scope of operation. When thinking of God's creation as an act of God, we think of the total dependence of everything on God. When we consider creation as a noun, as what God in fact has made and is making, we are struck more by the total independence it enjoys, right to the point, in the case of freedom, of standing for or against God. The Creator has thereby risked, as it were, the true freedom of the creature. While this is an insoluble enigma, both sides of the reality of creation must be affirmed if we are to appreciate its mystery. For, by creating, God is committed to having time for creation, for letting it be itself, and for making space for what has come from the divine hand. God is not a big reality mixed in with multiplicity of creation. For in its own domain, the world of creation is intelligible in its own right and on its own terms. Herein lies the foundation for the integrity of all scientific exploration. Indeed, no idea of God can be allowed to distract the mind from exploring what God has made.

More practically, cosmology, physics, chemistry, biology, psychology, and so on have their own subject matters. They are not to be confused with a theology of creation even if such "subject matters" are aspects of the one creation and are the activities of human consciousness. Ideally, all human modes of exploration properly exist in a conversational interaction, each and all with a sense of the one overwhelming manifold mystery. Given this growing multiplicity of specializations, how to prevent confusion, how to promote interaction and collaboration within the one great, all-involving event of the universe are exciting questions. The task of the theology of creation is to remind science that, in exploring any kind of reality, it is not edging out the reality of God. God is not part of creation. The Creator acts both within and from beyond the scientifically accessible structures and dynamisms of the material world. On the other hand, in exploring ultimate reality, there is no need to demean or ignore any aspect of reality that is scientifically accessible to human investigation. To be created is to be given to exist, in its own right and with its own self-organizing powers.

If all beings are given into existence out of the generosity of Infinite Be-ing, God is never foreign to creation. Everything is essentially related to God as its abiding source, sustenance, and goal. In the limited and varied being of the created universe, the sheer, unlimited Be-ing of God is, so to speak, materialized, embodied, expressed. The incarnation of the Word is, in the sense we suggested above, a culminating incarnation of God—the Word coming into his own, as the full, personal self-communication of God (John 1:11).

We can therefore suggest that believing in creation frees the mind to be completely untrammelled in its explorations of reality. While intelligence delights in what is achieved through the scientific explanation of the universe on intraworldly terms, it must also appreciate the genuine creative reality of mind in the midst of creation. The mind can keep expanding as the reality it explores brims with questions: What is the explanation of all the explanations? What is the sufficient reason for all our sufficient reasons? What is the ultimate value of everything we have found worthwhile? Before what or whom we do we finally stand? What does the consciousness of being a self suggest, a self that enjoys so much, that thinks, explores, acts, creates, cares, and wonders? Belief in creation, then, inspires the ultimate adventure in thinking, as the mind and heart refuse to rest in anything but the ultimately intelligible, the finally good, and the unified whole.

And yet creation includes the astonishing variety of real things, in all their interrelationships, processes, and levels of existence. Why is this *all*, this *whole*, so intricately varied and differentiated? Evolutionary biology gives its answer in terms of the history of life's emergence. Physics and chemistry point to all the elements and forces and patterns necessary for the universe to be what it is.

Modern ecological awareness appreciates the wondrous diversity and interconnectedness of life, so as to warn the human generations against carelessly tearing or upsetting the web of life on this planet. In pondering the question of why there is such variety in creation, St. Thomas Aquinas gives a deceptively simple answer. God chooses a varied creation to express more fully the richness of divine Be-ing:

> God is...the most perfect agent. Therefore, it belongs to him to induce his image in created things in the most perfect way in a manner that befits created nature. But created things cannot attain to the perfect image of God in a single form: the cause exceeds the effect; for what exists in the cause in utter simplicity, is realised in the effect in a composite and pluriform manner....It is fitting, then, that there be a multiplicity and variety in created things so that God's image be found in them perfectly in accord with their mode of being.[6]

However, interwoven with the varied wonder of creation is the force of evil as was mentioned earlier. Disease, catastrophe, the perversions of human freedom, death itself permeate what God has created. If belief in creation excludes any evil principle in rivalry with God, why then is evil such a force, and such a presence? Why is creation burdened with such a problem of evil?

THE EXCESS OF CREATION

The history of Christian thinking largely leads to silence, hope, and waiting. We human beings would have more chance of hearing silence and seeing darkness than of understanding evil. It is the oppressive absence of the good we need and seek. In the face of the excess of evil, faith does not attempt a philosophical answer. It offers no solution except that of opening the way to a more complete surrender to the mystery of love, in order to participate in the transforming and healing power of love and mercy. For the "almighty" source of love is also an excess beyond human comprehension. The excess of God's love is displayed as it exposes itself to our problem of evil in the incarnation, suffering, and death of the Son. Such love is not turned to vengeance but keeps on being love in its ultimately transforming power. It has already triumphed over evil in the resurrection of the crucified, thereby anticipating an ultimate victory. God's love shows its patience in having time for the whole of human history against the day of a final universal judgment when evil will be revealed for what it is. In the meantime, the omnipotence of love assures us of the forgiveness of sins and promises an ultimate transformation in "the life in the age to come."

There is, then, no instant solution for the conflicts and clashes, the destruction and limitations, the disease and ambiguity we experience. Nonetheless, God the Father Almighty promises an ultimate universal judgment to justify his way of creating and redeeming, and so, to allow time and history to follow their course. As faith waits for this final evidence, it is summoned to stand with the Son, who "for us and our salvation" has immersed himself in the cosmic process, thereby making himself vulnerable to the risk and tragedy of human history. A suffering creation finds its hope in the knowledge that God suffers our sufferings even more than we do ourselves.

The Canticle of Daniel calls us back from cosmic sadness to the defiant affirmation of universal praise. The inspired writer summons all "the works of the Lord to bless the Lord." In our present knowledge of the wonder of the universe and emergence of life within in, such praise can be extended into a thousand other forms. The biblical prayer of praise runs through the realities of the natural world—sun, moon, and stars; night and day; heat and cold; sea and dry land; wind and rain; animals, birds, and fish; angels and human beings. But today the contemplative appreciation of the universe leaps to new possibilities. God can be glorified in the uncanny providence that guided the universe through its astoundingly improbable journey to this present moment. It now brings forth to awareness of the vast, intricate scope of the universal event.

"All you works of the Lord, O, bless the Lord!"—cosmic forces, galaxies in their billions, matter in all its varied forms, consciousness in all its glimmerings, both the sturdy predictabilities and the strange randomness of nature, its order and its chaos, in all the ten million species of living things with whom we share this planet, in every instant of the billions of years that have gone into our making, in all the elements of the stardust from which we are made: "To him be highest glory and praise forever."

Faith in creation is not limited to the "invisible," that is, to what is outside the immediate range of human experience. It includes "the visible." To know the Creator means not to reject any aspect of creation. Prayer, contemplation, and intelligence itself cannot exist save as earthed in what we see and hear, touch and taste, smell, hear, and feel. Sense, feeling, imagination, and all delight in this world serve to bring home to the human mind and heart the mystery pervading all creation. Every level of our human awareness has its place in faith's experience of the one creation in which everything is related.

This sense of universal interconnection is the foundation of all analogical knowledge of God. The *invisible* is known through the *visible*. What is immediately accessible as, say, food and drink, as light and fire, as water and earth, as sexual love and family intimacy, is, in its largest frame of reference, a symbol of the beyond, of what is present but inexpressible. Above all, the humanity of Jesus is the incarnation of the divine, for the Word made flesh is the ultimate analogy: "In him we see our God made visible, and so are caught up in love of the God we cannot see" (First Preface of Christmas). Flowing from the climactic event of the incarnation is the special sacramental awareness of faith. Familiar human symbols become "visible signs of invisible grace." More provocatively, our neighbor, whom we can see, must be loved as condition of loving God whom we cannot see (cf. 1 John 4:20).

The creed's confession of God the Creator, far from permitting a disjunction in our experience, unites the visible and invisible domains of reality as the one self-expression of God in creation. The visible is a path to the invisible, not a distraction from it. The Word is incarnate in the visible, and not concealed behind it. As St. Augustine preached, "Through the invisible made visible, we pass from visible things to the invisible."[7]

The result is a distinctive kind of Christian realism. When ultimate reality is disclosed in the earthly, familiar realities of immediate experience, the world cannot be treated as a mirage. It is not a veil behind which an unknowable and unknown reality is concealed. In the native patterns of human experience, reality is accessible, to be known and revealed in its ultimate dimensions. In this respect, the created totality in which the visible and invisible are related is the condition for the development of Christian civilization. The world of the senses, the expanding horizon of the human meaning and value, and the reality of the spiritual are all united in the one universe of God's creation. The instinct of Christian faith to embody itself in a given culture is, at root, a refusal to let the visible, the native element of our experience expressed in work, art, and imagination, be consigned to noncreation, or to the nondivine. Faith is a public matter, a cultural fact, and not an individual private refuge, nor a private revelation. It is a social communication. The revelation of God occurs in the rough and tumble of actual history, not merely in the inner domain of the spiritual. That is to say that faith can never desert the visible for some disembodied realm.

In treasuring the visible, faith claims the world of the senses. It has eyes, just as it hears, tastes, inhales the presence of God. It senses the mystery in realities of the world, in the symbols of its sacraments, in the form of its words, in the face of its neighbor. The invisible comes to us through the visible as the *icon* of the one "who is." It follows, then, that both the experience of the senses and the creativity of imagination are integrated into the ecstasy of faith. Signs, symbols, sacraments, the incarnation itself—all point beyond themselves to what transcends our world. Since faith is never a mere matter of having a good look at the visible, believers never simply see God—either in themselves or in others, nor, for that matter, in the entire event of the universe. Nonetheless, the invisible domain is not unfelt; it too is experienced. The realm of the invisible stirs in the depths of our consciousness, in all the dynamics of knowing and loving, judging, deciding, and relating to the other and to the whole. It turns consciousness into conscience, and lifts that conscience to its ultimate height in the experience of being loved, and of being called to share in the life of love: "No one has ever seen God; if we love one another, God lives in us, and his love is perfected in us" (1 John 4:12).

There is, therefore, an interior dimension of creation. In that invisible *within*, God's Spirit stirs in the manifold activities of our conscious selves, as well as in creation as a whole. Creation is going on; it happens both in the scientist's understanding the universe and in the physical universe itself. Creation includes both the artist's self-expressive activity and the objective work of art. It contains both the mind at work and the reality it understands or produces. It is there in the silence of the mystic and in inspired words of faith and devotion, in the integrity of good conscience and in the good deeds that are done.

In other words, creation is not simply "already out there," as though we are spectators. It is also "in here," making us participants through the creativity of human consciousness, in all the modes of its loving, praying, exploring, acting, dreaming, and communicating. In that way, creation occurs, as the *visible* becomes conscious of itself in the *invisible* reality of mind and heart and spirit. And this *invisible* expresses itself in the visible domain of the material, public, social world. Adoration of the Creator leads to a truly bodily indwelling in the wonder of creation: matter and spirit, senses and mind, the exterior and the interior are interrelated as in the one created universe.

To inhabit the world with a vivid sense of its being God's creation is to live with an awareness of everything as sheer gift, as we have previously stressed. Thanking becomes the condition of true thinking. All creative thinking and acting, all the loving and doing—all likewise participate in God's creation. The creativities of mind and heart, of eye and hand, of word and art communicate in the unfolding of what is coming to be. The divine Spirit is at work in the scientist and the scholar, in the inspired productions of the artist, in the contemplative and the mystic, and most of all, in the moral activity of good men and women working together in love and justice to make the world both a human place and a biosphere hospitable to life in all its forms. And so, to be part of creation and to adore the Creator brings both a gift and a responsibility. We live the wonder of existing, belonging and acting in the universe of God's creating.

To believe in one God is to turn to the infinite Light that cannot be fully known within the bat-like vision of human knowledge:

"No one has ever seen God" (John 1:18). Yet faith in Christ makes us familiar with what, to human vision, is the blinding glare of too much light, and that, for human intelligence, is an impenetrable darkness. Hence, the need to appreciate what has been given from beyond: "It is God the only Son, who is close to the Father's heart, who has made him known" (John 1:18). The Word incarnate reveals the human face of God, and the Spirit enables faith to hear the inexpressibly fullness of that Word (John 16:12–14).

In the confession of the One God, the faith of Israel and the faith of the Church are united: "You shall love the Lord your God with all you heart, and with all your soul, and with all your mind, and with all your strength" (Deut 6:5; Mark 12:30; Matt 22:34–40; Luke 10:25–28). God is to be loved with the best energies of our being, with all our powers of knowing, loving, and doing. In God, our minds adore the all-surpassing truth that summons them, and our actions find their scope and fulfillment. In adoring, loving, and entrusting ourselves to this One, we belong together most fully as "we," and enter a community of love and forgiveness. The commandment connected to the summons to love God unreservedly is this: "You shall love your neighbor as yourself" (Mark 12:31). There is no going up to God unless it includes going out to our neighbor. Consequently, we cannot come to God, isolated, alienated from others, and loveless in their regard. It remains, however, that all our capacities to explore this present world, and to be drawn beyond it into the fullness of life, find their point of rest in the One God: "For with you is the fountain of life; in your light we see light" (Ps 36:9).

Certainly, the Christian experience of God is shaped by the disconcerting vision that Jesus brings into the situation. He comes, looking upward to his origin with the Father, and outward—to the scope of what the Father is bringing about through the mission of the Son. His entry into the historical scene opens it to dimensions of "spirit and truth" (John 4:23). The Samaritan woman's God of our "fathers" is now revealed as "the Father," loving the whole world and seeking true worshipers "in spirit and truth" (John 4:24), in a way that cannot be limited to Mount Gerizim or Jerusalem, or to Rome or Rio, Melbourne, or Tokyo—a realm defined only by God's life-giving love.

If true worshipers of God are not limited to any particular time and place, that is because, within the mystery of creation, God can no longer be "kept in his place." The world itself is newly defined as that into which the Father has sent his Son. The world has lost its self-made boundaries through the coming of the Son and the sending of the Spirit. Union with God does not mean, therefore, losing oneself in an infinite solitude, since this One God does not live in self-contained isolation. God lives in the vitality of interpersonal love and relationship. The life of God, Father, Son, and Holy Spirit, is communication and endless giving to the other, so that God is one as a unity-in-communion. The divine communion enfolds believers into itself—that they may dwell in God and find their unity within the divine life:

> The glory that you have given me I have given them, so that they may be one, as we are one, I in them and you in me, that they may be completely one. (John 17:22–23)

THE INTELLIGENCE OF FAITH

Belief in creation and faith in the Creator do not mean that believers are always trying to "prove the existence of God." The opposite seems to be the case when believers are more intent on proving, not God's existence, but the genuineness of their own existence in the light of the mystery into which they are drawn, as their origin and end. Still, to live the gift of faith does not entail intellectual paralysis. Faith cannot be isolated from the intellectual or moral concerns of life, nor cut off from the sheer wonder of existing at all, and the wonder of the universe itself. In this respect, faith is to be lived, not as stupidity or ignorance or indifference to the real world, but as the wisdom that can integrate every dimension of life—in surrender to God and in the service of our neighbor.

On the other hand, out of its long experience of the ways of God, Christian tradition does recognize some proofs or arguments for God's existence, as previously mentioned. Perhaps the word *proof* is far too cut and dried. It may suggest that the existence of

God could be established as one more fact, pinned down by rational control—one factor among many, within a philosophic or scientific system. But God is outside any system, and beyond the reach of any mind. Proof, in a naive, superficial, and logical sense, cannot conclude to the reality Christians adore as *God*. Even "arguing" to God's existence, while more modest in its connotation, is still all too heady a description of the "searching and groping" of which St. Paul speaks of (Acts 17:27). The word *intimation* suggests something of heart and mind moving together to what must remain beyond our grasp, even if "not far from each of one of us." It connotes both God's action—intimation in an active sense—and our experience of it—intimation in a passive sense. Human beings cannot evade questions arising out of the depths of what and who they are in this world. Such questions arise within human consciousness as it unfolds through all the relationships that make up an individual, personal life. When life is fired at us point blank, the uncanny fact of the sheer existence—of the universe and of ourselves within it—demands explanation.

Believers, therefore, take part in the time-honoured exercise of attempting to give reasons why "God" can mean in fact what faith already lives. As faith expands its capacities to reflect and understand, it expands with a growing appreciation of the universe as God's creation. The more believers gather to themselves the diversified wonder of the universe, the more inclusive is their cosmic praise:

> Bless the Lord, all you works of the Lord;
> sing praise to him and highly exalt him forever. (Dan 3:57)

Arguments for God's existence were traditionally based on the objective inexplicability of the world. For instance, there had to be a first cause since no one element of reality, nor all of it together, is a sufficient explanation of why anything exists, nor why the universe has emerged in the astonishing way it has. True, this is not so much "proving the existence" of God as arguing that the world is ultimately not self-explanatory. Intelligence owes itself an intelligent explanation, and so asks why any such explanation is truly ultimate in not presupposing anything else.

In recent times this line of argument has been taken further as the billions of years of cosmic time and space have been gradually explored through a series of astonishing discoveries. The Big Bang, the formation of the galaxies, and the appearance of our tiny planet Earth, the emergence of life, and the way the universe is aware of itself in the consciousness of the human mind and heart—all suggest a richer context. In fact, the wondrous event at the origin of our universe has made science itself remarkably open-minded on the possibility of an original, provident, and limitless Mind behind it all. After pondering such possibilities, an outstanding modern philosopher suggests some fascinating questions facing the modern thinker about the character of God as charged not only with unfathomable wisdom, power, and exuberant generosity, but also with dazzling "imaginative" creativity,[8] working through a creative synthesis of both law and order, on the one hand, and chance, risk, spontaneity, on the other.

Faith in God does not exclude believers from the conversation that makes up human culture. They share in the adventure of intelligence, wonder, and creativity, to insist, however, that the ultimate question must not be suppressed. Moreover, they point to a special kind of data drawn from the millennial experience of religious people in their adoration of the One God and with which their own experience resonates. Believing in God, therefore, does not mean surrender to absurdity. In fact, for believers, at least, faith is the supremely meaningful act. The question that aches in all our efforts to understand concerns the final meaning of everything we understand. We hunger for meaning and cannot live without it. It is the essential sustenance of the mind. In this search for meaning, human knowledge has expanded in a myriad of ways, above all in the "knowledge explosion" of our times. Our minds unfold in this world of meaning. We are plunged into a limitlessly intelligible world that emerges ever more brightly as the human mind explores it. We are participating in a universe of meaning and existing in an intelligible world that cannot be explained by repressing intelligent questions. Science and scholarship collaborate in celebrating the fact that questions *do* have answers, and that reality overbrims with meaning to an astonishing degree. To believe in, and to adore, the One God is to have a sense that there is a meaning, an ultimate, all-comprehending meaning implicit in all that we have found meaningful.

Faith in God, then, is not an option for absurdity. It is, rather, a celebration of meaning and a confirmation of our restless search for truth. Intelligence ponders on the "sufficient reason" for something being *this* rather than *that*, for intelligence feeds on meaning and sufficient reason. A sense of being beholden to truth pervades all intellectual activities as the mind seeks to find a point of rest in a sufficient reason that is truly sufficient. In this respect, the absolute is the intelligence and love of God, the truth that grounds all truth, the sufficient reason for all sufficient reasons, the solid ground and foundation of truthful existence.

Moreover, believing in God is not immoral, but an assent to absolute good and value, the source and foundation of everything we most prize and of all that we find worthwhile. The fact that conscience can find peace only in honesty, justice, and generosity suggests that we live in a universe based on value and the truly good—a universe grounded in an original goodness—indeed, occurring as the gift of primordial love. Hence, believing in the One God implies that moral decisions really count in a value-friendly universe.

Believing in God, then, is not a self-destructive option, nor a form of self-enclosure. It is not moving away from who or what we are, individually, socially, and culturally. Believing means living in the presence of the mystery for which our personal being, individual and social, most hungers for its confirmation and fulfillment. Our hearts are home to the supremely personal reality, to the One in whom we are most alive, in whose embrace each of us is named and recognized and destined for the fullness of life. Human existence means being involved in an elemental "love affair," as the English Benedictine Sebastian Moore writes, with the infinite Good. This has been described as a "natural desire to see God" so that to be human means to be waiting on the Mystery to manifest itself. Faith occurs when the Word is spoken in the hearing of creation, and when the Spirit gives a listening creation the power to listen further and respond. In that sense, to exist is to stand on holy ground in the presence of the Infinite mystery that summons and attracts. St. Anselm, in the first chapter of his *Prosologion*, prays in words applicable to us all:

> Teach me to seek you, and reveal yourself to me as I seek, because I can neither seek you if you do not teach me how, nor find you unless you reveal yourself. Let me seek you in desiring you; let me desire you in seeking you; let me find you in loving you; let me love you in finding you.[9]

TWO OBSTACLES: "FATHER" AND "ALMIGHTY"

There are two designations of the one God that today have proved problematic. First, to name God as "Father" seems, in the context of the current critique of patriarchy, especially when intensified by feminist concerns, to open the way to patriarchal idolatry. Second, the creedal invocation of God as Almighty and omnipotent raises modern suspicions of totalitarianism and psychological oppression. A word, then, of each of these.

"Father"

To name God as "Father" without the awareness of context is to risk reducing its meaning to some cultural sense of fatherhood, either ancient or modern. That would project onto God a cultural idol in some form. In contrast, the Christian meaning of "our Father" is revealed only through the incarnation of his Son and through the gift of his Spirit dwelling within us. Adoring and invoking God as "Father" manifests faith's conviction that God, the Father, is the absolute "beginning." Divine initiative precedes all creation, all time, and all human action—even the action of Jesus himself.[10] For Paul, "the Father of our Lord Jesus Christ" is the original actor "who has blessed us in Christ with every spiritual blessing," who has chosen us in Christ "before the foundation of the world" to be present to him in love (Eph 1:1–4). In the vision of faith, everything comes into being out of God's generative and creative love. God creates the universe "out of nothing." When God creates, nothing is first "there," as it were, as some kind of raw material. More positively, God creates purely "out of love," so that all creation is loved into being, the manifestation of sheer loving on the part of God.

God is Father first as the inexhaustible fount of all life—both within God, in the life of the Trinity, and in the universe of divine creation. God is, therefore, invocable as "Father," not merely as the source of creation, not only in his gracious relationship to us in time, but also in the eternity of his loving self-expression in the Son and in the grace of his Spirit, named and adored, therefore, as "the Father of our Lord, Jesus Christ."

Everything derives from this divine personal source as a gift. The Father's love precedes all creation, all time and all human action; it enfolds all becoming, and is the end of all fulfillments. Faith's relationship to God as Father cannot be determined by sacred sites or ethnic loyalties: "you will worship the Father neither on this mountain nor in Jerusalem" (John 4:21). God the Father is beyond all the limits and boundaries the historical world imposes.

Naming God as "Father" in a Christian sense is the culmination of the experience of all the gifts of God, especially in the sending of the Son and in the further gift of the Spirit. Consequently, thanksgiving (in Greek, *eucharistia*) offered to the Father precedes and accompanies all religious thinking. Paul accordingly encourages the early Christian community to move forward,

> joyfully giving thanks to the Father who has enabled you to share the inheritance of the saints in the light. He has rescued us from the power of darkness and transferred us into the kingdom of his beloved Son, in whom we have redemption, the forgiveness of sins. (Col 1:11–14)

When notions of God's fatherhood congeal into oppressively patriarchal patterns, part of the remedy is being aware of the genesis of faith's confession of God as Father. Although the Father is "the first divine person" in the trinitarian formulation of faith, it is the Holy Spirit, usually referred to as "the third divine person," who comes "first" in our experience of God. For the Spirit reveals Christ to faith so that, in the words of the liturgical doxology, "through him and with him and in him, in the unity of the Holy Spirit, all glory and honor" is offered to the Father Almighty. The circle is complete, since the Father is the One from whom Jesus, the Son, comes, in whose presence he lives, and to whom he has returned. And so, as sons and daughters in the Son, we are freed to be free with God:

> For you did not receive the spirit of slavery to fall back into fear, but you have received a spirit of adoption. When we cry, "Abba! Father!" it is that very Spirit bearing witness with our spirit that we are children of God. (Rom 8:15–16)

"Almighty"

Equally ultimately revealing and presently problematic is the confession of the Father as "almighty." Just as the faith undermines any idolization of God as a patriarchal figure, it likewise subverts any notion of divine power as brute power or caprice. In contrast, God's "glorious power" (Col 1:11) can be understood only in terms of the reality of Christ and the Holy Spirit, and in relation to the free creation that the Father calls into being.

Nonetheless, the "almighty" character of God (in Latin *omnipotens*; *pantokrator* in Greek) does mean that there is nothing outside God's creative and providential scope. The whole of history unfolds before the Father's gaze and is brought to its climax in the life, death, and resurrection of Jesus, the only Son. Confessing "the Almighty" in these terms, therefore, is an act of limitless hope:

> Now to him who by the power at work within us is able to accomplish abundantly far more than all we can ask or imagine, to him be glory in the church and in Christ Jesus to all generations, forever and ever. Amen. (Eph 3:20–21)

In short, the Father's omnipotence is not an unbridled force aiming to stun and shock all lesser powers with some kind of superenergy. In contrast, the power of God acts, as Elijah experienced it, "as the sound of sheer silence" (1 Kgs 19:12), and, as history unfolds, in the Word made flesh. In the incarnation, divine power surprises creation with the revelation of God's own involvement in our humanity, beyond the scope of what eye can see, what ear can hear, or what the human heart can conceive. That kind of power is compatible with a divine vulnerability. God refuses to appear in our world save in the form of the crucified humanity of the Son. In this sense, the crucified Christ is both "the power of God and the wisdom of God" (1 Cor 1:24).

In short, the almighty character of God is primarily instanced in the supremely personal gift of the divine Word becoming flesh. Only God can communicate in this way. In the world of finite persons, despite the generosity evident in our various forms of gift-giving, there are limitations. We have to acknowledge a limit beyond which human giving is either destructive for oneself or oppressive and manipulative of the other—or even both. In contrast, such is the power of the Father's love that it does not diminish his divinity or overwhelm our humanity. His Word becomes flesh with us (in Hebrew *Emmanuel* means "God-with-us"), to offer believers the fullness of God's gifts. The Spirit comes to be, as it were, God-within-us, to enable our free and ever-growing acceptance of the Word. In these gifts of the divine Word and Spirit, the "almighty" character of God is displayed in the unreserved character of the Father's giving. Divine omnipotence, therefore, does not enter into competition with human freedom, as though the more of the one means less of the other. Rather, God acts to create, enlarge, and fulfill our liberty, as the Creator and fulfillment of freedom. Where the human autocrat exercises power over "subjects," the Almighty Father works within the freedom of the children of God, in order to bring about true liberty of spirit and true autonomy. The greater our freedom, the more creative our response, the more the omnipotent freedom of God is displayed.

Another aspect of the omnipotence of God is patience. God has time and, indeed, *makes* time for the whole of human history to grow into its true grandeur and scope. The patience of the Almighty is not defeated by human evil. The power of God is incalculably at work, despite the reality of evil, healing, forgiving, and leading to an ever-greater good. Though the patience of God is manifested in time, it is not endlessly frustrated or resisted. The will of God *will* be done. God acts, however, not as a brute force or grandiose display, but out of the inexhaustible imagination of love. Beyond all human limits, conditions, and calculations, such love achieves its own success. The crucified Jesus is raised from the dead. The evidence of this all-transforming event is such that it discloses to faith the triumph of God over evil, and yet allows for the freedom of each one to surrender in hope to the life-giving power of God, the Father Almighty.

The omnipotence of God is a life-giving and person-forming power. It works beyond the tiny limits of our own self-making. To confess the Father Almighty, therefore, is to enter the realm of true life, only to receive it as a gift and a grace: "All things can be done for the one who believes" (Mark 9:23). Though we might long for the eternities of life, love, and universal communion, reaching such fulfillment is impossible in terms of any human abilities. But such limitations are not imposed on the almighty love at work through the universe: "For mortals it is impossible, but not for God; for God all things are possible" (Mark 10:27). Consequently, faith in God, the Father Almighty, is the foundation of hope. The last word on the human predicament is not swallowed up in the dark silence of suffering, guilt, death, and failure. Working within, with, and through that groaning totality of the way things are is God's limitless and loving power.

The almighty, all-comprehending compass of God's power is not contradicted by an evolutionary understanding of the world, which can be entirely appropriate from a scientific point of view. It remains, however, that the "almighty" power of God does not compromise any cosmic forces or evolutionary processes. The dynamics of emergence and evolution are indifferent to individual fate, and even to the continuance of the species—perhaps even to the continuance of planetary life itself. In contrast, the almighty power that is the object of faith and the ground of hope is intensely personal. In God's creative intention, no one is left out or left behind, and, in terms of human history, no one generation is closer to God than another, and no self-sacrifice for others is lost. Those who have died out of the world, those who have given their lives for the sake of others, are not mere raw material for progress. They have died into the depths of the mystery at work and are embraced by the healing and creative action of the almighty Father.

Admittedly, the totality of what is in the making cannot be known to the human mind. It must be left to the omnipotent wisdom that operates in God's way and in God's time. The central icon of the emerging wholeness of creation is the risen Christ. The Spirit's transforming power is manifested in the crucified and risen Jesus, overflowing into the whole of creation and the whole of history. Nothing and no one is outside its universal care: "We know that all things work together for good for those who love God, who are called according to his purpose" (Rom 8:28).

In the face of evil, omnipotent goodness is displayed in a new intensity. The divine capacity to turn evil into good is manifested as mercy and forgiveness. The inexhaustible resources of God's love thus break the vicious circle of revenge and domination by inspiring the spiritual and moral risk of being "merciful, just as your Father is merciful" (Luke 6:36). Christian hope grows in a world where the limitless power of divine goodness, though seemingly defenseless, is the ultimately decisive factor:

> If God is for us, who is against us? He who did not withhold his own Son, but gave him up for all of us, will he not with him give us everything else?...No, in all these things we are more than conquerors through him who loved us. For I am convinced that neither death, nor life, nor angels, nor rulers, nor things present, nor things to come, nor powers, nor height, nor depth, nor anything else in all creation, will be able to separate us from the love of God in Christ Jesus our Lord. (Rom 8:31–32, 37–39)

God's omnipotence confronts the omnipotent pretensions of human culture—"the principalities and powers" of this world. The almighty character of God's love subverts the totalitarian pretensions that lie at the root of the world's self-destructive pride. In this regard, the loving power of God works to exorcise our most familiar demon, the lust for power that infests human history. God alone can topple the idols that distract us from the one thing necessary, to obscure our true finitude and to mask our dependence on the Other. The Father, the Almighty, acting in the subversive force of love, leaves us with nothing but the disarmed reality of our own humanity—yet as always loved by God, and offered true life as a gift. The humbling outcome is a new awareness: "God's foolishness is wiser than human wisdom, and God's weakness is stronger than human strength" (1 Cor 1:25).

The active experience of prayer makes us familiar with the manner in which God's almighty power works in our world. God does not act as one more vector of force among countless others. Rather, God works in all causes, and acts in all activities. However, the almighty power of divine love does not act from the outside, but from within the reality and dynamics of the world of divine creation. The seeming powerlessness of prayer works within, as the most life-giving and ultimate of all energies. In this respect, God is not changed by our prayers, as though our Father is made aware of some aspect of our needs or some detail of possible good that previously escaped his notice. The opposite is the case: the sheer bounty of God's love inspires human freedom to express itself in prayer in order that the heart be made more open to the gift-giving God. In this manner, God's power changes believers into intercessors, as they open their lives and the lives of others, and the life of the world itself, to the ultimate gift.

In all this, God acts as Creator and Redeemer by being intimately self-involved. As already mentioned, the climactic instance of God's self-involvement is the incarnation of the Word and the outpouring of the Spirit. This is to say that God is with us, within, behind, and before us, in all the pushes and the pulls that determine our lives. God acts in all influences from above and from below, in the formation of the structures that determine our being, in the intelligence that guides us, and in the transformation that awaits us in the life of the world to come. Everything issues from the Almighty, but with the gentleness of light, and in both the patience, and the impatience, of love.

When all is said and done, God is almighty, not in the sense of being capriciously at work from beyond our world, but as integrating all that makes up our world so as to make it serve an ultimate and all-inclusive purpose—to communicate the divine self-gift to creation.

To sum up, the words of the ancient sage of Israel cannot be bettered:

> We could say more but could never say enough;
> let the final word be: "He is the all."...
> For he is greater than all his works....
> Glorify the Lord and exalt him as much as you can,
>   for he surpasses even that....
>   Do not grow weary, for you cannot praise him enough.
>   (Sir 43:27–30)

To conclude: The power of God's love is revealed in patience and respect for the structures and dynamisms of the created world. The power of God has had time, indeed, made time and made space for us, in the billions of years needed for the universe to unfold, for life to emerge, and for human consciousness to awake in wonder. Dante wrote of the "the love that moves the sun and the other stars" (*L'amor che muove il sole e le altre stelle*). Today, we can think of that love creating and moving the universe from the first moment of the Big Bang, to the formation of the galaxies and the stars, planets, and finally of our Earth. There followed the emergence of primitive life three and half billion years ago, until it eventually broke through in human life. And in the human mind and heart, the universe became aware of itself as a gift of limitless wonder. Omnipotent love has time for the whole of human history to grow to its own grandeur and to reach its fulfillment.

Chapter 6

BY WAY OF NEGATION

Biblical and Philosophical Perspectives

Any exploration into God cannot bypass the dark or hidden character inherent in the notion of God. Though we might be attracted to the boundless Light of God, there is the way of negation. It resides in the inherent limitation and darkness of the human mind, and finds traditional expression in "the threefold path" of affirmation, negation, superaffirmation, and in the dynamics of analogical thinking.[1] That may sound rather foreign and philosophical when compared with the confidence of living faith, the words of Scripture, and the celebration of the sacraments and the liturgy. Nonetheless, there is an inevitable darkness.

AN ESSENTIAL NEGATION

Hans Urs von Balthasar makes a basic point when he speaks of the self-surrender inherent in the movement of faith. It implies a certain self-dispossession and expropriation:[2]

> In faith and through it, rather, I am made open and dispossessed of self....The important thing is the movement away from myself, the preference of what is other and greater, and precisely the person who has been expropriated for God does not want to become fully secure with regard to this Other and Greater.[3]

The way of negation affects the whole person, not only the mind and its cognitive scope and ability. In this chapter, we would like to bring together a number of aspects of our notion of God and divine revelation, and its relation to human experience. The classic theological tradition insists that any theological knowledge has to be content with telling us what God is not—compared to human imagination and expectations. Divine Be-ing infinitely exceeds every mode of the being found within the immediate world of our existence. The notion of the all-actual fullness of divine Be-ing functions as a kind of clearing space in which the mystery of God can be explored and affirmed, even though never to be fully known. We are like bats flitting through the sunlight and never able to look at the source of light. But even if we find our way around like the bat through radar-like auditory signals, the beatific vision and its "light of glory" seem an impossibility. However, God does not frustrate the human effort to know him, but respects the creaturely mode of our present existence, and the limitations to human knowledge that result.[4] The human mind must proceed by way of analogy—of likeness and greater unlikeness.[5] Clearly, there is a continuous play of language in the biblical witness to God. The Judeo-Christian tradition is most familiar with references or descriptions of God as "light," "the fountain of life," "the Good Shepherd," and so forth. But even the simplest affirmation of the goodness of God implies three stages in its meaning. First, there is the affirmation "God is good." Second, this is followed by an immediate awareness of the limitations of thinking and speaking in this manner, so that God is not "good," in the ordinary limited ways we experience what we call "good" in things or persons of our world. And then, third, after that moment of healthy hesitation, the mind can spring forward into the open free air of what God must be, even if how that is so remains unknown: God is good in a boundless, inexpressible manner, beyond our capacities to understand or imagine. Though present in all that is, God is not like anything in the world, and the kingdom of God surpasses the projections of human imagination: "No one has ever seen God" (1 John 4:12).

When it comes to exploring the Mystery of God, any approach must include prayer and reverence, especially when confronted with the now-conventional irreverence of modern speech. The beginning and end of exploration must be more personal, engaging one's sense of life's direction and value. That self-investment offers a preliminary anticipation of "God," the One to whom we pray. The personal *we* is important at this point, for it implies a certain other-directed solidarity, a sense of common purposes and destiny. The great family of humanity, one way or another, faces life and death, suffering, and hope for the future, in the overwhelming contingency of its existence, with the religious conviction of a future fulfillment given in the intimacy of union with God, and finally seeing God, face-to-face. In a lapidary description of that experience, Bernard Lonergan writes,

> That fulfilment is not the product of our knowledge and choice. On the contrary, it dismantles and abolishes the horizon in which our knowing and choosing went on and it sets up a new horizon in which the love of God will transvalue our values and the eyes of that love will transform our knowing....Though not a product of our knowing and choosing, it is a conscious dynamic state of love, joy and peace that manifests itself in acts of kindness, goodness, fidelity, gentleness and self-control.[6]

The Jewish tradition refrained out of reverence from pronouncing the sacred name, *YHWH*.[7] Other names and titles for God were employed, such as the *Lord*, the *Holy One*, the *Most High*, and so forth. While it is true that Christian faith in the incarnation introduced into human history a new kind of familiarity with God, there is still the need for Christians to constantly refresh their sense of reverence and wonder in regard to the infinities of God's love, wisdom, and power. Without such awe, religious activities become increasingly banal.

THE NEW TESTAMENT PARADOX

The Bible presents privileged data from the past concerning God's self-revelation. In the experience of Abraham, of Moses, of the whole people of Israel, especially in the great prophets and sages, God was self-revealed as "the Lord," the Holy One to be adored and loved, trusted and obeyed. In the experience of John the Baptist, of Jesus himself, and in the different experiences of Mary, Peter, Paul, and all the disciples and apostles numbered among the earliest followers of Jesus, and the different communities of the early Church, the One God is present in a climactically personal way—loving, merciful, self-giving. Though the writings of the New Testament witnesses to the light of divine revelation, they are not afraid of the darkness in which faith and hope must operate. The resurrection of the crucified One occurs in a world where the innocent still die, and the ways of God are beyond human comprehension. Hope must maintain itself in patience. Take the case of the earliest witnesses to Christ. After his crucifixion and death, Jesus "presented himself alive to them by many convincing proofs" (Acts 1:3). Yet they could still ask, "Lord, is this the time when you will restore the kingdom to Israel?" (Acts 1:6). Jesus's answer is instructive: "It is not for you to know the times or the periods that the Father has set by his own authority" (Acts 1:7). Judgments, calculations, and desires based on the proportions of time or place or culture—that is, anything less than God's transcendent freedom—are precluded, even if the disciples are to witness to Christ "in Jerusalem, in all Judea and Samaria, and to the ends of the earth" (Acts 1:8). There is simply no clear blueprint.[8] Let us look more closely at a number of instances of the negative style of the rhetoric of hope as we sample it in the Letters of Paul, in the Synoptic Gospels, and in the Gospel of John. Here we make a brief remark on each of these and the role of negativity in their writings.

Paul, for example, knows no hesitation in declaring that the resurrection of Jesus is the focal point of Christian existence. Nonetheless, he emphasizes the need for a patient openness in regard to what God is bringing about. In reference to Isaiah, he writes,

> No eye has seen, nor ear heard,
> nor the human heart conceived
> what God has prepared for those who love him.
> (1 Cor 2:9; see also Rom 11:33)

Paul's references to the future are more like descriptions of what is being left behind. A rear-view mirror does not map what lies ahead. The Apostle's impatient reply to a Corinthian query is noteworthy: "How are the dead raised? With what kind of body do they come?" (1 Cor 15:35). He answers in predominantly negative terms. The risen body is contrasted to what is "perishable," "sown in dishonor," "sown in weakness," "physical" in our present experience. Yet in the light of Christ's resurrection, he anticipates that the risen body of each one will become "imperishable," "raised in glory," "raised in power," "spiritual" (1 Cor 15:42–44). Hope for a risen existence reaches beyond any capacity to determine or even to represent the future. It awaits a fulfillment in the God who, "by the power at work within us is able to accomplish abundantly far more than all we can ask or imagine" (Eph 3:20). Paul contrasts the straining after a controlling knowledge of the future with surrender to the transcendence of God's wisdom. Here, he quotes both the Prophet (Isa 29:14) and the Psalmist (Ps 33:10) alike: "I will destroy the wisdom of the wise, and the discernment of the discerning I will thwart" (1 Cor 1:19). He goes on to say, "For since, in the wisdom of God, the world did not know God through wisdom, God decided, through the foolishness of our proclamation, to save those who believe" (1 Cor 1:21). The Apostle points to the source of true wisdom that lies beyond all human measure and control: "And we speak of these things in words not taught by human wisdom but taught by the Spirit, interpreting spiritual things to those who are spiritual" (1 Cor 2:13).

In this reversal of values, a certain negation or "deconstruction" of routine expectations and desires is demanded. The ever-new gift is not a simple *datum*, a "given," but an incalculable *donum*, a "gift." What God gives cannot be represented in the calculations and categories of present experience.[9] It comes from beyond the horizons formed by prevailing religious or philosophical projections. If "Jews demand signs and Greeks desire wisdom" (1 Cor 1:22), the cross of Christ will be a stumbling block to the expectations of the traditional religion, just as it will appear to the philosophers—and to any imperial ideology—as an extravagant or subversive folly: "For God's foolishness is wiser than human wisdom, and God's weakness is stronger than human strength" (1 Cor 1:25).

Even though Paul himself is justified in claiming the riches of the tradition of Israel as his own—"a Hebrew born of Hebrews; as to the law, a Pharisee," he has come to regard all this as "loss" and "rubbish," so that he might gain Christ and find justification in him alone (see Phil 3:4–11; see Matt 10). Hope in Christ has meant for him a "deconstructed" life, intent on the ways of God, rather than relying on an inherited intellectual or traditionally religious assurance. When Christian hope in any age is focused on the resurrection of the Crucified as its luminous center, something like Paul's vertiginous "loss" of past assurances is a sign of its health and authenticity.

The Christian imagination must not be allowed to rest in any image drawn from the present sphere of human experience. In his letter to the Romans, Paul states, "Now hope that is seen is not hope. For who hopes for what is seen? But if we hope for what we do not see, we wait for it with patience" (Rom 8:24–25). Hope comes into its own only by yielding to what only God can bring about. Even praying for the fulfillment of hope must not be constricted to the limitations of human desire. Our desiring needs the guidance and direction of the Spirit: "For we do not know how to pray as we ought, but that very Spirit intercedes with sighs too deep for words" (Rom 8:26). An extraordinary paradox runs through the whole of Christian experience. Despite the clarity of its faith in the risen Christ, Christian hope must learn to live not only with not-understanding and not-representing, but also with a certain not-willing. It must yield its mundane desires and expectations to the incalculable dimensions of the Spirit. Thus, the mundane ego, even in its most religious expressions, is radically disturbed in its desires and projections. This is a point at which Buddhist and Christian cannot but agree—and learn from each other.[10]

For their part, the Synoptic Gospels do nothing to lessen the distinctive Christian sense of negativity and provisionality. Despite the evidence that the Gospel writers were dead sure that the all-deciding event of God's action had occurred in Christ, they left plenty of room for what is yet to be revealed and further assimilated. Though Jesus preached the kingdom of God, its growth and seasons are not in human hands, nor subject to human law or prediction (Mark 4:26–29). Moreover, the scope of God's reign allows for wild aspects of undecidability. It nets fish of all kinds and qualities (Matt 13:47–50) and permits the weeds to grow alongside good grain (Matt 13: 24–30). To enter into this kingdom is to treasure new things and old in a proportion that remains unclear (Matt 13:51–52). For Luke especially, if one is to be included in the incalculable scope of God's mercy (Luke 6:37–42), it means refraining from judgments and the condemnation of others. The true relatives of Jesus are not those represented by blood relationships, but those who do the will of God (Luke 8:19–21). Most notably, the separation of the sheep and goats in Matthew 25 is disconcerting to all believers—and nonbelievers too—who have allowed a cultural form of religion to obfuscate the inclusiveness of God's reign (Matt 25:31–46).

Then there is the Johannine perspective. Even though Jesus encourages his disciples to accept his word, he allows that they cannot yet bear the full reality of what he has to say: "I still have many things to say to you, but you cannot bear them now" (John 16:12). His followers must go beyond their present apprehension to await an as yet incalculable future: "When the Spirit of truth comes, he will guide you into all truth...and will declare to you the things that are to come" (John 16:13). Earlier in the Gospel, Jesus declared to the Samaritan woman that "you will worship the Father neither on this mountain nor in Jerusalem" (John 4:21). The true worship of

God is not tied to sacred sites marking the particularities of religion and culture, but must be conducted in the space proportioned "in spirit and in truth" (John 4:23–24). Neither geographically, ethnically, nor conceptually bounded, the only horizon that remains is the indefinable reality of the Father himself, who is seeking out true worshipers.

Clearly, John is confident of the continuing revelatory power of the Spirit. But that confidence does not preclude his warning against believing every kind of spirit: "Beloved, do not believe every spirit, but test the spirits to see whether they are from God....By this you know the Spirit of God: every spirit that confesses that Jesus Christ has come in the flesh is from God" (1 John 4:1–2).[11] Such a demand for discernment is not without its difficulty. When faced with the elusive and opaque human reality of "the flesh" in which Jesus has come, discernment becomes complex. Only to a lofty Gnostic system is everything clear, pure, and untroubled by the presence of the utterly other. But true discernment points in another direction: "We know love by this, that he laid down his life for us—and we ought to lay down our lives for one another" (1 John 3:16). This demand is insistent: "For those who do not love a brother or sister whom they have seen, cannot love God whom they have not seen" (1 John 4:20). John's letter has a stark, but not altogether surprising, conclusion: "Little children, keep yourselves from idols" (1 John 5:21).

Some kind of orientation beyond neat religious notions or consoling interpretations seems to have been envisaged all along: "Let us love, not in word or speech, but in truth and action" (1 John 3:18). This is the original emphasis of the gospel itself. To know God is not a matter of "seeing" the divinity in some immediate evidence. Following of the other-directed "way" of Jesus (John 14:6), however, is the essential requirement, for "no one has ever seen God. It is the God only Son, who is close to the Father's heart, who has made him known" (John 1:18). Believers are reminded not to settle for any provisional version of human identity, no matter how secure the promise of eternal life, for "what we will be has not yet been revealed" (1 John 3:2). Though Jesus is "the resurrection and the life" (John 11:25), the risen Lord is never an object of matter-of-fact description. Experiences of his presence and absence interweave in the lives of these early witnesses to faith (see John 20:29–31).

The great prayer of Jesus (John 17) strikingly expresses the dynamic of Jesus's return to the Father and his involvement with all who believe in him: "I glorified you on earth by finishing the work that you gave me to do. So now, Father, glorify me in your own presence with the glory that I had in your presence before the world existed" (John 17:4–5). The heavens are so opened (see John 1:51) as to enfold the world into that relationship that exceeds all created forms of belonging, namely, the communion existing between the Father and his Son. As a result, as Jesus is going to the Father, the disciples will begin to inhabit the world in a new way—as witnesses to what God is bringing about: "And now I am no longer in the world, but they are in the world, and I am coming to you" (John 17:11a). Jesus asks the Father to protect his followers so "that they may be one, as we are one" (John 17:11b). Because of who his disciples already are, and because of what they will later do, a new community based in the unity of the Father and the Son comes into being (John 17:20–21). Jesus prays that the disciples given to him by the Father will be transported into a new sphere of existence—to be where he is and to share in his vision and glory (John 17:24a).

This prayer in the Gospel of John is not dealing with some distant existence in the future, but has immediate impact on Christian consciousness. By ascending to the Father and leaving the familiar world of his disciples, Jesus has in effect relocated them. Their world is changed. They live now in the heavenly realm of life and communion to which Christ has ascended, breathing the atmosphere of the Father's house of many dwelling places (John 14:2–3). The Father's original love for Jesus is now overflowing to those identified with him: "that the love with which you have loved me may be in them, and I in them" (John 17:26b). United with Jesus in his return to the Father, the disciples are drawn into the universe of mutual love and self-giving communion (John 13:34–35; 15:12, 17). It follows that not only is Jesus ascended, but also the disciples themselves are in a profound sense now "ascended" with him, and share in his communion with the Father. By ascending to "my Father and your Father, to my God and your God" (John 20:17), the ascended and glorified

Jesus transcends all worldly realities, categories, and previous conceptions. He now belongs to his followers in the deepest intimacy of his relationship to the Father.

Nonetheless, the invisibility of God remains, along with the impossibility of reducing the divine to an object or a particular factor within the world. Though the Johannine writings speak in strikingly intimate terms of our coming to know God (John 17:3; 1 John 4:7), being born of God (John 1:13; 1 John 3:9), and dwelling in God (1 John 4:16), there is a certain reserve when it comes to speaking about "seeing God." In fact, the Gospel states the opposite (e.g., John 1:18; 1 John 4:12).[12] Aquinas continues this tradition by speaking of being joined to God as to one radically unknown, who always transcends limited human knowledge. God is known only through the contemplation of the "effects" of his action. In other words, God is known in what he does, not directly, and never comprehensively.[13] Still, loving familiarity with God is possible, since love for God can go further than knowledge,[14] to "join" us to what always exceeds our knowing.[15]

The Prologue of the Gospel ends by directing its readers from the gift to the giver. If God has uttered his Word in the flesh, if the Father has sent his only Son, if God is so unreserved in giving, how are we to imagine the God who is the source of such grace? The answer is to be found in the gift. The invisible mystery of God the giver is made known in the flesh of history. By initially focusing on the Word, the Prologue suggests that God is to be heard, rather than seen. Even though faith rejoices in "gazing" on the glory of the only Son, the visibility in question is of the Son *from* the Father (John 1:14cd). God is invisible and the Father inexpressible—save by becoming visible and expressible through his Word and Son. Because Jesus Christ alone is turned toward God as the Word (John 1:1), and turned toward the Father as the only Son (John 1:18), he embodies the gift of the truth and unfolds the character of the Father.

The remarkably direct denial of any human capacity to see God, with which the Prologue concludes, is not only an affront to the Jewish piety of the day. It also undercuts prevalent Gnostic pretensions of knowing the absolute "One and the True." Yet the negativity of this denial serves the positive plenitude of God's self-revelation in Jesus Christ. The negation works in the believer to inspire a sense of receptivity and surrender to the mystery of the Father and his will. Faith brings no controlling knowledge of God. What it does bring is a relationship to Jesus Christ—soon to be revealed as the way, the truth, and the life (see John 14:6). To know him is to know the Father (John 14:7, 9–11). In his "heart-to-heart," Father-ward relationship (John 1:18), the only Son is unreservedly receptive to the divine will, and to all that God is, and is doing in the world. The eternal character of Jesus's identity as Word is thereby acted out in a relationship extended in time through his whole historical existence. Through this dialogical relationship the Father will be revealed, and his love for the world (John 3:16) will be enacted and expressed in the events that make up the Gospel story.

The Gospel Prologue has not aimed primarily to teach a new idea on God, but to introduce a story leading to an all-surpassing new experience of God—who is yet to be disclosed in the glory of Jesus. Thereby, it stands as declaration demanding to be countersigned by innumerable generations of others in their experience of the life, the light, and the love that has come to them.

This is to say that, though the Word does not reduce human speech to silence, it does affect human powers of expression with a kind of unrelenting negation in the light of the excess that marks the glory to be revealed. It subverts any overconfident pretensions to knowledge on the part of the disciples (see John 1:41, 45; 3:2, 9–10; 5:37b), and is always outside the horizon of human anticipation and experience. Until there is the hearing and seeing of faith, all lesser levels of hearing and seeing are radically called into question. However, neither previous revelation nor the original coherence of all things in the Word are negated. The great positives remain. Jesus will still be numbered among "the Jews," from whom comes salvation (John 4:22). The Word he embodies and communicates is still the fulfillment of the Scriptures (John 1:23; 6:45; 17:12; 19:24, 36). The world continues to be the object of God's love (John 3:16). Even with his historical departure, Jesus is still present to "the advantage" of his disciples, in the gift of the Spirit (John 16:7), and in the blood and water of the sacraments (John 19:34–35). Above all, the original glory that was proper to the Son "before the foundation of the world" (John 17:24) breaks on that world in the final hour of fulfillment. And the genesis of all creation in the Word is climaxed in his exultant cry, "It is finished" (John 19:30).

THE REVELATION EFFECT

There is a multidimensional impact of each of these revelatory aspects of the Christian mystery on the life and imagination of the Church. An overbrimming excess of the images, symbols, narratives, and interpretations of the Christ event finds expression in the New Testament. His ascension is at once a looking back and a looking forward. It looks back in order to amplify faith's comprehension of the meaning of Jesus's life, mission, death, and resurrection. However, it also looks forward. The disciples are not left impotently gazing into the heavens, but looking outward into the life and mission of the Church in its outreach to all peoples and all ages. As a result, Christian existence, retrospectively and prospectively, is deeply marked with the character of surrender, waiting, and hope. Jesus has gone before us. But in the present time, the faith of his followers must now wait, longing for his return as the Lord and judge of all. Though no longer in the world as he was before, he is neither absent nor disengaged from it. The numinous cloud accompanies his departure and his promised return (Acts 1:9–11). But he is carried upward to this divine realm with arms extended in blessing (Luke 24:50–53)—a gesture of effective solidarity with all who will follow him (see Luke 22:42–43). It does not represent Jesus turning away from the community of faith, but rather an all-embracing turning to them from the height, depth, and breadth of the mystery of God.

Necessarily, all believers follow Paul's directive words, whatever their respective situations: "Forgetting what lies behind and straining forward to what lies ahead, I press on toward the goal for the prize of the heavenly call of God in Christ Jesus" (Phil 3:13–14). Today, however, anyone sharing the Apostle's eagerness "to press on toward the goal" cannot but be affected by the mood of hesitation and disillusionment characteristic of this present historical period. It is often referred to as a "postmodern" era—a suitable tag to evoke the disconcerting fluidity in the ways of thinking and living in an increasingly complex world. *Postmodern* obviously means a period coming after what is assumed to be the solid style and clear certainties of the lengthy "modern" era. In this regard, it suggests a slippage from the classical forms of philosophy, theology, art, and even social and political organization. The classic forms that shaped the formative traditions informing the modern world up to the present were held in place by implicit philosophical commitments. There were shared assumptions concerning the nature of reality, the human person, the human capacity to know, the existence of God, as well as values of religion, beauty, and virtue. But a great change has taken place. Opinions may well differ in describing the present situation or in diagnosing its problems. But all agree that this is a changing world. Consequently, the Church, being part of that world, is not spared exposure to the seismic shifts that have occurred in human and historical experience.

In this postmodern context, faith, though it knows a deeper darkness, is spurred into a fresh creativity—to be bolder and more confident in its commitment to the distinctive character of Christian revelation—including the sense of reality it communicates and the moral conduct it inspires. When the shape of reality in all its guises has become so fluid, it is a good time to rise to the challenge of witnessing to the singular reality of the God revealed in the Christ event, and to explore it in the largest hermeneutical and contemplative space—cosmic, ecumenical, interfaith, and eschatological. To that degree, all this is a stimulus toward a more creative catholicity.

A new focus on the singularity of the Christian phenomenon brings its own costs. When faith is concentrated on the concrete and the singular, it can lose the universal connotation of the more philosophical abstract outlook. However, a clear sense of the distinctive and singular character of Christian reality and the particularity of its revelation must be critically cherished. There is a singularity to be respected—the divine, freely chosen economy of God's self-revelation in this particular manner. It could have been otherwise, but this is how divine wisdom determined it—as enacted in Christ, and in his life, death, resurrection, ascension, in the outpouring of his Spirit, and in the promise of his return at the end of time.

By defending the singularity of Christian revelation against the abstract universals of religion, spirituality, universal revelation, and so forth, a deeper negativity and darkness can result. The Word became flesh and, it can seem, can be left out of the general, ever-fluid, and inconclusive exchanges of the human conversation. Christian belief in the incarnation does not mean a contradiction of the human, but a new appreciation of humanity and a new way of belonging to it. It is here that some philosophical aspects of phenomenology can throw light on the negative-positive character of theological statements.

A critically elaborated account of the radically "given" but paradoxically hidden quality of what is disclosed is found, for instance, in Jean-Luc Marion's influential trilogy, *Reduction and Givenness, Being Given*, and *In Excess*.[16] In a way that combines the negative and positive aspects of revelation, Marion speaks of a "saturated event." In the experience of revelation, the overbrimming or "saturated" significance of the phenomenon imposes itself on the subject. It is given to such an extent that the subject is more like a witness to an event rather than an agent of its construction.[17] The believer is a recipient, more passive than active. In this respect, the gift of God's revelation is expressed most of all in the grammar of the dative case, for the gift is given *to* the believer. Revealed truth is not simply "there" to be inspected or possessed, as something taken for granted. It is rather as aspect of the divine self-giving, and self-communication to the receiving subjects, to reconstitute them in a new awareness: "If anyone is in Christ, there is a new creation" (2 Cor 5:17). In this instance, what is given is primary—not the conditions laid down by our rational capacities. "Positive" revelation demands the negation of rationalistic presuppositions and conditions. To think truly is to be aware of how thinking begins in response to something given. It is less thinking "about" something, and more thinking from *within* what is given, by responding to it, and by allowing to appear what is arrestingly "other." This phenomenological return to the given provokes a kind of theological conversion in method and style so that a theology of revelation is beholden, humbly and reverently, to what is given. It is marked by contemplative receptivity to the data of faith as disclosing the mystery of God and divine self-revelation. True, there is the danger of collapsing everything into a fideistic subjectivism that would be an obstacle to the full development of the theological intelligence and wisdom. At the other extreme, some may be rightly wary of an objectivism that overwhelms the role of the believing and thinking subject. But the biggest problem for theology is to think that the believing subject is already established before anything is given. When phenomenological style puts the emphasis on the self-giving "object," any activity on the part of the subject is marked by receptivity and responsiveness to what is given so that rationalistic pretensions no longer occupy center stage. What is radically precluded is a notion of the subject as a detached, all-knowing monad projecting itself onto what is other.[18] For the subject is the one who is "subjected" to what is overwhelmingly other, by witnessing to it and being stripped of all pretensions to comprehend or constitute what is given.[19] The healthy negativity here implied in this receptive role makes the mind of the believer into a luminous indicator of what is given.[20] Paradoxically, the sight of faith finds its focus in disclosing the "visibility" of what has been given from beyond its vision.

Yet intelligence and further exploration are not thereby put to sleep and left in the dark. Take, for example, the phenomenon of one's own birth. A response of gratitude is called forth for whatever it was, and whatever it led to. It occasions an endless effort of interpretation of the personal and communal meaning of such an unobjectifiable event.[21] It provokes an exploration of both the past that preceded it, the time in which it happened, its outcome in the present as it occurs, and of the future it gives rise to—even though the event of my "being born" fits into no prior project on my part—and perhaps not on the part of my parents!

The subject-object polarity inevitably shapes discussion, despite the extremes of both objectivism and subjectivism being spurious totalities. Rigid polar categorizations are incapable of appreciating what is given or the manners in which it provokes the response of thought or action. An approach to the given can be so overloaded by preconceptions and concerns that it is immediately subjected to one's own interests. In that case, the given experience would be merely raw material to be reduced to an acceptable conceptual and rational form by the self-contained subject. However, in the sense of Marion and others, the phenomenon is "saturated," not by one's prior attitudes, notions, and tastes, but in its overbrimming significance. Its inexhaustible freshness leaves thought ever at a loss to objectify what has so disclosed itself. The excess of the "saturated phenomenon" calls into question any prior limitation to the event of the self-revelation of God. In that light, all else is darkness.

As a phenomenon of revelation, the incarnation represents a culminating moment in the self-revelation of God. As an event it saturates in its intensity and expansiveness our sense of God, our view of the world, and our view of the universe itself. As the manifestation of divine beauty, the incarnation contests the world made ugly by despair and evil. In the flesh of the risen One, our own enfleshed or incarnate lives have already entered the realm of an eternal life of communion with God. On the face of Jesus, we discern, in a clouded way, God's glory and our true selves. The Word incarnate in Christ Jesus is a phenomenon that saturates our perceptions. Admittedly, on the one hand, a phenomenology restricted to clearly determined philosophical limits will contest this theological extension of what are otherwise regarded as mundane phenomena. On the other hand, the Church is a phenomenon in world history, and it would seem unrealistic not to appreciate it as such, and to explore its manifold influences. Further, a theology more habituated to a propositional and systematic exposition, may find this exposition too primitive. Yet what is at stake is not only the distinctiveness of the focal Christian phenomenon but also the play of light and darkness inherent in it. There is no intention of bypassing the critical demands of systematic theology and its ordered explorations of the meaning of God, but to awaken such theology to a new freshness.

Inevitably, the more phenomenologically specific and concrete Christian faith is in its singularity, the more it is likely to experience itself as the "foolishness" that Paul speaks of (1 Cor 1:18–25). The erudite "scribe" or the rationalist "debator of this age" (1 Cor 1:20) will find that the actuality or possibility of the event of Christ crucified cannot be rationally entertained. But a genuine Christian sense of God does not apologize for the particularity of what has been given to faith. Nor must it concede that it is "irrational"—when it is only such to a "rationality" that cannot allow God to exist and to act in this particular way, as in the scandalous bodiliness of raising the crucified Jesus from the dead.

TRANSCENDENT MYSTERY

The category of saturated phenomenon attempts to appreciate the complex play and many-sided character of the Christian experience of God. It, therefore, is not unrelated to the polyvalent and originally biblical word *mystery*. In current common usage, it refers to a puzzling phenomenon that demands investigation even though leaving us in the dark; and, for the adept investigator, the anticipation of detecting an eventual solution. Then, the mystery is solved, all questions are answered, and the plot ends when the "mystery" is no more. In contrast, Paul can speak of "the mystery that has been hidden throughout the ages and generations but has now been revealed to his [God's] saints...Christ in you, the hope of glory" (Col 1:26–27). The language of Christian doctrine refers to the "mysteries of faith"—the Trinity, incarnation, grace, and the beatific vision. These are the revealed objects of faith, for reason unaided could not deduce them. On a more devotional level, there are the "mysteries" of the life of Jesus, for example, the once fifteen and now twenty mysteries of the rosary, as various aspects of Christian revelation are become the subject of contemplation. On a more theological plane, say in the theology of Karl Rahner, "mystery" is fundamental notion expressive of God's self-communication to the human spirit.[22] In this sense, the mystery is not something to be solved, but something so given, so self-giving in its power to attract and fulfill the human heart that it constitutes the basic horizon of life and existence itself. The many "mysteries" of faith are aspects of the one self-giving mystery of God, which even as it communicates itself in the Word and Spirit, remains ever beyond any finite grasp. Human destiny culminates in the "beatific vision," God seen in a face-to-face vision, and yet in the inexhaustible infinities of the divine reality. Even though the blessed participate in the life of God, the divine mystery is not lessened, but more positively appreciated in its boundless excess.

Why not speak more simply, then, of the "mystery" of the revealed God rather than make this phenomenological detour? Would not that word say more than any quasi-philosophical term could suggest and say it better? In response, I would simply suggest that that the term *mystery* and its specific Christian and theological meaning is best recovered, and even intensified, by appreciating it as a saturated phenomenon. To the degree we treat the phenomenonality of divine revelation in this manner, there will be less likelihood of reducing a particular truth of faith to the ambit of the rationally acceptable. It is one way of locating the events of revelation outside the consciousness of the believer/theologian by making it an object of some kind to be inspected at will and assigned a place in some larger scheme of interpretation. In this sense, a genuine phenomenological approach restores a sense of mystery, and more so, in the instance of saturated phenomena, but most of all in the event of God's self-revelation.

The *chiaroscuro* of our knowledge is intensified in what we previously referred to as "limit situations or experiences."[23] Any effort to speak of God is earthed in fundamental human experiences of limits and frontiers—the limit of our capacity to understand or express, and the frontier of something given from beyond the horizon of our experience.[24] This kind of experience of excess is so fundamental in fact that without them we could not speak of God at all. Touched by the altogether Other, we human beings experience limitation. Not only do we confront out own mortality, but also all other limitations to our existence in mind or in action, and in all the ways we might experience human fragility and sinfulness. Great simple words, such as *love*, *joy*, *peace*, *beauty*, and *insight*, try to convey a certain range of elemental experiences. At the other extreme, there are moments or states when the words like *guilt*, *powerlessness*, *suffering*, *despair*, and *absurdity* resonate as more honest expressions. These expressive words indicate the positive or negative situations in which, one way or another, we are taken to the limit, to the edge. We are brought to the frontier of something else and something quite "other"—to touch the fringe of inexpressible mystery. It is to touch on "another world" as when one is entranced by great art or struck with the goodness, beauty, or wisdom of another person. Ordinary horizons suddenly expand to new dimensions in the presence of what cannot be contained, an inexpressible something or Someone. Quietly or dramatically, life draws us to such limits, to the beyond. Such experiences refresh what the word *God* can mean. Whether such occurrences are felt as unsettling edges of this world or as the frontier of another world, they are "God events" and direct mind and heart into the darkness of the inexpressible. They are windows both into what God has meant in the past, and what God can mean now. This experience of limits shapes our deepest selves and make us face into the dark. The ecstatic self is ever moving on, out, and toward what is Other. Exposure to other religions, spiritual traditions, and cultures intensifies the darkness of the human search. Our experience of struggling and hoping and loving, of living and dying, puts us in fruitful contact with all witnesses to God, as they have experienced the holy mystery in different ways and know the darkness and light in which it is wrapped.

Though faith enlists its own range of images, it employs them precisely *as* images, not as idols or as mere fabrications of human sentiment. To that degree, the images of faith are not idols but *icons*—precisely designed to let the mystery disclose itself on its own terms. The images of faith shine with a light from beyond, evoking the infinity of the mystery that has expressed itself in our world. The images employed by faith are not projections onto the blank screen of human aspiration, but in the darkness of human existence they are backlit, as it were, by the revelation of a love not of this world. In short, an authentic faith is intent on letting God be God!—in the scandal of the cross; in a humble invocation of the Spirit; in the shared celebration and witness of those who make up the people of God, saints and sinners alike.

A purified faith can refresh the notion of God, even in what appears to be a postreligious and "godless" phase of culture. The myth, not the science, of evolution tended to undermine human dignity and to rob the world itself of its mysterious depth within God's creation. As naive notions of how God acts in nature are surpassed, faith is free to explore how God is ever creative, the great attractor drawing the immense, groaning, manifold totality of the world toward its goal.

In this respect, Israel's invocation of the Lord as *YHWH* was a kind of gracious riddle. God gave his name as "I will be who I will be" (cf. Exod 3:14). Subsequent generations of faith have invoked God named in such terms, and then found faith in God self-revealed in Christ and the Spirit. However unreserved God's gracious communication, it can be received only through the gift and in the receptivity of faith. The Word of God is spoken from a great silence, so to provoke an attitude of listening in the human heart. The attentive mind is ever searching for words, the better to serve the truth revealed. The Word of God and the Spirit of God cannot be contained or constricted, nor reduced to anything less than God's own self-communication. With the prophet Elijah, all believers must struggle against the false gods, to know the one, true God only in humble self-surrender to the "sound of sheer silence" (1 Kgs 19:12). Such is the awesome silence of the mystery within which the whole world groans, hopes, and prays for fulfillment (see Rom 8:18–27).

In the silence and darkness of the mystery, God is experienced as "No-thing"—for God is not like anything else occurring within the horizon of human experience or knowing. God is beyond the range of our words and outstrips all ideas and concepts. Gregory of Nyssa, one of the great mystical doctors of the Church, wrote long ago, "The unlimited divine nature cannot be accurately contained by a name."[25] However intimately present to the heart of faith, God infinitely surpasses all human capacities of understanding and expression. Speech about God, therefore, must always favor the language of analogy, as was mentioned above. The scope of religious expression shuffles between what is known within our experience, on the one hand, and the unknowable, inexpressible reality of God, on the other. All our words lead into the divine silence, just as the holy darkness surrounds what little clarity our ideas might have. In comparison, therefore, with the clearly defined world of particular realities, God is "No-thing" and "No-where," never contained within any category or concept or image. Although the Creed certainly intends to affirm the true reality of God, it does not disclose it, but directs faith to the full dimensions of the mystery. Every profession of faith, every formula of belief, all alike fall short and await the evidence that only God can give. The mystery eludes all human language and does not encourage religious chatter. Nonetheless, the words of faith reach forward in adoration and love: "Beloved, let us love one another, because love is from God; everyone who loves is born of God and knows God...for God is love" (1 John 4:7–8). To have faith is to be plunged into the depths of the Mystery we can never objectify nor stand back from. To exist, to live, and finally, to love, is to be drawn into the homeland our hearts immediately recognized as more real than the air we breathe.

While the way of negation is a theoretically subversive and demanding way of knowing, a larger context is always to be borne in mind. All worthwhile knowing has, in some way, a negative dimension because it is personal and participative in a self-involving manner. As mentioned before, a couple cannot look up the meaning of their marriage in a textbook, for it is found only in the living and the loving. A work of art is not produced by simply following a book of instructions. Artists know what they have to offer only by doing it. The greater the reality, it would seem, the more our knowledge is tacit, and the more we feel our way forward. It means living on the inside of experience and being content with a participative knowledge that we can never stand back from.

Still, it is possible to have the meaning—understood as a series of concepts or logical formulations—and yet to miss the experience. Unless the distinctive experience of God to which the Gospels invite us is appropriated, theological language must appear abstract and general. What was once universally unquestioned, namely, the existence of God and the spiritual dimension of human beings, is now widely problematical. When "the truths of faith" drift free from traditional moorings, a sea of relativity seems to be the only option, while the question of meaning is endlessly deferred.[26]

Moreover, many predict that future Christianity will be increasingly in spiritual dialogue with the great religions of the East.[27] In a key article,[28] Rahner emphasizes the importance of the experiential grounding of faith. He writes,

> Today it is becoming clearer, and that too within Christianity at the doctrinal and institutional level, that this experience of God...really constitutes the very heart and center of Christianity itself and also the ever living source of that conscious manifestation which we call "revelation."[29]

It will be necessary to reclaim the Christian experience of God as it is documented in the New Testament. Without a reclamation of the God-ward movement of conversion inscribed in the singularity of that experience, the formulations and doctrines of faith cannot but appear abstract and exotic, while theology will look like a more or less sophisticated distraction from the singular personal form which the Gospel witnesses to. The evangelists were not intent on providing material for conciliar definitions; nor were Jesus and his disciples theologians giving seminars. In their respective ways, they were witnessing to the all-transforming gift of God. The more believers are refreshed in their experience of God, the more doctrines of faith will be seen as signposts pointing into the inexpressible mysteries they are meant to serve, and the more theology will be continually reinvigorated in its exploration of what has been historically revealed.

To conclude: this note on "the way of negation" in both its biblical and philosophical versions is meant to amplify, in a positive manner, the inevitable and desirable component of negativity in referring to God. There is no negativity in the Light that God is, in the divine intelligence and intelligibility. But the human mind unaided cannot in this life be exposed to the light, but is rather batlike in its experience and understanding of the divine Light. It is well to keep both these polarities in mind.

Chapter 7

GOD AND DIALOGUE

There is no going to God without reaching out to others: exploring *the* Other requires a continuing path of interacting with the others who cross our path, including, embracing, and learning from them.

Perhaps the term *dialogue* is overused today. It can connote a mere fallback position in just about any attempt to establish good relations. To that degree, it can be a symptom of timidity in those who have lost the courage of their religious convictions, especially when the criterion of objective truth is weakened, or when there is no recognition of the positive claims of divine revelation. In such cases, appealing to dialogue would be simply a form of repression of real differences, as well as an implicit acknowledgment of common defeat regarding the possibilities of ultimate reconciliation. However, fresh clarity and conviction lie in exploring more deeply the theological or "God dimension" of the meaning of genuine dialogue.

DIALOGUE AS EVENT

Everyone admits that research into traditions, key doctrines, and culturally determined ways of life are essential. Likewise, the patient drafting and sifting of documents is inescapable, along with critical interpretations of classic religious writings and commentaries. But, with the growing emphasis on dialogue among persons, faiths, and traditions, along with a shared willingness to enter the risk and exposure involved, there is a shift of consciousness.

Exclusive concentration on the objectively articulated expression of religious truth must recognize the intersubjective field of communication. In an open horizon of interaction, participants in dialogue meet in order to discover further reaches of the reconciling truth. In this intersubjective field, truth exercises its attraction primarily by being lived and incarnate in a communication with the "other." While sacred writings and classic doctrines emerge from the past,[1] dialogue is above all an encounter in the present. It takes place between living "others" who, in this instant, breathe the same air of this planet in these times of unprecedented pluralism.

Dialogue, therefore, is better described as an *event* enacted in this critical moment of history, that is, in this *Now* of the historical moment. For each act of dialogue is a new event within the common search for truth—a "moment of truth" within interpersonal communication. It occurs, too, as possessing the character of a gift, the grace of something newly or surprisingly given. Those who were in many cases previously estranged now come together in a shared search for something more. When the event character of dialogue is appreciated in this way, there is something of indefinable excess.[2] The outcome is unpredictable. It is never reducible to the expression of a common policy or articles of doctrinal or moral agreement, and so forth—however welcome such outcomes might be.

RECEPTIVITY TO THE OTHER

In the exchanges of dialogue, different registers of affectivity come into play. The "other" is welcomed into communication, not in order to suffocate that otherness, nor to reduce it to a projection of more of the same and the familiar, but actively to allow for it. The other is welcomed within the boundless horizon of God's action in the world. In that horizon, the real other is not a projection of "me" or "us," but enjoys an irreplaceable, specific, and objective dignity in the universe of God's love, even if the eschatological realization of one living communion including all is beyond imagination. As a consequence, dialogue enacts the creative catholicity of faith, hope, and love.[3]

Our deepest God-ward commitments can be fully lived out only in an interpersonal space and field of communication. Interreligious dialogue, therefore, does not envisage participants merely episodically overhearing the respective religious positions of others. A common attitude of listening means that the other is encountered, not, first of all, in an intellectual, ethical, or doctrinal capacity, but in a personal and historical particularity. The actual, personal other emerges from the anonymity inevitably associated with typical generalizations regarding individuals or communities. He or she is encountered as a *you*, however disconcertingly in the *here and now* of a particular event. In this respect, dialogical openness, particularly to the hitherto estranged other, contrasts with a projection of "more of the same." What is asymptotically envisaged is a unity-in-difference, rather than the homogenized sameness. If the ideal is uniformity, it precludes the promise of anything new. A hidden ideology is repressively at work, prescribing that the other must be converted to *us*, rather than *all of us* being converted to the radically new in our communal history. The postmodern situation, along with its deconstructionist philosophies, calls for an appreciation of the previously disowned. Ideologically imposed systems of uniformity and immobility are radically shaken by a freshly appreciated *alterité*.[4]

But there is also an interreligious basis of a more theological kind. A more generous openness to the human other takes place within the horizon of the utterly Other, namely, God.[5] The human other exists, or is *here*, not simply by chance, or because of an outreach of a particular religious tradition or community, but, most radically, because of the grace and giving of the transcendent God. To that degree, a genuine dialogical overture is a result of God's action in the world. The transcendent and all-inclusive Other has not ceased to act. In the wide world of divine creation, the Creator is to be neither possessed nor controlled, but adored and praised in all and as the God of all.[6] Interreligious dialogue, therefore, must leave the ineffable Other both free to act and free to give, in ways always hidden to human comprehension.

In terms of dialogical activity and attitude, the terms *interfaith* or *interreligious* can give the impression that the faith or religion concerned is a fixed entity, a body of religious positions and practices, with clearly defined goals, boundaries, doctrines, and so forth. The implication, therefore, is that discussions occur from behind fixed positions, so that each faith or religion tends to be reduced to a body of its clearly articulated doctrines and beliefs. Admittedly, it would be destructive for all concerned to argue that dialogue demands that those participating in it must hold all such beliefs in suspension. Nonetheless, it might be more realistic, and even more promising, not to speak of *interfaith* communication, but to refer to a God-centered *interhope* dialogue, in regard to the other—and, indeed, to the universe itself. Admittedly, hope is sustained by faith and articulated in beliefs. However, "interhope dialogue" suggests an eschatological overture that brings a larger, future-oriented dimension to the exchange. The result is a more self-involved and properly open communication. For example, I might say with all the weight of Christian and Catholic tradition that I hope to share eternal life, in a transformed creation already anticipated in the risen Christ, with *you*, and all peoples as the beneficiaries of God's limitless love, with all who are destined, as I believe and hope, to see God face-to-face. At least, it would suggest something wonderfully indefinable, a horizon of excess that reduces the force of present religious, spiritual, or philosophical differences. Exchanges on the level of hope, we suggest, cannot but engender a more engaged and lively dialogical attitude.[7]

A CHRISTIAN STANDPOINT

In a more formally institutional manner, dialogue with the other is structured into Christian faith through Vatican II's *Nostra Aetate*—and more explicitly, in *Gaudium et Spes*. What appeared over fifty years ago as a rather formal pastoral and ecclesial overture to other faiths has become a practical imperative these decades later in the light of the Church's mission to the world. It has borne fruit in such documents as *Dialogue and Proclamation*.[8] The mission of the Church "*to* all peoples" (*ad Gentes*) is now a mission to be conducted "*among* all peoples" (*inter gentes*). Many Christians in their hometowns and cities live with neighbors and fellow citizens who are Indigenous, or Muslim, Hindu, Buddhist, and so on. Add to this plurality a growing proportion of those admitting to "no religion" in the more secularized countries of the West, even while professing that they are still "spiritual." The Catholic Church's secretariats for dialogue at least have the advantage of keeping the ideal of dialogue institutionally structured in a rapidly expanding situation. Demographic developments caused by mass migrations, and refugees fleeing from inhospitable regions of political, religious, economic, or environmental threat, add to the challenge and contribute to the resources for a deeper understanding and solidarity.

At this point, we can dwell on a specifically Christian quality of dialogue. Whatever their personal positions, all participants in dialogue might well attempt this kind of "recollection," in ways appropriate to their own faith, religious tradition, or spirituality, be it Jewish, Muslim, Hindu, Buddhist, humanist, and so on.[9] To do so would require a certain heightening of awareness of what is involved—both in relation to God and in relationship to others.

True, dialogue has been very much a Christian thing. It is now pervasive in the rhetoric of how the Church relates to the world and, for that matter, how Christians should related to one another and to members of other faith traditions. There is something about Christian existence that makes it imperative to reach out to the other in an expanding catholicity of communication. In an authentically *Cat-holic* position, the *-holic* suggests an open horizon. It is as though a postmodern sensibility has been quietly absorbed into the Church's classic doctrinal and proclamatory modes of discourse. As such, dialogue with the other is recognized as a vital ingredient in the Church's living tradition. And if it is to be a living tradition, it has to be more than a massive bank of spiritual capital, containing in its vaults answers to questions never asked before.

Genuine dialogue must be alert to the differing worlds and specific horizons in which each religion lives. After all, *religion* is an abstract term, but religions are particular. This is well said by the Spanish American philosopher George Santayana:

> Any attempt to speak without speaking a particular language is not more hopeless than the attempt to have a religion that shall be no religion in particular. Thus, any living and healthy religion has a marked idiosyncrasy. Its power consists in its special and surprising message and in the bias which that revelation gives to life. The vistas it opens up and the mysteries it propounds are another world to live in; and another world to live in, whether we expect ever to pass wholly over into it or not, is what we mean by having a religion.[10]

In these new times, seemingly without precedent, believers are well advised to let God be God, in the hope that the true God will be revealed in the way and on terms determined by God alone. Such an attitude introduces into faith a new intensity of surrender and adoration. In that context, Christian dialogue must be at the service of the Holy Spirit, who works to "declare to you the things that are to come" (John 16:13). The Spirit is given beyond any human measure (John 3:34) compared to the limits set by previous failures, current evils, formal policies, cultural expectations, historical conflicts, and even doctrinal formulations. The appearances of the risen One take place in the context of a mission into the larger world of the nations (Matt 28:19; John 20:21). In the Fourth Gospel, God is referred to as the Father who seeks "true worshipers," beyond traditional sacred sites: "neither on this mountain nor in Jerusalem" (John 4:21). For Paul, encountering the other is located within the expanding horizon of God who is "gather[ing] up all things" in Christ (Eph 1:10). It takes place in the universe created in Christ, "through him and for him" (Col 1:15–16). The Prologue of John's Gospel is more protological with its hymnic affirmations: "All things came into being through him" (John 1:3)—the "life" and the "light" of all (John 1:4).

This sense of the universality of Christ, however, need not compromise the sincerity of true dialogue. Understandably, it can seem that Christian dialogue with the other must be inherently totalitarian and imperialistic. Must Christians, therefore, stand back from the ultimacy and unreserved character of their faith, and bracket out, or even deny, the inclusive universality of their own standpoint for a more accommodating and egalitarian inclusiveness? The only way out of such a dilemma is to go deeper into what is involved and to refine a sense of the "absolute" and "relative" registers of faith. Faith must remain *absolute* in its unqualified commitment to God's revelation in Christ. But it is *relative* in regard to the indefinable dimensions of the Christian mystery yet to be realized. The intersubjective realizations of that mystery are immeasurably more extensive than the Christianity of the present, or Christendom in the past. In the unimaginable extent of God's free action, Christ is given as "the image [in Greek, *eikon*] of the invisible God" (Col 1:15)—and not as an idol erected by the projections of Christian ideology. Faith's surrender to the eschatological extent of the mystery of Christ demands an outreach to the other, and to all others, as already known and loved by God, whatever the limitations of present attitudes and understanding. Hope faces into the eschatological future as the space in which the other is welcomed as *you*, as a unique person. It envisages the ultimate *we* that hope desires and love already begins to anticipate. In this perspective, the salvific will of God inspires the theoretical and practical inclusiveness that finds its proper expression in dialogue. In that respect, three relationships are fundamental, namely, in regard to the neighbor, the enemy, and in prayerful intercession. Each of these relationships disrupts the tendency to self-enclosure and to the reduction of the other to the closed circle of "family member."

First, the *neighbor*. The neighbor is never a theoretical entity, but precisely the other who occurs, as it were, as a disturbance to the closed circle of familial or communal life. The other is there, not immediately as an object of love, but as a reproach to the narrowness of love, and as an appeal to a more self-transcending and other-directed way of loving. The Jewish philosopher Levinas has given what is now a classic expression to the ethically provocative appearance of the neighbor.[11] The face of the neighbor turned to any of us embodies the question, Where were you when I needed you? The New Testament offers numerous variations of such disruptive experience, principally in the parables of the Good Samaritan (Luke 10:29–37) and the last judgment (Matt 25:31–46). Further suggestive instances are the scandal resulting from Peter's entering the house of Cornelius (Acts 10:1–48), Philip's encounter with the eunuch of the court of Queen Candace (Acts 8:26–40), and the somewhat ironic report of Ananias's reaction to the converted Saul (Acts 9:10–19), who, much to the surprise of Ananias, has been chosen to be the future Apostle to the nations. In the background of any understanding of Christian dialogue is the incident of Jesus's own encounter with the Samaritan woman at the well (John 4:7–15). In the name of God, the distant or disowned other comes to be recognized as "neighbor," for God is to be worshiped "neither on this mountain nor in Jerusalem," but "in spirit and in truth" (John 4:21, 23).

Second, the *enemy*. Paradoxically, the presumed presence of the "enemy" in the Gospel makes it clear that the life faith is ill-advised to envisage a serene world of gently conducted dialogue. The world that God loves, and that Christ comes to save, will be in neuralgic reaction against anyone who disturbs the prevailing human condition with a summons to love, to forgive, to be reconciled, and to renounce oneself (Luke 6:27–31; John 16:1–4). The world, and even its religions, is the milieu in which the crucified Jesus is a scandal to the Jews, a folly to the Greeks (1 Cor 1:22–25), and a subversive of imperial authority. The imperative to Christian dialogue does not mean repressing this uncomfortable ingredient in Christian witness in the world. It is presumed, then, in actual situations that dialogue can entail an encounter with hitherto powerful "enemies." As a result, dialogue comes to have a sharp edge of urgency and risk—when intent on fostering communication between all parties and disarming the murderous animosity that has often prevailed. But even in such an uncomfortable encounter, as Luke 6 attests, the "enemy" and the "persecutor" are encountered in the realm of a limitless mercy (Luke 6:36). Christ has come, in the words of John's Gospel, not to condemn the world but to save it, and thus to make even erstwhile enemies cosharers in eternal life.

There is a risk. Dialogue with the antagonistic other in the domain of God's grace treads a fine line between provoking further anti-Christian animosity and appearing weak, vulnerable, and exploitable. Christian realism can expect no less; but, under the sign of the cross and following the example of the Suffering Servant, it cannot foreclose on the limitless range of God's mercy, nor, despite past antagonisms, to foreclose on the possibilities of reconciliation. The experience of conflict is no reason to deny the divine intention to bring all to salvation (1 Tim 2:3–4). How this is to be worked out is not given to the mortal mind or imagination to conceive (Rom 11:33–34). What must remain clear in Christian dialogue is that it must move forward both in an unreserved commitment to Christ, and in the service of the inclusive scope of God's salvific love.

Third, *intercession*. Dialogue with the other occurs within the Christian prayer of intercession:

> First of all, then, I urge that supplications, prayers, intercessions, and thanksgivings be made for everyone....This is right and is acceptable in the sight of God our Savior, who desires everyone to be saved and to come to the knowledge of the truth. (1 Tim 2:1–3)

The Christian sense of God in this basic instance of prayer cannot forget that "God our Savior...desires everyone to be saved." Salvation is destined for all; and the gift that Christian faith witnesses inspires a relationship to all others—even to those who are "kings and all who are in high positions" (1 Tim 2:2). At the heart of such prayer is a sense of the other, not as defined by one's present relationships, but as indefinable within the universality of God's saving intention. And yet there is a relationship—within this transcendent horizon—between oneself and the other, with both parties identified "in the sight of God." The implication is that our lives are "right and acceptable in the sight of God" to the degree we are open to the other precisely in the realm of God's saving grace. Once the unpredictable and patient activity of dialogue is understood as an aspect of the intercessory relationship of Christian prayer for all, its intentionality is broadened and deepened; it is both prayer and an answer to prayer.

After mentioning these three basic relationships, we can go on to make further reference to a Johannine perspective. The Prologue of the Gospel focuses on the incarnation of the Word *Logos* (John 1:14a). As the Gospel unfolds, it evokes an ever-shifting *dia-logical* space. The Word enters into conversation with all the *dramatis personae* who will figure in the dramatic unfolding of John's narrative. In the presence of this Word, they will evince either acceptance, incomprehension, hesitation, doubt, questioning, or rejection, or any combination of such attitudes. The Word, dwelling among us (John 1:14), thus opens a unique field of communication. The "God-ward" (in Greek, *pros ton theon*) status of Word in the first verse of the Prologue presumes a certain dialogical relationship within the divine mystery itself. In John 17, this Word-God relationship is unfolded in the prayer of the Son to the Father. Coming out of this original communion, the Word enters the world to make it an expanding field of dialogue.[12] The living "flesh" of the world includes communication with others. It reaches out to believers in every age. God's unrestricted love for the world, therefore, provokes the full play of human conversation on the meaning of life, human identity, the destiny of the world itself, and the character of God.[13] As the Word is the life and light of all peoples (John 1:3–5, 9), it radiates interreligious dialogue so as to open the possibilities of communication to a new register of meaning. It is not the time to forget that the first words of the Word in John's Gospel are, "What are you looking for?" (John 1:38).

A DEEPER THEOLOGICAL CONTEXT

All of the above remarks suggest aspects of the intentionality of Christian interreligious dialogue. The quite traditional notion of "the divine missions" moves into a fresh relevance, even though it is somewhat neglected in the theology of dialogue and deserves more development than can be indicated here.[14]

The "visible mission" of the Word occurs in the incarnation. It spans the depths and heights of human existence, namely, through Christ's death and resurrection. The visible mission of the Word is related to the "visible mission of the Holy Spirit,"[15] the manifestation of the Spirit at the foundation and in the continuing existence of the Church through history. Here, the Church is that identifiable part of the world that has become intentionally alive to the mystery of God's self-communication to the world as a whole. What tends to be overlooked, however, is the realm of the "invisible missions," as they have been elaborated by Augustine and Aquinas. Now, the "visible" missions of the Word and the Spirit manifest what has been going on throughout all human history. The "invisible" communications of the Word of wisdom and in the Spirit's gift of self-transcending love have been occurring. That is to say, the historical events of the incarnation and the outpouring of the Spirit disclose what takes place within the interior realm of human consciousness through the "invisible" workings of grace.[16] In such a perspective, the invisible mission of the Word reaches its expressive apex in the life, death, and resurrection of Jesus. Likewise, the invisible mission of the Spirit is explicitly experienced in the witness of Christian believers, their Scriptures, their sacraments, and their doctrinal beliefs. But here we call attention to that more diffuse and vast realm of divine communication that in principle is limitless and unrestricted to the past or present limits of the Christian community. In this regard, Christian dialogue presumes what has been going on for everyone throughout all time, in the interiority of human consciousness. Aquinas describes this in experiential terms associated with the intentionality of knowing and loving God, however incognito such a God may be. God sends the Word into the realm of human intelligence to enable it to attain a transcendent wisdom and light. Likewise, the Father breathes the Spirit into the human heart in its desire for union with the ultimate good. Thus, there results a quasi-experience of God through an enlightening of the mind and the transformation of the heart (in Latin, *instructio intellectus et inflammatio affectus*)—a sense of divine indwelling, and an experiential participation in the divine mode of knowing and loving proper to God's own life.[17] In this mystical and theological horizon, God dwells in creation in as many ways as there are persons: the Father's house has many rooms (John 14:2).

The intentionality of Christian dialogue can fittingly be located in the field of trinitarian missions by which God is present and active in the lives of all. At that point, Christian dialogue comes to an awareness of an immeasurably vaster world than that of explicitly Christian history. In the special history of revelation,

God is self-defined in terms of the incarnation and in the gift of the Spirit of Pentecost. But in the larger world of the invisible missions, the Word of God is incognito as far as history goes; yet, at the same time, it is experienced as the infused wisdom that bathes the self-transcending search for truth in a light not of this world. Likewise, the Holy Spirit is incognito, as the love that sustains and fulfills all our loves for God and the world, all its rejection of evil and love for the good, however it is named.[18]

A theological assessment of religions as systems, traditions, or spiritual philosophies and their status in the sweep of God's saving providence cannot be hurried. In the meantime, dialogue is between persons. Only in persons do religions or philosophies of life exist. In that perspective, Christian dialogue operates at the interface of what theology has termed "the visible and invisible missions" of the Word and the Spirit.

In all this, *dialogue* is not primarily a noun, but a verb. It expresses a conscious, intersubjective activity, a passing over to the other, and a return to oneself in a limitlessly expanding sense of the *We* of all humanity in God. Interfaith dialogue intensifies and extends our consciousness of the grace of God operating in all the events that make up "the way of all the earth."[19]

Chapter 8

EXPLORATION UNENDING

An Open Conclusion

In *An Exploration into God*, as was said at the beginning of this project, the preposition *into* is important. If the mystery of God is infinite, then any exploration is necessarily open-ended, and, in the deepest sense, inconclusive. Indeed, theologians have long stressed that even in the beatific vision of God face-to-face, one aspect of that vision is to see that God is absolutely uncontainable and never fully graspable by any finite mind. Indeed, only God can really "get" God. Even in the bliss of the blessed, the infinite mystery can never be exhausted, for it calls forth an endless kind of joyous exploration. It gives a knowledge that leads into an ever-continuing knowing, a love that keeps on being love for the infinite goodness and beauty that are revealed, a delight that draws ever more fully from the divine joy and bliss.

SUMMARY AND SIGNPOSTS

True, part of the motivation for writing these pages was a lament over the strange kind of amnesia that can come into cultures and even creep into religious studies and theological systems, church communications, and interreligious dialogue—a forgetfulness of God, even though the light that God is underpins all searchings for meaning, value, and beauty. After these steps along the way of our exploration into God, I would like to bring the different perspectives opened up to some kind of conclusion. I am under no impression that any concluding statement can be definitive. After all, we have been dealing with the darkness and light of God, the analogical character of our knowing, the singularity of revelation, and the absolute and limitless Be-ing of God. The words of the Fourth Lateran Council continue in the Christian exploration of the mystery of God as a wholesome reminder: "Between creator and creature no similarity can be noted without a greater dissimilarity being noted."[1] Nonetheless, there are some conclusions that may be drawn, following this particular exploration into God, not so much as summing up what has been said, but as pointing the way forward into a greater sense of the mystery into which believers have been drawn.

By briefly retracing our steps we can arrive at a clearer sense of direction in our exploration into God. We began by drawing attention to the absent frontier in so much of our religious and even theological conversation, with the result that references to God become stale and banal. Cultural conditioning plays a part in making the frontier seem so distant and, indeed, absent. Further, our very familiarity with religion, theology, liturgy, and religious expression, theoretical and practical, can desensitize us to the most radical and crucial of all questions, "Where is your God?" (Ps 42:3). One question begets many: How is God to be found? What are we looking for? And why bother? The first chapter of John's Gospel, after hymning the incarnation of the Word of God among us, prepares believers to receive the whole message of the Gospel. It is worth noting, therefore, that the first words of the Word addressed to the disciples who have begun to follow Jesus, are a question, "What are you looking for?" (John 1:38). Questions keep recurring in every time and culture as to where God is to be found, and how God is the fulfillment of all we long for. Such questions lose none of their edge in our present situation when they are ignored.

The pressures of culture from without, and our oppressive familiarity with religious practices and expressions from within, make it necessary to refresh, as best we can, the boundless God-horizon in which we think and act and pray—all aspects of an orientation to the mystery that attracts us as nothing else can. In Nietzsche's vivid language, cited in chapter 1, God is not meant to be a spider sucking the vitality out of human existence, but the mystery that is the "transfiguration and eternal Yes" to what life is about. Problems remain. The culture is in a state of flux. It has entered into a postmodern situation in which the phrase *God is dead* sounds all too certain, while affirming the opposite in this pluralist age has value only as a personal conviction, leaving the wider world untouched.

There are problems of expression. A literal-minded age may not recognize the flexibility and range of reference in language attempting to name all dimensions of reality. Hence, the special character of analogical language: words and ideas born of experience in the routine world can be stretched, as it were, toward what is other. When that evocative and creative character of language wanes, words drown in the flood of advertising and media chatter.

There are problems also as to the character of knowledge itself. If theology is traditionally described as "faith seeking understanding," it might be considered as an odd type of knowledge, at best as an emotive or mythological rhetoric. Things look different with the realization that a form of faith—and love, too—pervades all efforts to understand. In a paradoxical sense, the more self-involved we are in mind, heart, and imagination, the more we come to know realities beyond the routine scope—as when the love of nature informs ecological and environmental sciences. It is not extreme to claim that a commitment to love God with all one's heart and mind and soul and strength results in a special kind of knowledge of God as it is expressed in the Bible and in the mystics, great and small.[2]

The second chapter attempted to clear the ground for such a consideration of God that excludes both idolatrous and mythological fundamentalism. There are classic resources to be retrieved in Aquinas's notion of God as sheer, all-actual, Be-ing, but not as a "supreme being" among many "beings." Such a notion need not distract from the personal and concrete sense of personal faith and replace it with a vague colorless abstraction. The sheer, all-actual Be-ing of God forms the horizon in which all biblical, doctrinal, and experiential data on the character of God can be appreciated in their depth and singularity. Not to attempt this can lead to a flat fundamentalism. Expressions of faith lack a sense of wonder and are incapable of speaking with conviction in the dialogical situation of faith today, especially concerning God as what Friedrich Nietzsche calls life's "transfiguration and eternal Yes."

After clearing the ground in this way, we moved onto to more specific topics, dealing with our consciousness of God, creation, the Trinity, the "Father Almighty," the negative character of our knowledge of God, and the sense of God implicit in true dialogue with the religious other.

The aim of chapter 3 was to reshape the question of God and creation as it resonates in human consciousness. We suggest that the idea of the Creator God is best considered "from the inside out," from the experience of consciousness and interiority. It entails attentiveness to the experience and dynamics of consciousness in everyone who experiences, imagines, asks questions, makes judgments, and responds in wonder, hope, and love. Such an approach contrasts with the more traditional perspective, "from the outside in," which can give the impression of already knowing God as a supreme object among the innumerable objects of our experience and knowledge, and, therefore, known in a way that is independent of the consciousness of the knower. This objective kind of knowing affected traditional discussions of the soul, its existence and classification. Such considerations can now be located on firmer ground by appealing to the experience of consciousness, that is, as that interior but personal dimension, the principle by which we are related both to the Creator and to the whole of creation.

Chapter 4, entitled "Trinitarian Connections: Inside Knowledge," sought to enlarge the trinitarian frame of reference while at the same time intensifying the distinctive Christian experience of God in Christ and the Spirit. The basic scriptural source is John's Gospel—on which the subsequent trinitarian doctrine and theology rely. With its implications of the primacy of relationality and communion, a trinitarian sense of God is well attuned to a contemporary understanding of the dynamics inherent in the emergent universe. It is likewise a fertile source for promoting interfaith dialogue. A renewed trinitarian vision, therefore, can prove a precious resource in the present era. Faith in the Trinity flows from an "inside" knowledge of God as believers are drawn into the movement of the life of God and are conformed to each of the diving persons.

In considering God, the Creator, "Father Almighty," we were able to emphasize the gifted character of creation in chapter 5. Creation is a gift and a giving since it originates in the divine freedom, and in a love unconditioned by anything outside itself—in that sense, God creates "out of nothing." Indeed, it is the equivalent of saying that God creates "out of love." This love is dependent on nothing outside of God, who freely calls and sustains all things in being. Given its divine origins, the created universe is a unified whole—"heaven and earth," the "visible and the invisible"—as the Creed expressed it. From this derives a particular biblical realism in which God is known, not despite, but in and through material creation. Furthermore, we stressed that God is invoked and confessed as "Father" only in relation to his self-gift in the Son and the Spirit—so that a critical understanding of the trinitarian communion is called for, with special emphasis on the gift of the Spirit—through whom we come to know Christ, and through Christ, dare to say, "our Father." Similarly, the omnipotence of the Creator is not reducible to divine caprice: for all the works of God are tempered by an infinite wisdom and intelligence, just as the self-giving love of God is the subversively "omnipotent" factor within God's creative and providential action, working through the death and resurrection of Christ.

Implicit in all the previously treated topics is the "way of negation." The negative character of our biblical and philosophical knowledge of God is not an obstacle to this exploration into God. It is rather the condition for its positive continuance. The aspect of negation works positively by intensifying and amplifying the inevitable (and desirable) *chiaroscuro* in any knowledge of God. Though this light-in-darkness is the condition of human knowledge in this life, there can be no negativity in the Light that God is, no shadow or limitation in the divine intelligence and intelligibility. But the human mind unaided cannot in this life be exposed to that Light. Our human knowledge is rather bat-like in its inability to look directly and immediately into the sunlight of who and what God is. The negative character of our knowledge of God has been remarked on in several contexts within the present "exploration," especially when it comes to analogical thinking and the threefold way of affirmation, negation, and eminence. It is often surprising to find this negative dimension woven into the biblical sources arising from witnesses who were utterly convinced of divine revelation and of the positive truth that had been so disclosed. The way of negation, therefore, does not belong merely to the history of philosophy or mysticism; it is intrinsic to the dynamism of knowing God in every context, be it liturgical, doctrinal, biblical, theological, or contemplative.

In this present era of interreligious dialogue, it is appropriate to conclude our exploration with a reflection on "God and Dialogue." Authentic dialogue is a unique event, an experience of disclosure and a renewed sense of divine transcendence. Given that implementation of such interreligious dialogue is a major current commitment for the Church, it is worth recalling the imperatives original to the Christian tradition that point in this direction: the mission to all nations, the practice of intercession, the love of neighbor, and even of enemies. In all this, *dialogue* is not primarily a noun, but a verb. It expresses a conscious, intersubjective activity, a passing over to the other, and a return to oneself in an expanding sense of the *We* of all humanity in God, an inexhaustibly promising event within God's communication to human history.

ORIENTATION TO TRANSCENDENT MYSTERY

We have already had occasion to point out that this exploration into God does not begin with a big idea of God, or even with an idea of a big God. There is no question of any demeaning of the divine mystery, or subjecting it to something outside itself. Rather, the intention here is to begin, not with a big idea, but with the fundamental orientation of our conscious being. Here, as elsewhere, we gratefully acknowledge the influence of Bernard Lonergan when he writes,

> Now an orientation to transcendent mystery is basic to systematic theology. It provides the primary and fundamental meaning of the name, God. It can be the bond uniting all men despite cultural difference. It provides the origin for inquiry about God, for seeking assurance of his existence, for endeavouring to reach some understanding of the mysteries of faith, at the same time it is quite in harmony with the conviction that no system we can construct will encompass or plumb or master the mystery by which we are held.[3]

The following seven points are worth noting:

1. An orientation to transcendent mystery is basic to theology. Such an orientation is based in that self-transcending movement of mind and heart as it looks beyond any present attainments to search for the ultimate meaning of all that is found meaningful, to find the ultimate worth of everything that is worthwhile, good, and valuable, finally to enjoy fully the beauty and the love that persistently filled the heart with longing.
2. This orientation based in the self-transcending dynamism of our conscious being provides "the primary and basic meaning of the name, God." In other words, and in a traditional idiom, God is named first of all as the One who alone can "save our souls," where "soul" means the self-transcending movement of existence toward fulfillment and ultimate rest only in absolute truth and absolute goodness.
3. This orientation is such that it can bring together those who are culturally divided and inspire interreligious dialogue in the light of the ever-greater God.
4. This orientation leads to limitless questions but also anticipates ultimate answers: we would not be seeking

God unless, in some way, we had already found him, or even more deeply, unless the grace of God had already found us.

5. From this orientation comes the search for a proof, or intimation or assurance, of the existence and presence of God in a world of meaning in which cultures can be hostile to religion, to what transcends the world and is opposed to what disturbs their self-containment.
6. This orientation finds explicit expression in faith, and faith as a self-transcending openness to the Other seeks understanding of the mysteries of God as articulated in the Scriptures, in the teachings of the Church, and as explored in the long labor of theology to enrich understanding with a deeper knowledge of what has been revealed.
7. The orientation toward God is dynamic and can never congeal into a closed system, lacking a sense of the limitless mystery of God and of the singularity of what has been revealed.

In his *Method in Theology*, Lonergan describes religious believers as drawn to a higher form of self-transcendence. They undergo a conversion in an event that "dismantles and abolishes the horizon in which their knowing and choosing went on and sets up a new horizon in which the love of God will transvalue our values and the eyes of that love will transform our knowing."[4] Consequently, we cannot but agree with Karl Rahner's more specifically theological statement that the "experience of God really constitutes the very heart and center of Christianity itself and also the ever-living source of that conscious manifestation which we call 'revelation.'"[5] For his part, Hans Urs von Balthasar further specifies a relation to God as "the movement away from myself, the preference of what is other and greater."[6] Such approaches find solid support in biblical accounts of the experience of the prophets and in the gospel's narrative of the challenges faced by Jesus's disciples in proclaiming the kingdom of God.

The question of God and of any exploration into God has suffered enormously by being cut off from religious experience, especially the mystical or "submystical" as the living field of reference. A muscle-bound rationality favoring (or attacking) objective doctrinal expressions tended to push to the margins any consideration of the experience out of which doctrines arose. As a result, knowing God became more and more to be regarded as an assent to a cerebral proposition regarding the divine existence and the Trinity of persons. The self-communication of God going on in the humble dress of ordinary experience was hardly registered. However, in the push and pull of daily experience, people feel the tug of truth in their dealing with one another and the insistent impulse to love and to keep on loving even to the point of continuing prayer and acts of forgiveness.

All exploration into God must encounter the problem of evil—as was mentioned on the first pages of this book. The encounter with evil, however stark, oppressive, and piercing, must take a larger picture into account, made up of the experience of many other aspects of reality and dimensions of human experience. The problem of evil collides always with the "problem" of goodness and beauty, of hope and moral goodness, the problem of why anything exists—including ourselves—and the character of that consciousness in which these "problems" occur. Moreover, a religious attitude intensifies the problem. The more there is a sense of God, the more that evil in all its forms and influences is felt to be grotesque and obscene. To that degree, there is a point in this oft-repeated adage: "Religion is the wound not the bandage!"

In the experience of the good and beauty—and of the parasitical presence of evil in whatever is good and beautiful—the great Mystery beckons, at once from within, and yet from beyond the time-and-space-bound limits of human existence. It is the conviction of faith that God acts in order that that human beings may find their ultimate fulfillment in the divine life. It is not as though our searching discovers God or somehow attracts his attention. The initiative is all on God's part. Paul, in his discourse to the Athenians, emphasizes that precise point:

> [God] allotted the times of their existence and the boundaries of their places...so that they would search for God

> and perhaps grope for him and find him—even though he is not far from each one of us. For "In him we live and move and have our being." (Acts 17:26–28)

In the face of the atheism of our day and the idolatries embedded in our culture, faith in the One God is a countercultural stance, as already mentioned.[7] Biblically speaking, faith in God is always a choice against obvious cultural deities—the "false gods," whatever they might be: "You shall have no other gods before me" (Deut 5:7). In biblical terms, God is not *Baal*, the deification of nature (see 1 Kgs 16—18), nor *Moloch*, the idol of political power (Lev 18—20; 1 Kgs 11:7), nor *Mammon*, the idol of greed and possessions (see Matt 6:24, etc.). True faith cannot serve both the One God and false gods. In the end, idols inspire, not the liberating self-surrender of faith, but the sacrifice of what is most properly human within us. And so, by contesting all forms of cultural self-enclosure, commitment to God is a source of creativity within history and society. In the face of the emptiness and universal doubt that hugely affect the modern era, faith in the One God lays the foundation for the continual renewal of hope. When there is a loss of the sense of the transcendent, a prevailing mood is that of cosmic despair while public agnosticism is presumed in the social, intellectual, and moral conversation of the time.

Despite the cultural incubus, commitment to God has a transformative effect. Lonergan, as referred to above, speaks of a fundamental God-ward orientation taking the form of a radical self-transcendence. A deep and far-reaching conversion is set in motion and leads one into "a new horizon in which the love of God will transvalue our values and the eyes of that love will transform our knowing."[8] In the language of tradition, charity informs all virtues, and works in human consciousness to produce wisdom, a depth and intimacy of knowing, that can savor the mystery of God. The path of exploration into God is necessarily accompanied by love, wisdom, and selflessness as notable gifts of the Spirit.

The metaphysical objectivity of the Scholastic tradition privileged theoretical precision and intellectual rigor in our knowledge of God. However, the rich account of affectivity that accompanied this highly intellectual approach has often been overlooked, specially the role of the Spirit permeating Christian consciousness:

> No one comprehends what is truly God's except the Spirit of God. Now we have received not the spirit of the world, but the Spirit that is from God, so that we may understand the gifts that are bestowed on us by God. (1 Cor 2:11–12)

A new field of communication is the result: "And we speak of these things in words not taught by human wisdom but taught by the Spirit, interpreting spiritual things to those who are spiritual" (1 Cor 2:13).

Faced with these and similar New Testament texts (such as 1 John 2:27), theological systems were somewhat at a loss. There is a gifted excess, in the gift of the Spirit and in the knowledge to which it leads. It gave rise to the tradition of "spiritual senses," as found with different emphases in the writings of Origen, Augustine, Bonaventure, and Ignatius of Loyola.[9] Such authors presumed that a lively expanded and embodied consciousness accompanies all knowledge of God.[10]

The love that informs faith not only unites believers to God, but also locates them in the community of faith. Faith is a social bond that gives rise to shared scriptural, doctrinal, institutional, and moral beliefs, expressive of a shared sense of what has been revealed and must now be passed on to future generations. In this shared awareness or sense of faith, faith makes its own the body of attestations, narratives, and judgments as found in the Gospels and other writings of the New Testament. That appropriation of the earliest written tradition can hardly be separated from the Church's liturgical action (as we will mention later). The common celebration in adoration and thanksgiving of what has been revealed in Christ is the site in which Word of God, in Scripture or proclamation, lives and works its transformative effect. Within the developments of its history, faith is further focused, and the beliefs that express it are more sharply articulated in the words of the creeds, in symbolic communications, in the witness of saints, doctors, and martyrs, in the rise of theologies, and in the development of the arts—musical, figurative, architectural, and so forth.

"LETTING GO"

Perspectives on how the reality of God is known and experienced lose nothing by being earthed in the deep cultural movements of our time. Martin Heidegger can instruct us on this level, even if he drew back from any theological or religious commitment. In his *Discourse on Thinking*,[11] we find the philosopher's notion of *Gelassenheit*—translatable as "releasement," with connotations of "abandonment," "detachment," and "letting go" in regard to everyday patterns of knowing and choosing. The goal is a receptive and courageous attachment to the real ground of existence.[12] For Heidegger, the modern malaise is a flight from "meditative thinking." This is akin to contemplative attunement to the wholeness and originality of being. The modern fragmentation of thinking and distraction from the wholeness of being is the product of a technological culture. What is needed is a refreshed openness and receptivity to counter the technological style of calculative thinking and the manner of existence it promotes. This entails a "letting go" of the compulsions, control, and preoccupations that have cramped existence into an alien pattern.[13] To be released from all this opens the possibility of dwelling in the world in a new and wholesome way. Consequently, true thinking is not locked in itself, but looks beyond itself to the mystery that already possesses us. It means entering the "region" of the whole truth of being that is really our home and native place, even if it cannot be represented or reduced to the categories of the routine world of ordinary perceptions and activities.[14] Compulsive manipulative habits of action must yield to a more centered and serene style. It manifests itself as a kind of nonacting compared to the preoccupations of routine busy-ness and control, just as it points to the need of receptivity and waiting for the whole truth to reveal itself. This whole truth is impervious to analysis or control, and yet constitutes the proportion in which the human being exists in a wholesome and thankful manner.[15]

The existential attitude that Heidegger evokes has remarkable similarities with the concerns of the eminent Christian thinkers referred to above. Lonergan presupposes a preconceptual orientation to God preceding and grounding all eventual expression, and working as an undertow in the consciousness of faith. Rahner placed consistent emphasis on the ever-present, incomprehensible mystery affecting all our knowledge and love and action. Von Balthasar interprets knowing God as demanding a continuous looking away from oneself and one's activities or abilities, for the sake of the inexhaustible mystery. How much these eminent thinkers drew inspiration from Heidegger is not for the present writer to say, except to observe a notable convergence of concerns, despite the differences in language and idiom. They all sought to allow for a transcendent horizon of self-transcendence in order that the human spirit might breathe.

GIFTS OF THE SPIRIT

Preceding all these is the traditional theology of the gifts of the Holy Spirit, which, in one way or another, influenced the theologians I have cited, and may have indirectly influenced Heidegger through the German mystical writers familiar with the writings of Aquinas, especially Meister Eckhart and his teaching, "All that God asks you most pressingly is to go out of yourself...and let God be God in you."[16] As regards Aquinas's *Summa*, despite its emphasis on objective intelligibility, logical precision, and systematic exposition, it is intriguing to note that it included, and repeatedly made room for, what could never be systematized, namely, the gift of the Spirit. For St. Thomas, the gifts of the Spirit lead to both an intimate knowledge of God and union with the divine will in every domain of action. These gifts work in a suprarational manner and enable heart and mind to have a sense of God in ways that can never be reduced to the routine frameworks in which we construct and understand our world.

The seven gifts of the Holy Spirit are traditionally enumerated as wisdom, understanding, counsel, fortitude, knowledge, piety, and fear of the Lord. Aquinas presents these gifts as saturating every aspect of our knowing and choosing, so enabling the faithful to respond to the movement of the Spirit and to act in a manner that is "beyond the human measure."[17] While the life of faith engages the hardy world of objective and rational theological discourse, the gifts of the Spirit represent a vertically given excess, extending, or even disrupting, the horizons of reason alone. Intelligence must be receptive and waiting, as it were, on the gift from above, in order to know and to act in a way that respects the transcendent character of the Spirit's action. Each gift is, therefore, an aspect of transforming grace of the Spirit and specifies a particular buoyant receptivity within Christian consciousness to the Spirit's "suprarational" action. They contrast, therefore, to the muscle-bound rational systems that can so easily take control of theological exploration. An appreciation of these gifts of the Spirit, therefore, leads to a healthy deconstruction of a one-dimensional rational or calculative mode of thinking, while suggesting other domains of spiritual perception.

The Thomist account of the gifts recognizes a certain strain or dislocation inherent in the life of faith and its present way of knowing God. There is an essential cloudiness and limitation in our mode of knowing. While there is a native aptitude for the pursuit of the good and the truth proportionate to this present mode of human existence in the world, such a proportionate attunement is lacking when it comes to knowing the revealed God and participating in the divine life. Hence, the gifts of the Spirit are a necessary complement to the life of faith in that they attune the mind and heart of the believer to the divine milieu in which faith must now live, guided by "an instinct and movement of the Holy Spirit."[18] A monodimensional rationality would tend to go against the kind of receptivity and surrender that the gift of the Spirit entails. The gifts of the Spirit have, therefore, a healing effect, for they equip the faithful with a special instinct. Faith can thereby reach beyond mundane patterns of calculation, to know God in a more intimate and experiential manner.[19]

Knowing God comes to mean more than having bright ideas or making correct deductions. There is the gift of Spirit-infused "wisdom" providing a special "taste" (*sapientia*, translated as wisdom, from the Latin *sapere*, "to taste") for the things of God.[20] "Knowledge" in this kind of savoring experience gives faith a "feel" for the totality of God's self-revelation in Christ. Then, there is the gift of "understanding" (*intellectus*) implying a clear-eyed perception of the uniqueness of divine revelation, and protecting it from the general impressions and projections that would dim its unique originality and reduce it to some general class of religious phenomena.[21] The gift of *scientia* ("knowledge") likewise bears on the singular uniqueness of divine revelation, saving its universal significance from being lost in an empty and meaningless contingency.[22] Then there are gifts of another type, more related to our choosing and loving. Through the further gift of *pietas* (often poorly translated as "piety"), Christian consciousness is disposed to live with an intimate sense of filial relationship with the God of love and mercy. The gift of *timor Domini* ("fear of the Lord") brings with it a radical poverty of spirit, along with a reverent sensitivity to the ways of God and a readiness to surrender to divine providence.[23] In the domain of moral action, the gift of *consilium* ("counsel") is the special Spirit-guided instinct for responding to the divine will in the details of individual and social life.[24] The spirit of "fortitude" is manifested in a vigorous choosing of the ways of God and in a rejection of the contrary.[25]

These brief remarks on the gifts of the Spirit suggest a certain buoyancy and assurance in any exploration into God. The gifts act in a suprarational way and surpass the scope of reason alone—what Heidegger would call "calculative thinking." The gifts are identified within the history of religious and Christian experience as enabling an attitude of "letting go" and self-surrender. The gifts allow the mystery of the ever-greater God to have its way in the mind and heart of the believer. Thus, the consciousness of faith is lifted to new levels. To that degree, knowing God entails being always open to the surprises that only the Spirit of God can give.

LITURGICAL ACTION

It might seem that this exploration is concluding in an eccentric mixture of metaphysics and mysticism, theology, philosophy, and some admixture of poetry—all leading to into a sphere of exalted abstractions. Any exploration worthy of the name, however, must come down to earth, and keeps its feet on the ground. A deliberate act of grounding occurs eminently in the liturgy. The *opus Dei* of the liturgy is not a matter of more thinking, nor a keener and more mystical manner of experiencing, nor living with a consciousness distracted into every transcendent possibility. Nor, for that matter, is attention so concentrated on the nameless Other that our exploration into God must exclude a wide and deep experience of life in this world. The liturgy is less to do with doing or producing something. Rather, the essential form of the liturgy is to enact, in time and space, and in the midst of all the contingencies of life, the real sense of God in all creation, and, indeed, of all creation in God. Liturgy is at once an earthed and englobing activity, not in the sense of reducing the manifold of the world to a narrow band of religiosity, but of opening the pluriform reality of the world to both its real depth and its ultimate future. And yet, positioned in the here and now, it is at once an affirmation and a hope. From that perspective, liturgical activity means resisting the sheer oppressive weight of what is often called the "secular" as opposed to the "religious." Yet this resistance is not with a calculation of greater strength or power, as though the religious dimension subverts or swallows the secular. The service is of God, if it is of *God*, and not of an idol of human construction. Nor, indeed, some kind of group-dynamic demonic possession or narrowly focused obsession. Liturgical action, in contrast, is possible only in poverty of spirit. It moves in a humility resulting from the openness and abandonment that arise from being left with nothing but God and what God can do. It is the conduct of patience, poverty, and surrender to God in the world, and of finding all we call "the world" in God. Indeed, from that point of view, the Church is that part of the world that brings to expression the universal mystery at work in every aspect of the world.

In this sense, liturgy is a refusal to allow the spirit of our common humanity to be suffocated by the spurious opposition of the religious and the secular: the secular is too important for that, situated as it must always be within the horizon of God's creative action; and the religious, in its explicit relationship to the Source of creation and salvation, is more real than a decorative addition to the rituals of a particular culture. To act liturgically is to "do God"—in word and symbol, in art and community, in the time and space of the here and now, even if in a way that is inescapably vulnerable to ideology and monodimensional secularism. Yet the liturgy humbly presses on in its daily, weekly, and yearly round. However poor and naked, it gives expression to the presence of God in the world, and of everything we call "the world," in God.[26] The liturgy "does" faith (and hope and love) in God—"doing God"—in the limitation and poverty of a moment in space and time. It means not holding to exalted moods, beautiful words, or noble sentiments, but being left with nothing but God, and with what God is doing as all creation anticipates its fulfillment in God. To that degree, liturgical action is the expression of a radical poverty and cultural nakedness, even a nonexperience compared to the vividness of ordinary secular experience. Nonetheless, the liturgy, as the service of God, is world forming, in its wholeness, and in its openness to the depths and heights of the present, and to the eschatological future. Liturgical acts are characterized by patience, poverty, and hope, taking place in time, but toward that future when God will be all in all.

From this point of view, Christian liturgy bears clear resemblances to all kinds of sacred rituals and their ways of offering participation in sacred space and sacred time. From a specifically Christian perspective, a number of particular features could be mentioned if the liturgy is to be presented in terms of an exploration into God—the inspired Scriptures, the sacraments, the real presence of Christ in the Eucharist, the transformations of grace, the communion of saints, and so forth. Although a conclusion to this exploration cannot suddenly become a new beginning, we can offer two remarks.

The first treats of the confession of sins, a typical introductory rite in all Christian liturgical activities. In this respect, the Christian liturgy concretely actualizes exploration into God, but not so as to present the faithful as conquering heroes or daring explorers. We are sinners who are confronted with the truth of evil we have caused or contributed to, and, therefore, unable to proceed further into God without invoking the divine mercy for healing and forgiveness.

Though such a confession is allied to the way of negation, the confession of sins and the prayer for mercy mark an exploration into the God who is "out of this world" in terms of its structures of identity and moral judgments. For in the present world, justice moderates society by declaring the accused guilty or not guilty. Courts of law have the power to draw conclusions from any finding of guilt or innocence. In a society armed with the laws and procedures of justice, it is dangerous to admit to moral guilt and to ask forgiveness, for that would be a form of public nakedness and vulnerability. Any such confession can be manipulated, perhaps to be portrayed as a symptom of weakness and lack of integrity. But in the liturgical confession of sins, the community of believers stands before God to acknowledge its resistance to the will of God in thought, word, deed, and omission, "through my fault, through my most grievous fault." To admit sinfulness in this way, publicly, even if with due discretion, is an intensely countercultural act. It establishes the liturgy as a movement into the God who cannot be contained in even the most respectable structures of the world.

Second, there is the liturgical focus on Christ. The readings from Scripture place the liturgical activity within the corporate history of Old and New Testaments. The Bible is not a compilation of information, but an invitation to enter through faith into the history of God's self-revelation. Divine revelation continues as an ongoing and inexhaustible event, centered in the promise and fulfillment that have occurred in Christ. In that frame of mind, the Eucharist is celebrated within the horizon of the universe of God's creation in Christ. Consequently, the liturgy occurs in a God-charged field in which the universe is being transformed into God's new creation, centered in Christ, "the firstborn of all creation" (Col 1:15).

In all its acts, the eucharistic liturgy envisions, and even enacts, the world "otherwise," as it is before God. Christ has occupied the depths and the heights of that world through his death, resurrection, and ascension to the fullness of his humanity with God. The liturgical doxology, "through him, with him, and in him" evokes the reality of the new creation in Christ as a field of communion and mutual indwelling. His disciples inhabit the world in a new way, as a community based in the unity of the Father and the Son: "that they may be one, as we are one" (John 17:11). Jesus's ascent to the Father relocates believers into a space of holy communion and mutual indwelling: "As you, Father, are in me and I am in you, may they also be in us, so that the world may believe that you have sent me" (John 17:21).

Each eucharistic liturgy realizes an answer to the prayer of Jesus, "that they may all be one. As you, Father, are in me and I am in you, may they also be in us....I in them and you in me, that they may become completely one" (John 17:21–23). By implication, the liturgical horizon unfolds in the interrelationships and mutual indwelling deriving from the union existing between the Father and the Son. Each is *in* the other for the life of the other. By being from the other, for the other, and so, *in* the other, the liturgical praise of the Father, Son, and Spirit arises from participation in God's own trinitarian life. This is to say that the Eucharist is not "virtual reality" in any sense. It is a Spirit-inspired form of actual reality, communicating Christ as the "real food" and "real drink" of eternal life. In this regard, the liturgy of the Eucharist brings together what is often kept apart—the reality of God, consciousness of the self in relation to others, and the emerging universe itself. As the sacrament centered on the "real" presence of Christ, liturgical consciousness is not a distraction from the reality, but an immersion into it. The liturgy, therefore, "re-members" and brings together in a new integrity the fractured experience of humanity on many levels. As holy communion, it joins believers to Christ's body, and summons them to participate in its growth. The risen and ascended Christ, he is not *here* in any sense of worldly location, but present beyond any worldly measure or containment. Christ is not located in the world because that world now exists in him (Col 1:16).

In liturgical consciousness, elemental notions such as *world*, *heaven*, *time* and *place*, *change*, and *body* need to be recast. If Christ is risen and ascended into heaven, then, in and through him, humanity, together with the world in which it is inextricably immersed, has entered into a new mode of existence. Liturgical experience is not shaped by Christ absent from the world, but as related to that world in a new way—just as humanity has not been discarded in the Christ risen from the tomb or ascended into heaven. Heaven, in

Christian terms, therefore, is not a vague celestial and unreal location, but communion with God in Christ in a creation transformed. By moving into God as revealed in Christ, humanity and the created universe find a new integrity. The liturgy, then, is an enactment of how, in Christ, the world has been irreversibly ascended into the life of God, and God descended into the life of the world. The liturgy is, therefore, not an imaginative attempt to fit Christ into an unredeemed world; nor is it a memorial to his past presence after his disappearance into a vaguely determined heaven. Rather, the liturgical synthesis or "reduction" consists in seeing both the world and heaven embodied in him: something new has irreversibly begun; time and space are newly configured in Christ. With him as the center and focus of God's action, the corporate faith of the Church grows, from one generation to the next, as an exploration into God.

We must come to the end of our exploration. It is not so much the end of the road, but looking back to a series of signposts, each pointing further into God. We begin to recognize more accurately the self-made frontier that we have allowed to bound our lives. It is also moving beyond it, to find a land and a region unbounded, our homeland. Yet always, the exploration into God goes on....

NOTES

INTRODUCTION

1. Christopher Fry, *A Sleep of Prisoners* (London: Oxford University Press, 1959), 47–48.

2. See the epilogue in Elizabeth A. Johnson, *Quest for the Living God: Mapping Frontiers in the Theology of God* (New York: Continuum, 2007), 228.

3. Augustine, *Ennar.in Psal.30*, PL 36, 252.

4. Anthony Kelly, *Eschatology and Hope* (Maryknoll, NY: Orbis Books, 2006), esp. the chapter on heaven, "The Homing of Hope," 159–78.

5. For example, Anne Hunt, *The Trinity: Insights from the Mystics* (Melbourne: ATF Press, 2010).

CHAPTER 1

1. I borrow this phrase from the stimulating work, Jean-Yves Lacoste, *La Phénoménalité de Dieu: Neuf études* (Paris: Cerf, 2008), esp. 15–32.

2. For valuable historical and cultural comment, see Terry Eagleton, *Culture and the Death of God* (New Haven, CT: Yale University Press, 2014), esp. 151–74.

3. Friedrich Nietzsche, *The Antichrist*, in *The Portable Nietzsche*, ed. and trans. Walter Kaufmann (New York: The Viking Press, 1972), 585–86.

4. William W. Hoye, *The Emergence of Eternal Life* (Cambridge: Cambridge University Press, 2013), 13–63.

5. David Bentley Hart, *The Experience of God: Being, Consciousness, Bliss* (New Haven, CT: Yale University Press, 2013), 32.

6. See Emmanuel Falque, *The Metamorphosis of Finitude: An Essay on Birth and Resurrection*, trans. George Hughes (New York: Fordham University Press, 2012), 30–36.

7. Gregory of Nyssa, *Commentary on the Song of Songs*, ch. 1, v. 3, trans. C. McCambley (Brookline, MA: Hellenic College Press, 1987), 53.

8. For the scope and variety of analogy, see Philip A. Rolnick, *Analogical Possibilities: How Words Refer to God* (Atlanta: Scholars Press, 1993); also, W. Norris Clarke, "Analogy and the Meaningfulness of Language about God," in *Explorations in Metaphysics: Being, God, Person* (Notre Dame, IN: University of Notre Dame Press, 1992), 123–49.

9. *STh* I, q. 5, a.5.

10. *STh* II-II, q. 23, a. 6, ad 1.

11. *STh* II-II, q. 27, a. 4.

12. *STh* I-II, q. 28, a. 2.

13. See Larry W. Hurtado, *God in New Testament Theology* (Nashville: Abingdon Press, 2010).

14. Hurtado, *God in New Testament Theology*, 1.

15. In an effort to strike the right balance, see Anthony J. Kelly and Francis J. Moloney, *Experiencing God in the Gospel of John* (Mahwah, NJ: Paulist Press, 2003).

16. Jean-Yves Lacoste, *From Theology to Theological Thinking*, trans. W. Chris Hacket, intro. Jeffrey Bloechl (Charlottesville: University of Virginia Press, 2014), 20–29.

17. Karl Rahner, "The Experience of God Today," in *Theological Investigations XI*, trans. David Bourke (London: Darton, Longman and Todd, 1974), 164.

18. Bernard Lonergan, *Method in Theology* (London: Darton, Longman and Todd, 1972), 106.

19. Hans Urs von Balthasar, *The Glory of the Lord: A Theological Aesthetics*, vol. 1, *Seeing the Form*, trans. Erasmo Leiva-Merikakis (New York: Crossroad Publications, 1982), 237.

20. Lacoste, *From Theology*; note the reference to Boethius's *The Consolation of Philosophy*, 31.

21. Lacoste, *From Theology*, 34–36.

22. Alasdair MacIntyre, *God, Philosophy, Universities: A Selective History of the Catholic Philosophical Tradition* (Lanham, MD: Rowman and Littlefield, 2009) provides further historical background into today's philosophy and its ways of raising the question of God.

23. Lacoste, *From Theology*, 3.

24. *Phaedo*, 67e. See Desmond Stewart, *Plato: A New Translation of the Phaedo* (London: Euphorion Books, 1972), 32.

25. Aquinas, in *STh* I, q. 6., a. 1, ad 2, distinguishes and connects two modes of wisdom, the "mystical" connaturality of love and the "rational" way of intellectual inquiry.

26. Points well made in Hart, *The Experience of God*, 275–90.

27. On this topic of analogy, current discussion might note that Derrida's whole deconstructionist project owes its origins to his desire to work out the terms of analogy. See Jacques Derrida, *An Introduction to Edmund Husserl's Origin of Geometry*, trans. John P. Leavey Jr. (Lincoln: University of Nebraska Press, 1989). "Husserl never ceased to appeal to the imperative of univocity. Equivocity is the path of all philosophical aberration. It is all the more difficult not to be hasty here, as the sense of equivocity in general is itself equivocal. There is a *contingent* plurivocity and multisignificance and an *essential* one" (100–101).

28. Useful methodological remarks are found in Elizabeth A. Johnson, *Quest for the Living God: Mapping Frontiers in the Theology of God* (New York: Continuum, 2007), 14–39.

29. See *STh* I, q. 20, a. 2.

30. A. N. Williams, *The Ground of Union: Deification in Aquinas and Palamas* (Oxford: Oxford University Press, 1999), 93–101.

31. Robert J. Spitzer, *New Proofs for the Existence of God: Contributions of Contemporary Physics and Philosophy* (Grand Rapids: William B. Eerdmans, 2010).

32. Lacoste, *From Theology*, 48–49. See, too, *Summa Contra Gentiles* (*SCG*), c. 52.

33. Lacoste, *From Theology*, 55–71.

34. Lacoste, *From Theology*, 52, 60.

35. See Lacoste, *La Phénoménalité de Dieu*.

36. See Bruno Latour, *Inquiry into Modes of Existence: Anthropology for Moderns* (Cambridge, MA: Harvard University Press, 2013).

37. Lonergan, *Method in Theology*, 290.

38. See Hoye, *The Emergence of Eternal Life*, 84–99.

39. See John F. Haught, *Christianity and Science: Toward a Theology of Nature* (Maryknoll, NY: Orbis, 2007), 24–29.

40. Hart, *The Experience of God*, 15.

41. Hart, *The Experience of God*, 225.

42. For limit experience in science, see John F. Haught, *Christianity and Science: Toward a Theology of Nature* (Maryknoll, NY: Orbis Books, 2007), 24–26.

43. Note different points of view: see Brendan Purcell, *From Big Bang to Big Mystery: Human Origins in the Light of Creation and Evolution* (New York: New City Press, 2011), and Latour, *Inquiry into Modes of Existence*.

44. Aquinas, *In Boet. de Trin.*, q. 2, a. 1, ad 6.

45. Augustine, *Confess.*, bk. 1, 4.

CHAPTER 2

1. Quoted in Deal W. Hudson, "The Future of Thomism: An Introduction," in *The Future of Thomism*, ed. Deal W. Hudson and Denis William Moran (Notre Dame, IN: University of Notre Dame Press, 1992), 7.

2. Michael J. Buckley, *At the Origins of Modern Atheism* (New Haven, CT: Yale University Press, 1987).

3. John Milbank, *Theology and Social Theory: Beyond Secular Reason* (Oxford: Blackwell, 1990).

4. Claude Romano, *L'événement et le monde. Épithée. Essais Philosophiques* (Paris: Presses Universitaires de France, 1998), 60–69.

5. For an outstanding contribution to this whole field, see W. Norris Clarke, *The One and the Many: A Contemporary Thomistic Metaphysics* (Notre Dame, IN: University of Notre Dame Press, 2002).

6. The literal translation of *esse* is, of course, "to be." I have tried to capture the sense of the verb designating the infinite, active plenitude of the divine "to be" by using the word *Be-ing*. I would be wary of using *existence*, not only because such a usage is foreign to Aquinas's vocabulary, but also because it is rather abstract, a noun instead of a verb.

7. *STh* I, q. 13, a. 11.

8. *Ipsum esse est perfectissimum omnium: comparatur enim ad omnia ut actus. Nihil enim habet actualitatem nisi in quantum est: unde ipsum esse est actualitas omnium rerum et etiam ipsarum formarum* (*STh* I, q. 4, 1 ad 3).

9. Eric Voegelin, *Order and History*, vol. 1, *Israel and Revelation* (Baton Rouge: Louisiana State University Press, 1969), 408–12.

10. *STh* I, q. 2, a. 3.

11. A movement that culminates in Christ as "the way": "our Lord Jesus Christ…demonstrated for us the way of truth in himself" (*Prol., Tertia Pars*). Note, too, how the incarnation "transvalues" our natural knowledge of God: e.g., *STh* III, q. 46, a. 3.

12. For a linguistic reading of Aquinas, see David Burrell, *Aquinas: God and Action* (Notre Dame, IN: University of Notre Dame Press, 1979).

13. *In Eph.* 1, Lect. 8; *In Heb.* 11, Lect. 1.

14. *STh* I, q. 12, a. 13, ad 1.

15. Note the remarkable text from one of Thomas's Aristotelian commentaries: "The divine will is to be understood as existing outside the order of beings, as a kind of cause which pours forth all being and its differences. The possible and the necessary are different ways of being; and so necessity and contingency in things and the distinction of the one from the other originate from the divine will in the context of proximate causes. According to the status of these causes effects are adjudged necessary or contingent—although they all depend on the divine will as from a first cause which transcends the order of necessity and contingency" (in *I Perihermenias*, c. 9, lect. 14, n. 22).

16. Cajetan, in *STh* I, q. 39, a. 1, *Edit. Leonina*. In this connection, note the remarks on the divine simplicity in David Bentley Hart, *The Experience of God: Being, Consciousness, Bliss* (New Haven, CT: Yale University Press, 2013), 135–37.

17. *STh* I, q. 1, a. 7, ad 1.

18. *De Potentia*, q. 7, a. 5.

19. *In Div. Nom.*, c. 7, Lect. 4.

20. Compare *I Sent.* d 2 a 1 ad 3 with *de Pot.* q. 7 a 5, and in *STh* I, q. 13, a. 2.

21. *STh* I, q. 13, a. 2.

22. This will be understood more and more in the history of thought as trinitarian communion.

23. *STh* I, q. 8, a. 1.

24. See Hart, *The Experience of God*, 152, 227.

25. Hart, *The Experience of God*, 30.

26. Hart, *The Experience of God*, 227.

27. *STh* I, q. 43, a. 5, ad 2.

28. *STh* I, q. 84, a. 5.

29. *Dicendum quod manifestatio quae fit per aliquod lumen, ad omnia illa se extendere potest quae illi lumini subiiciuntur* (*STh* II-II, q. 171, a. 3).

30. With an emphasis on the Spirit typical of the *Secunda Pars*, Thomas remarks that "whatever its source, truth is of the Holy Spirit" (*omne verum a quocumque dicatur a Spiritu Sancto est*) (*STh* I-II, q. 109, a. 1, ad 1).

31. *STh* I, q. 12, a. 1.

32. *STh* I, q. 12, a. 13, ad 1. On the relationship of negation to affirmation in our knowledge of God, see *De Pot.* q. 7, a. 5. Note also ch. 6, "By Way of Negation," in this volume.

33. *STh* I-II, q. 112, a. 5.

34. *STh* I-II, q. 112, a. 5, ad 3.

35. *STh* I, q. 13, a. 2.

36. *STh* I, q. 13, a. 8, ad 2.

37. *STh* I, q. 13, a. 7.

38. *STh* I, q. 13, a. 11.

39. *STh* I, q. 13, a. 11, ad 1.

40. *STh* I, q. 13, a. 2.

41. This is not to say that the *via eminentiae* is ultimately negative—as we shall see in ch. 6.

42. *STh* I, q. 1, a. 8.

43. *STh* I, q. 1, a. 7, ad 1.

44. *STh* I, q. 1, a. 7, *sed contra*.

45. *STh* I, q. 84, a. 5. On participation, see Clarke, *The One and the Many*, 72–91, and "The Meaning of Participation in St. Thomas," in *Explorations in Metaphysics: Being, God, Person* (Notre Dame, IN: University of Notre Dame Press, 1992), 89–101.

46. *Dicendum quod manifestatio quae fit per aliquod lumen, ad omnia illa se extendere potest quae illi lumini subiiciuntur* (*STh* II-II, q. 171, a. 3).

47. *STh* I, q. 13, a. 5. As previously mentioned, on this topic of analogy, current discussion might note that Derrida's whole deconstructionist project owes its origins to his desire to work out the terms of analogy. See Jacques Derrida, *An Introduction to Edmund Husserl's Origin of Geometry*, trans. John P. Leavey Jr. (Lincoln: University of Nebraska Press, 1989): "Husserl never ceased to appeal to the imperative of univocity. Equivocity is the path of all philosophical aberration. It is all the more difficult not to be hasty here, as the sense of equivocity in general is itself equivocal. There is a *contingent* plurivocity and multisignificance and an *essential* one," 100–101.

48. *STh* I, q. 20, a. 2.

49. A. N. Williams, *The Ground of Union: Deification in Aquinas and Palamas* (Oxford: Oxford University Press, 1999), 93–101.

50. *STh* I, q. 12, a. 13, ad 1.

51. *STh* I, q. 43, a. 6.

52. Jean-Pierre Torrell, *Saint Thomas d'Aquin, maître spirituel* (Paris: Cerf, 1996), 31.

53. For a constructive suggestion within the current problematic of the gift, see Robyn Horner, *Rethinking God as Gift: Marion, Derrida and the Limits of Phenomenology* (New York: Fordham University Press, 2000).

54. *STh* I, q. 43, a. 5, ad 2.

55. Jacques Derrida, *Of Spirit: Heidegger and the Question*, trans. Geoffrey Bennington and Rachel Bowlby (Chicago: University of Chicago Press, 1989). In Thomist terms, we could say that, just as the Word is not any kind of word, neither is the Spirit any kind of spirit, let alone the *Geist* of the Nazi era.

56. *STh* II-II, q. 1, a. 2.

57. *STh* II-II, q. 1, a. 2, ad 2.

58. *STh* I, q. 2, prol.

59. As previously mentioned, "Our Lord Jesus Christ…demonstrated for us the way of truth in himself" (*Prol., Tertia Pars*). Note, too, how the incarnation "transvalues" our natural knowledge of God: e.g., *STh* III, q. 46, a. 3.

60. *STh* I, q. 13, a. 8, ad 2.

61. *STh* I, q. 2, prol.

62. See, e.g., *STh* I, q. 45, a. 7, ad 3.

63. *STh* I, q. 2, a. 1, ad 1.

64. Torrell, *Saint Thomas d'Aquin*, 32–34.

65. *STh* I, q. 2, a. 3.

66. Williams, *The Ground of Union*, 40–41.

67. *STh* I, q. 13, a. 9.

68. *STh* I, q. 13, a. 8, ad 2.

69. *STh* I, q. 1, a. 1.

70. *STh* I, q. 12, a. 2.

71. *STh* I, q. 13, a. 7.

72. "Having considered the matters which pertain to the divine unity, it remains to what pertains to the trinity of persons in God" (I, q. 28, *prol.*): "after considering the divine persons, it remains to consider how creatures come from God" (I, q. 44, *prol.*); "Because, as Damascene says, the human is said to be made in the image of God...it remains to consider the human as the image of God" (I-II, q. 1, *prol.*); "Because the Saviour, our Lord Jesus Christ, showed forth to us the way of truth in himself...it is necessary, to bring the whole business of theology to a head, to follow with a consideration of the Saviour of all" (*Tertia Pars, prol.*).

73. The best reference here is found in the *Summa contra Gentiles*, bk. II, ch. 12—14. For an early discussion of this issue, see Anthony Kelly, "God: How Near a Relation?" *The Thomist* 34 (1970): 191–229.

74. For a discussion of the complexities of Aquinas's analogical use of "causality," see George Klubertanz, *St. Thomas Aquinas on Analogy: A Textual Analysis and a Systematic Synthesis* (Chicago: Loyola University Press, 1960), 24–26, 46–48, 70–73.

75. *STh* III, q. 4, a. 1, ad 2.

76. *STh* I, q. 43, a. 5, ad 2.

77. *STh* I, q. 43, a. 5, ad 2.

78. The transposition of traditional metaphysical and theological categories into the experiential and the personal is a major achievement of Bernard Lonergan, in his *Method in Theology* (London: Darton, Longman and Todd, 1972). For example, note his treatment of sanctifying grace, 120–24.

79. Elizabeth A. Johnson, *Quest for the Living God: Mapping Frontiers in the Theology of God* (New York: Continuum, 2007), 188–89.

80. See Hart, *The Experience of God*, 139–41.

81. Rudi Te Velde, in his *Aquinas On God: The "Divine Science" of the* Summa Theologiae (Aldershot, UK: Ashgate, 1996), makes this point: Aquinas is not a "theist" in the modern sense, but more a realist in his affirmation of God as sheer Be-ing (177–78).

82. Hans Urs von Balthasar, *The Glory of the Lord*, vol. 5, *The Realm of Metaphysics in the Modern Age*, trans. Oliver Davies et al. (Edinburgh: T. and T. Clark, 1991), 656.

83. In contrast to such dogmatic materialism, see Bruno Latour, *An Inquiry into Modes of Existence: An Anthropology for Moderns* (Cambridge, MA: Harvard University Press, 2013).

84. See Anthony Kelly, *Upward: Faith, Church, and the Ascension of Christ* (Collegeville, MN: The Liturgical Press, 2014).

85. Paul Imhof, Hubert Biallowons, and Harvey D. Egan, eds., *Faith in a Wintry Season: Conversations and Interviews with Karl Rahner in the Last Years of his Life, 1982–84* (New York: Crossroad, 1990), 163.

86. Te Velde, *Aquinas on God*, 177–79.

CHAPTER 3

1. On the American scene, see Michael H. Behe, Joseph Fessio, David W. Opderbeck, Richard L. Cleary, Michael Egnor, Fred Hutchinson, Jack D. Elliot, and Charlie Mae—in response to Robert D. Miller, "Design, Intelligence and Philosophy: An Exchange," *First Things* 164 (June–July 2006): 5–11.

2. The discovery of quantum mechanics and especially its Copenhagen interpretation (Bohr and Heisenberg) begins to touch on the radical philosophical problem of the relation between objective reality and the role of the subject exploring it. Michael Frayn's play, *Copenhagen* (New York: Anchor Press, 2000), gave dramatic expression to the issues.

3. Neil Ormerod, *A Public God: Natural Theology Reconsidered* (Minneapolis: Fortress Press, 2014), 70–76.

4. See Bernard Lonergan, *Method in Theology* (London: Darton, Longman and Todd, 1972), 292–93.

5. Lars Thunberg, *Man and the Cosmos: The Vision of St. Maximus the Confessor* (Crestwood, NY: St. Vladimir's Seminary Press, 1985), 71–92.

6. *STh* I, q. 14, a. 1; q. 16, a. 3; I-II, q. 80, a. 2.

7. Quoted by Gabriel Daly in his stimulating *Creation and Redemption* (Dublin: Gill and MacMillan, 1988), 116.

8. Difficulty 41, 1305B as translated in Andrew Louth, *Maximus the Confessor* (New York: Routledge, 1996), 157.

9. *STh* I, q. 90, a. 3; *Summa Contra Gentes*, bk. 2, ch. 87. Hereafter, cited as *SCG* bk. 2, c. 87.

10. *STh* I, q. 20, a. 2.

11. See James Alison, *The Joy of Being Wrong: Original Sin through Easter Eyes* (New York: Crossroad, 1998), 287–89.

12. John Polkinghorne, *The God of Hope and the End of the World* (New Haven, CT: Yale University Press, 2002), 103–7.

13. Polkinghorne, *The God of Hope and the End of the World*, 107–13.

14. See, for instance, Warren S. Brown, Nancey Murphy, and H. Newton Maloney, eds., *Whatever Happened to the Soul? Scientific and Theological Portraits of Human Nature* (Minneapolis: Fortress Press, 1998).

15. See A. Ganoczy, "Cerveau et conscience en anthropologie théologique," *Recherches de Science Religieuse* 92, no. 3 (2004): 349–81.

16. For an outstandingly informative treatment, see Brendan Purcell, *From Big Bang to Big Mystery: Human Origins in the Light of Creation and Evolution* (Hyde Park, NY: New City Press, 2013).

17. J. C. Eccles, *Brain and Conscious Experience* (Berlin: Springer Verlag, 1962), 327.

18. Cf. *SCG* bk. 2, c. 93. For an imposing specialized study, David Keck, *Angels and Angelology in the Middle Ages* (New York: Oxford University Press, 1998). On some aspects of contemporary discussion, Thomas F. O'Meara, *Vast Universe: Extraterrestrials and Christian Revelation* (Collegeville, MN: The Liturgical Press, 2012).

19. For further comment, see Stanley Grenz, *Theology for the Community of God* (Nashville: Broadman and Holman, 1994), 213–42, and Amy Plantinga Pauw, "'Where Angels Fear to Tread,'" *Modern Theology* 16, no. 1 (January 2000): 39–59; Robert Ombres, "God, Angels, Us," *New Blackfriars* 86 (January 2005): 48–61. For a brief study of the patristic tradition, Jean Danielou, *The Angels and Their Mission*, trans. David Heimann (Allen, TX: Newman Press, 1957).

20. Christoph Schönborn, *From Death to Life: The Christian Journey*, trans. B. McNeil (San Francisco: Ignatius Press, 1995), 95–97.

21. See James Alison, *Raising Abel: The Rediscovery of the Eschatological Imagination* (New York: Crossroad, 1996), 193–94.

22. See William W. Hoye, *The Emergence of Eternal Life* (Cambridge: Cambridge University Press, 2013), 144–57.

23. See Stephen M. Barr, *Modern Physics and Ancient Faith* (Notre Dame, IN: University of Notre Dame Press, 2003), 16, 183.

24. Thomas Aquinas, *Sermo V, in Dom 2 de Adventu* (Vives XXIX), 194.

25. Lonergan writes, "Genuine objectivity is the fruit of authentic subjectivity. To seek and employ some alternative prop or crutch invariably leads to some measure of reductionism"; *Method in Theology*, 292.

26. Thomas Aquinas, *STh* I, q. 88, a. 2, ad 3.

27. Melvin Konner, *The Tangled Wing: Biological Constraints on the Human Spirit* (New York: Harper and Row, 1982), 435.

28. For an instructive probe into the deep cultural conditions that have affected the question of God, see Neil Ormerod, "In Defense of Natural Theology—Bringing Transcendence to the Public Realm," *Irish Theological Quarterly* 71 (2007): 227–41, and, more fully, *A Public God: Natural Theology Reconsidered* (Minneapolis: Fortress Press, 2015).

29. For different ways in which the topic of creation can be approached, see Burrell, "Creation or Emanation: Two Paradigms of Reason," in *God and Creation: An Ecumenical Symposium*, ed. David B. Burrell and Bernard McGinn (Notre Dame, IN: University of Notre Dame Press, 1990), 27–37.

30. From the preface of John L. Mahoney, ed., *Seeing into the Life of Things: Essays on Religion and Literature* (New York: Fordham University Press, 1998), xiii.

31. Michael Polanyi, "Faith and Reason," *Journal of Religion* 41 (1961): 244. For a fuller treatment, see his *Personal Knowledge* (Chicago: University of Chicago Press, 1958).

32. Denis Edwards, *Jesus and the Cosmos* (Mahwah, NJ: Paulist Press, 1991), 44–54. From a philosophical point of view, see the outstanding Mark Wynn, *God and Goodness: A Natural Theological Perspective* (London: Routledge, 1999).

33. Admittedly, this more philosophical understanding does not go back to Genesis, which speaks more of a primal chaos. The *ex nihilo* character of creation was explored more in reaction to later

Gnostic and Manichean teachings that supposed a noncreated evil, material principle.

34. See Robert Sokolowski, "Creation and Christian Understanding," with response from David Tracy, in Burrell and McGinn, *God and Creation*, 178–96.

35. Lonergan, *Method in Theology*, 341–43.

36. See Thomas Aquinas, *STh* I, q. 12, a. 13, ad 1: "we are united to God as to one unknown."

37. For the original article, see Herman Muckermann, "Evolution (History and Scientific Foundation)," in *The Catholic Encyclopedia*, vol. 5 (New York: Robert Appleton Company, 1909), http://www.newadvent.org/cathen/05655a.htm.

38. Carl Sagan, *Cosmos* (New York: Random House, 1980), 23.

39. Jacques Monod, *Chance and Necessity* (New York: Knopf, 1970), 180.

40. Werner Heisenberg, "Scientific and Religious Truths," in *Quantum Questions*, ed. Ken Wilber (Boston: Shambhala, 1984), 39.

41. Though others who could be mentioned are Stephen Hawking, P. W. Atkins, Robert K. Adair, and Harald Fritsch.

42. Paul Davies, *God and the New Physics* (New York: Simon and Schuster, 1983), ix.

43. Etienne Gilson, "En marge d'un texte," in *Louis de Broglie, Physicien et Penseur* (Paris: Michel, 1953), 153.

44. As an indication of the medieval fascination with science, see Walter Principe, "'The Truth of Human Nature' according to Thomas Aquinas: Theology and Science in Interaction," in *Philosophy and the God of Abraham: Essays in Memory of James A. Weisheipl*, ed. R. James Long (Toronto: Pontifical Institute of Medieval Studies, 1991), 161–77.

45. Quoted in Michael J. Buckley, "Religion and Science: Paul Davies and John Paul II," *Theological Studies* 51, no. 2 (June 1990): 313.

46. Judith Wright, "The Forest," in *A Human Pattern: Selected Poems* (Sydney: Angus & Robertson, 1990), 104.

47. Thomas Aquinas, *STh* I, q. 65, a. 3.

48. Thomas Aquinas, *SCG* bk. 2, c. 2.

49. *SCG* bk. 2, c. 45.

50. Apart from an abundance of exciting documentation and marvelous instances of the variety of the past, Stephen Jay Goulding, *Wonderful Life: The Burgess Shale and the Nature of History*

(London: Penguin, 1989) is a striking model of scientific reconstruction, even as it poses profound philosophical questions.

51. Herbert McCabe, *God Matters* (London: Geoffrey Chapman, 1987), 2–9.

52. George Steiner, *Real Presences* (Chicago: University of Chicago Press, 1989).

53. Kathryn Tanner, *God and Creation in Christian Theology: Tyranny or Empowerment?* (Oxford: Basil Blackwell, 1988). This work studies the deep grammar of the classical theological tradition.

54. *SCG* bk. 1, c. 25.

55. *STh* I, q. 8, a. 1.

56. Edwards, *Jesus and the Cosmos*, 53–55. For a different context, see Jürgen Moltmann, *The Way of Jesus Christ* (London: SCM, 1990), 297–301.

57. *SCG* bk. 3, c. 69.

58. W. Norris Clarke, "Is Natural Theology Still Viable Today?" in *Prospects for Natural Theology*, ed. Eugene Thomas Long (Washington, DC: The Catholic University of America Press, 1992), 181.

59. John Paul II, "Letter to the Reverend George V. Coyne, S.J., Director of the Vatican Observatory," *Origins* 18, no. 23 (November 1988): 378.

60. W. Norris Clarke, *The One and the Many: A Contemporary Thomistic Metaphysics* (Notre Dame, IN: University of Notre Dame Press, 2001), 245–60.

61. Particularly stimulating in this area is Ilia Delio, *The Unbearable Wholeness of Being: God, Evolution, and the Power of Love* (Maryknoll, NY: Orbis, 2013).

62. For a compendious and concise point of reference, see George Coyne et al., *A New Physics and a New Theology*, trans. Michael Heller (Notre Dame, IN: University of Notre Dame Press, 1997), 25–40, 81–101.

63. Matthew Ogilvie, "New Evolutionary Theory and Catholic Theology," *Australian EJournal of Theology* 7 (2006): 1–11, http://aejt.com.au/__data/assets/pdf_file/0003/395130/AEJT_7.4_Oglivie_Evolution.pdf.

64. David Bentley Hart, *The Experience of God: Being, Consciousness, Bliss* (New Haven, CT: Yale University Press, 2013), 154–60.

65. Bentley Hart, *The Experience of God*, 300.

66. Bentley Hart, *The Experience of God*, 226.

CHAPTER 4

1. David Bentley Hart, *The Experience of God: Being, Consciousness, Bliss* (New Haven, CT: Yale University Press, 2013), 42–43.

2. Bentley Hart, *The Experience of God*, 44.

3. See Larry W. Hurtado, *God in New Testament Theology* (Nashville: Abingdon Press, 2010) for the section, "The Triadic Shape of God-Discourse in the New Testament," 99–109. Also Richard Bauckham, *Jesus and the God of Israel* (Grand Rapids: William B. Eerdmans, 2008), 127–51.

4. See Francis J. Moloney, *Love in the Gospel of John: An Exegetical, Theological, and Literary Study* (Grand Rapids: Baker Academic, 2013), esp. 37–69, 201–10.

5. On the necessity of understanding this divine reciprocity of relationships in an active and "verbal" sense, see G. Lafont, *Peut on connaître Dieu en Jésus-Christ* (Paris: Cerf, 1969), 272–77.

6. As Aquinas notes, in reference to John 10:30: "[A] twofold error is here excluded: that of Arius who divided the divine essence, and that of Sabellius who confused the persons. We escape both Charybdis and Scilla, because when he [Jesus] says '*one*', he frees you from Arius, because if 'we' are '*one*' there is no diversity. But in that he says '*we* are', he frees you from Sabellius, for as 'we', the Father and the Son are different subjects [*alius et alius*];" *In Evang. B. Joannis Expositio*, c. 10, 4. For an Athanasian treatment of these issues, Thomas F. Torrance, *Trinitarian Faith* (Edinburgh: Continuum, 2003), 110–45.

7. *Apology*, 38A.

8. For a thorough survey and comment, see Gary D. Badcock, *Light of Truth and Fire of Love: A Theology of the Holy Spirit* (Grand Rapids: William B. Eerdmans, 1997), 35–82; 145–70. Rowan Williams, in his *On Christian Theology* (Oxford: Blackwell, 2000), insightfully compares Johannine pneumatology with the Pauline and the Lucan types. See esp. pp. 115–21.

9. John 3:32–35; 7:16–18; 8:26–29, 42–43; 12:47–50; 14:10.

10. For an illuminating account of the Holy Spirit in the immanent Trinity, drawing on Eastern and Western positions, see Badcock, *Light of Truth*, 234–56.

11. For a considerable bibliography and a fuller expression of my own approach, see Anthony Kelly, *The Trinity of Love: A Theology*

of the Christian God (Wilmington, DE: Michael Glazier, 1989) and *An Expanding Theology: Faith in a World of Connections* (Sydney: E. J. Dwyer, 1993); "A Trinitarian Moral Theology," *Studia Moralia* 39 (2001): 245–89.

12. On the necessity of understanding this divine reciprocity of relationships in an active and "verbal" sense, see G. Lafont, *Peut on connaître Dieu...*, 272–77.

13. For an excellent account of the theological development involved, see Torrance, *Trinitarian Faith*, 47–75.

14. Paul Celan, *Poems*, trans. M. Hamburger (Manchester: Carcanet, 1980), 202–3. (EIN DRÖHNEN: "es ist / die Wahrheit selbst / unter die Menschen / getreten, / mitten ins / Metapherngestöber." For further comment, see John Milbank, *The Word Made Strange: Theology, Language, Culture* (Oxford: Blackwell, 1997), 131.

15. For a rigorous examination of the theme of divine eternity, see John C. Yates, *The Timelessness of God* (Lanham, MD: University Press of America, 1990).

16. I do not think this distinction is sufficiently appreciated. When it is not, "process" becomes the ultimate reality, but not "procession" in the trinitarian sense. There is a big difference between deifying the process and adoring the "proceeding" divine persons. Even a survey of such towering expertise as Ian G. Barbour, *Religion in an Age of Science* (San Francisco: HarperOne, 1990) does not mention the relevance of the trinitarian mystery to current evolutionary and genetic understandings of reality. Remaining only with the category of process strikes me as being theologically far too timid.

17. Quoted in Rupert Sheldrake, *The Rebirth of Nature: The Greening of Science and God* (New York: Bantam Books, 1991), 198. Noteworthy, too, is the influence of Sheldrake on the deep trinitarian structure of Bede Griffiths, *A New Vision of Reality* (Victoria Park, Australia: Association for the Blind of W.A., 1993).

18. See also Aquinas, *SCG* bk. 2, c. 45.

19. Here I have adapted three terms taken from John Macquarrie, *Principles of Christian Theology* (London: SCM Press, 1977), 195–202.

20. For a creative treatment of the divine missions, see Robert M. Doran, *The Trinity in History: A Theology of the Divine Missions* (Toronto: University of Toronto Press, 2012).

21. For an overview of Aquinas's approach to theology, see Anthony J. Kelly, "A Multidimensional Disclosure: Aquinas' Theological Intentionality," *The Thomist* 67, no. 3 (July 2003): 335–74.

22. *STh* I, q. 43, a. 1.

23. *STh* I, q. 43, a. 5, ad 2.

24. Thomas also speaks of the Father as given and indwelling through grace, but not as "sent." The first divine person is present precisely as the source of all divine life and love, the Father who is "above all and through all and in all" (Eph 4:6); (*STh* I, q. 43, a. 3).

25. *STh* I, q. 43, a. 5, ad 2.

26. *STh* I, q. 43, a. 1. For further treatment of the missions, Jean-Hervé Nicolas, *Synthèse dogmatique: de la Trinité à la Trinité* (Paris: Beauchesne, 1985), 231–65.

27. See Kelly, *Trinity of Love,* 168–69; 195–202.

28. See *STh* I, q. 43, a. 7; q. 88, a. 3.

29. *De Trinitate* VI; VIII–XV.

30. Servus Gieben, "Traces of God in Nature according to Robert Grosseteste," *Franciscan Studies* 24 (1964): 154–56.

31. For the analogical shift in our understanding of God's relationship to the world, see Carol Jean Vale, "Teilhard de Chardin: Ontogenesis vs. Ontology," *Theological Studies* 53, no. 2 (June 1992): 313–37.

32. Bonaventure, *Intinerarium Mentis in Deum* c. 3, n. 5.

33. *STh* I, q. 45, a. 6, ad 2.

34. *STh* I, q. 32, a. 1, ad 3.

35. *STh* I, q. 39, a. 7.

36. Jean-Pierre Torrell, *Saint Thomas d'Aquin, maître spirituel* (Paris: Cerf, 1996), 208–13.

37. *STh* I, q. 39, a. 7, ad 1.

38. For a recent treatment of this topic, see Timothy L. Smith, "The Context and Character of Thomas' Theory of Appropriations," *The Thomist* 63 (1999): 579–612.

39. Anne Hunt, *The Trinity and the Paschal Mystery: A Development in Recent Catholic Theology* (Collegeville, MN: Liturgical Press, 1997).

40. Anne Hunt, "Psychological Analogy and the Paschal Mystery in Trinitarian Theology," *Theological Studies* 59 (1998): 197–218.

41. On this point, see Carl N. Still, "'Gifted Knowledge': An Exception to Thomistic Epistemology?" *The Thomist* 63 (1999): 173–90.

42. *STh* I-II, q. 68, a. 1–2.

43. For example, Thomas Berry, *The Dream of the Earth* (San Francisco: Sierra Book Club, 1988), 44–46.

44. Beatrice Bruteau, "Eucharistic Ecology and Ecological Spirituality," *Cross Currents* (Winter 1990): 504.

CHAPTER 5

1. Jean-Yves Lacoste, *From Theology to Theological Thinking*, trans. W. Chris Hacket, intro. Jeffrey Bloechl (Charlottesville: University of Virginia Press, 2014), viii.

2. Werner Jeanrond, *A Theology of Love* (London: T&T Clark, 2010), is a valuable resource in the discussion of love in its divine and human forms, esp. 239–59, for a concluding summary.

3. *STh* I, q. 20, a.2.

4. See Brendan Purcell, *From Big Bang to Big Mystery: Human Origins in the Light of Creation and Evolution* (New York: New City Press, 2011), 316–30.

5. For an abundance of scriptural comment, see Larry W. Hurtado, *God in New Testament Theology* (Nashville: Abingdon Press, 2010), 38–47.

6. Aquinas, *SCG* bk. 2, c. 45.

7. Christmas Day Sermon (ca. AD 410, *Sermo* 190.2.

8. W. Norris Clarke, "Is Natural Theology Still Viable Today?" in *Prospects for Natural Theology*, ed. Eugene Thomas Long (Washington, DC: The Catholic University of America Press, 1992), 181.

9. The source for this quote is found in "Medieval Sourcebook: Anselm (1033–1109): Proslogium," accessed October 7, 2019, https://sourcebooks.fordham.edu/basis/anselm-proslogium.asp#CHAPTER%20I.

10. For example, see John 1:18; 3:16, 35; 4:23, 34; 5:18–21, 26–28, 30, 36–37; 6:32–33, 37–40, 44–45, 57, 65; 7:16.

CHAPTER 6

1. A standard reference here is William J. Hill, *Knowing the Unknown God* (New York: Philosophical Library, 1971), esp. 163–219. For a deeply philosophical, interfaith, and historical discussion, see David B. Burrell, *Knowing the Unknowable God: Ibn-Sina Maimonides, Aquinas* (Notre Dame, IN: University of Notre Dame Press, 1986).

2. Hans Urs von Balthasar, *The Glory of the Lord: A Theological Aesthetics*, vol. 1, *Seeing the Form*, trans. Erasmo Leiva-Merikakis (New York: Crossroad Publications, 1982), 228.

3. Urs von Balthasar, *The Glory of the Lord*, 22.

4. *STh* I, q. 13, a. 7.

5. See Francis X. Clooney, *His Hiding Place Is Darkness: A Hindu-Catholic Theopoetics of Divine Absence* (Stanford, CA: Stanford University Press, 2014), esp. 22–31.

6. Bernard Lonergan, *Method in Theology* (London: Darton, Longman and Todd, 1972), 106.

7. See "God" in the biblical Jewish tradition in Larry W. Hurtado, *God in New Testament Theology* (Nashville: Abingdon Press, 2010), 31–43.

8. Kevin Hart, *Kingdoms of God* (Bloomington: Indiana University Press, 2014) is an outstanding phenomenological illustration of the different and sometimes conflicting theological and philosophical approaches to God and the kingdom of God.

9. As Kevin Hart writes in a larger frame of reference: "Conversion is always needed; it is a perpetual turning toward God, not away from the world but away from being enthralled by it....On my analysis, this turning to the *Basileia* has two moments: the first is... *kenosis* in which the 'I' empties itself out in order to receive the Holy Spirit. But Christianity, to my mind, does not stop here....There is a second moment of...*epektasis*, in which one stretches out in the love of God and neighbour"; Hart, *Kingdoms of God*, 3.

10. See Anthony Kelly, "Eschatological Hope: A Christian Perspective," in *Hope: A Form of Delusion? Buddhist and Christian Per-*

spectives, ed. Elizabeth Harris (Munich: Editions of Sankt Ottilien, 2013), 229–50.

11. See Christopher Morse, *Not Every Spirit: A Dogmatics of Christian Disbelief* (Valley Forge, PA: Trinity Press International, 1994).

12. Though 3 John 11b does associate doing good with "seeing God," it is most likely that the author is speaking in reference to God's revelation in Christ.

13. *STh*, I, q. 12, a. 13, ad 1; *SCG* bk. 3, c. 48. For his extended comment on John 1:18, see *In Evangelium B. Johannis...*, c. 1, lect. 9.

14. *STh*, I-II, q. 27, a. 2, ad 2.

15. As an explicitation of the Johannine experience of God ("everyone who loves is born of God and knows God") (1 John 4:7b), this medieval position is far from irrelevant, as will be seen—especially when linked to the Thomist analyses of grace as an "interior instinct" (*In Evangelium B. Johannis*, c. 6, lect. 5, n. 3), as a conformity to the divine persons (*STh.*, I, q. 43, a. 3–6), of charity as a participation in God's own love (II-II, q. 24, a. 2), and of the rules for the discernment of the state of grace (I-II, q. 112, a. 5).

16. Jean-Luc Marion's influential trilogy, *Reduction and Givenness: Investigations of Husserl, Heidegger, and Phenomenology*, trans. Thomas A. Carlson (Evanston, IL: Northwestern University Press (1998); *Being Given: Toward a Phenomenology of Givenness*, trans. Jeffrey L. Kosky (Stanford, CA: Stanford University Press, 2002); *In Excess: Studies of Saturated Phenomena*, trans. Robyn Horner and Vincent Barraud (New York: Fordham University Press, 2002). For further elaboration and background, see *God without Being: Hors-Texte*, trans. Thomas A. Carlson (Chicago: University of Chicago Press, 1991); "Le possible et la revelation," in *Eros and Eris: Contribution to a Hermeneutical Phenomenology; Liber Amicorum for Adriann Peperzak*, ed. P. van Tongeren, P. Sars, C. Bremmer, and K. Boey (Dordrecht: Kluwer Academic, 1992), 217–31; "The Saturated Phenomenon," *Philosophy Today* 40 (1996): 103–24.

17. Marion, *Being Given*, 216.

18. Marion, *Being Given*, 261.

19. Marion, *Being Given*, 216–17.

20. Marion, *Being Given*, 264–65.

21. Marion, *Being Given*, 289; *In Excess*, 33, 42.

22. For a seminal article, see Karl Rahner, "The Concept of Mystery in Catholic Theology," in *Theological Investigations IV*, trans. Kevin Smyth (Baltimore, MD: Helicon Press, 1966), 36–73.

23. See John F. Haught, *Christianity and Science: Toward a Theology of Nature* (Maryknoll, NY: Orbis, 2007), 24–29.

24. See Lonergan, *Method in Theology*, as in n. 6 above.

25. Gregory of Nyssa, *Commentary on the Song of Songs*, ch. 1, v. 3, trans. C. McCambley (Brookline, MA: Hellenic College Press, 1987), 53.

26. With regard to the range of problems—and challenges—associated with postmodernity and the "deconstructive" methods associated with it, see Graham Ward, ed., *The Post-modern God: A Theological Reader* (Oxford: Blackwell, 1997). The editor's "Introduction" is particularly stimulating, see xv–xlvii.

27. The need to be attuned to the experiential dimensions of Christian truth is challengingly brought out by Joseph O'Leary, *La vérité chrétienne à l'âge du pluralisme religieux* (Paris: Cerf, 1994).

28. Karl Rahner, "The Experience of God Today," in *Theological Investigations XI*, trans. David Bourke (London: Darton, Longman and Todd, 1974), 149–65.

29. Rahner, "The Experience of God Today," 164.

CHAPTER 7

1. On these points, see Raimon Panikkar, *The Intra-religious Dialogue*, rev. ed. (Maryknoll, NY: Orbis Books, 1998), 61–71.

2. For a phenomenology of the event, see Claude Romano, *L'événement et le monde. Essais Philosophiques* (Paris: Presses Universitaires de France, 1998), 60–69.

3. Panikkar, e.g., describes this kind of dialogue as "a religious encounter in faith, hope and love," *The Intra-religious Dialogue*, 69–70.

4. For a valuable reflection in this context, see Georges de Schrijver, "The Derridean Notion of Hospitality as Resource for Interreligious Dialogue in a Globalized World," *Louvain Studies* 31 (Spring–Summer 2006): 79–104.

5. For different perspectives, see Elizabeth A. Johnson, *Quest for the Living God: Mapping Frontiers in the Theology of God* (New York: Continuum, 2007), 161–73.

6. For a specifically Thomist account, see Anthony J. Kelly, "A Multidimensional Disclosure: Aquinas' Theological Intentionality," *The Thomist* 67, no. 3 (July 2003): 335–74.

7. See Anthony J. Kelly, *Eschatology and Hope* (Maryknoll, NY: Orbis, 2006), 15–17; 25–28.

8. For full reference, see n. 4 above.

9. See Panikkar, *The Intra-religious Dialogue*, 73–83, for a telling criticism of any phenomenological method of *epoche* in regard to one's own faith.

10. Cited by Clifford C. Geertz, in M. Banton, ed., *Religion as a Cultural System: Anthropological Approaches to the Study of Religion* (London: Tavistock, 1985), 31.

11. See Jill Robbins, ed., *Is It Righteous to Be? Interviews with Emmanuel Levinas* (Stanford, CA: Stanford University Press, 2001), 171. Here, he states, "When I speak to a Christian, I always quote Matthew 25: The relation to God is presented there as a relation to another person. It is not a metaphor; in the other, there is a real presence of God. In my relation to the other, I hear the word of God."

12. In reference to an influential Jewish philosophy of dialogue, see L. Augustine Brady, "Martin Buber and the Gospel of John," *Thought* 201 (September 1978): 283–92.

13. For the hermeneutical (and human) importance of the play of conversation, see David Tracy, *The Analogical Imagination: Christian Theology and the Culture of Pluralism* (New York: Crossroad, 1981), 101, 446–55, and *Pluralism and Ambiguity: Hermeneutics, Religion, Hope* (San Francisco: Harper and Row, 1987), 16–27.

14. See B. Pottier, "Note sur la mission invisible du Verbe chez saint Thomas d'Aquin," *Nouvelle Revue Théologique* 123, no. 4 (October–December 2001): 547–57.

15. *STh* I, q. 43, a. 2.

16. *STh* I, q. 43, a. 6, ad 1.

17. *STh* I, q. 43. q. 5, ad 2.

18. For specific mention of significance of the three divine persons for interfaith dialogue, see Anthony Kelly, *The Trinity of Love: A Theology of the Christian God* (Wilmington, DE: Michael Glazier, 1989), 228–48.

19. John Dunne, *The Way of All the Earth: Experiments in Truth and Religion* (Notre Dame, IN: University of Notre Dame Press, 1978), is now something of a classic in its profound exploration of the intentionality of dialogue.

CHAPTER 8

1. *DS* 806.

2. For example, Anne Hunt, *The Trinity: Insights from the Mystics* (Collegeville, MN: The Liturgical Press, 2010).

3. Bernard Lonergan, *Method in Theology* (London: Darton, Longman and Todd, 1972), 342.

4. Lonergan, *Method in Theology*, 106.

5. Karl Rahner, "The Experience of God Today," in *Theological Investigations XI*, trans. David Bourke (London: Darton, Longman and Todd, 1974), 164.

6. Hans Urs von Balthasar, *The Glory of the Lord: A Theological Aesthetics*, vol. 1, *Seeing the Form*, trans. Erasmo Leiva-Merikakis (New York: Crossroad Publications, 1982), 237.

7. Note the following remark of Bernard Lonergan on authentic religion: "A religion that promotes self-transcendence to the point, not merely of justice, but of self-sacrificing love, will have a redemptive role in human society inasmuch as such love can undo the mischief of decline and restore the cumulative process of progress"; Lonergan, *Method in Theology*, 55.

8. Lonergan, *Method in Theology*, 106.

9. Von Balthasar, *The Glory of the Lord*, 1:365–80. For a variety of historical perspectives, see Paul Gavrilyuk and Sarah Coakley, eds., *The Spiritual Senses: Perceiving God in Western Christianity* (Cambridge: Cambridge University Press, 2012).

10. See, for instance, Pierre Rousselot, *The Eyes of Faith and Answers to Two Objections*, trans. Joseph Donceel and Avery Dulles (New York: Fordham University Press, 1990).

11. Martin Heidegger, *Discourse on Thinking: A Translation of Gelassenheit*, trans. John M. Anderson and E. Hans Freund (New York: Harper Torchbooks, 1969).

12. Heidegger, *Discourse on Thinking*, 53–56.

13. Heidegger, *Discourse on Thinking*, 58–61.

14. Heidegger, *Discourse on Thinking*, 64, 73, 80.

15. Heidegger, *Discourse on Thinking*, see esp. 81–90. The text is so highly evocative as a whole that attempts to give precise references seem like relapsing into calculative thinking!

16. *Meister Eckhart: The Essential Sermons, Commentaries, Treatises and Defense*, trans. Edmund Colledge and Bernard McGinn (Mahwah, NJ: Paulist Press, 1981), 184. For an excellent chapter on Eckhart, see Hunt, *The Trinity: Insights from the Mystics*, 73–98.

17. *III Sent.* d. 34, q. 1, a. 1; *STh* I-II, q. 70, a. 4.

18. *STh* I-II, q. 68, a. 2.

19. In the activity of the theological virtues is found the radical condition for the operation of the gifts. The movement of the Spirit is recognized in charity: "faith is about what is not seen, hope is concerned with what is not possessed, but the love of charity concerns the one who is already possessed, for the beloved is somehow within the lover, and also the lover is affectively attracted to be united with the beloved" (*STh* I-II, q. 66, a. 5). The work of Francis X. Clooney, *His Hiding Place Is Darkness: A Hindu-Catholic Theopoetics of Divine Absence* (Stanford, CA: Stanford University Press, 2014), invites further applications of the gifts to interfaith dialogue, as it accents the primacy of love, the darkness and absence that affect knowledge of the Beloved, and the need for a theopoetics to evoke the full reality of the particularity of Christian revelation. See his concluding remarks, 140–41.

20. *STh* II-II, q. 45, a. 1–6.

21. *STh* II-II, q. 8, a. 1–8.

22. *STh* II-II, q. 9, a. 1–4.

23. *STh* II-II, q. 19, a. 1–12.

24. Cf. *STh* II-II, q. 52, a. 1–4.

25. Cf. *STh* II-II, q. 139, a. 1.

26. I am indebted to an as-yet unpublished lecture of Kevin Hart, "'Poverty's Speech': On Liturgical Reduction," especially in reference to Jean-Yves Lacoste, *Experience and the Absolute: Disputed Questions on the Humanity of Man*, trans. Mark Raferty-Skeban (New York: Fordham University Press, 2010).

BIBLIOGRAPHY

Alison, James. *The Joy of Being Wrong: Original Sin through Easter Eyes*. New York: Crossroad, 1998.

———. *Raising Abel: The Recovery of Eschatological Imagination*. London: SPCK, 2010.

Badcock, Gary D. *Light of Truth and Fire of Love: A Theology of the Holy Spirit*. Grand Rapids: William B. Eerdmans, 1997.

Banton, M., ed. *Religion as a Cultural System: Anthropological Approaches to the Study of Religion*. London: Tavistock, 1985.

Barr, Stephen M. *Modern Physics and Ancient Faith*. Notre Dame, IN: University of Notre Dame Press, 2003.

Bauckham, Richard. *Jesus and the God of Israel*. Grand Rapids: William B. Eerdmans, 2008.

Behe, Michael H., Joseph Fessio, David W. Opderbeck, Richard L. Cleary, Michael Egnor, Fred Hutchinson, Jack D. Elliot, and Charlie Mae, in response to Robert D. Miller. "Design, Intelligence and Philosophy: An Exchange." *First Things* 164 (June–July 2006): 5–11.

Berry, Thomas. *The Dream of the Earth*. San Francisco: Sierra Book Club, 1988.

Brady, L. Augustine, "Martin Buber and the Gospel of John." *Though*t 201 (September 1978): 283–92.

Brague, Remi. *On the God of the Christians (and on One or Two Others)*. Translated by Paul Seaton. South Bend, IN: St. Augustine's Press, 2013.

Brown, Warren S., Nancey Murphy, and H. Newton Maloney, eds. *Whatever Happened to the Soul? Scientific and Theological Portraits of Human Nature*. Minneapolis: Fortress Press, 1998.

Buckley, Michael J. *At the Origins of Modern Atheism*. New Haven, CT: Yale University Press, 1987.

Burrell, David B. *Aquinas: God and Action*. Notre Dame, IN: University of Notre Dame Press, 1979.

———. *Knowing the Unknowable God: Ibn-Sina, Maimonides, Aquinas*. Notre Dame, IN: University of Notre Dame Press, 1986.

Burrell, David B., and Bernard McGinn, eds. *God and Creation: An Ecumenical Symposium*. Notre Dame, IN: University of Notre Dame Press, 1990.

Celan, Paul. *Poems*. Translated by M. Hamburger. Manchester: Carcanet, 1980.

Clarke, W. Norris. *Explorations in Metaphysics: Being, God, Person*. Notre Dame, IN: University of Notre Dame Press, 1992.

———. *The One and the Many: A Contemporary Thomistic Metaphysics*. Notre Dame, IN: University of Notre Dame Press, 2009.

Clooney, Francis X. *His Hiding Place Is Darkness: A Hindu-Catholic Theopoetics of Divine Absence*. Stanford, CA: Stanford University Press, 2014.

College, Edmund, and Bernard McGinn, eds. *Meister Eckhart: The Essential Sermons, Commentaries, Treatises, and Defense*. Classics of Western Spirituality. Mahwah, NJ: Paulist Press, 1981.

Collot, Michel. *La poésie modern et la structure d'horizon*. Paris: Presses Univeritaires de France, 2005.

Daly, Gabriel. *Creation and Redemption*. Dublin: Gill and MacMillan, 1988.

Danielou, Jean. *The Angels and Their Mission*. Translated by David Heimann. Allen, TX: Newman Press, 1957.

Davies, Paul. *God and the New Physics*. New York: Simon and Schuster, 1983.

Delio, Ilia. *The Unbearable Wholeness of Being: God, Evolution, and the Power of Love*. Maryknoll, NY: Orbis, 2013.

Derrida, Jacques. *An Introduction to Edmund Husserl's Origin of Geometry*. Translated by John P. Leavey Jr. Lincoln: University of Nebraska Press, 1989.

———. *Of Spirit: Heidegger and the Question*. Translated by Geoffrey Bennington and Rachel Bowlby. Chicago: University of Chicago Press, 1989.

Doran, Robert M. *The Trinity in History: A Theology of the Divine Missions*. Toronto: University of Toronto Press, 2012.

Dunne, John. *The Way of All the Earth: Experiments in Truth and Religion*. Notre Dame, IN: University of Notre Dame Press, 1978.

Eagleton, Terry. *Culture and the Death of God*. New Haven, CT: Yale University Press, 2014.

Eccles, J.C. *Brain and Conscious Experience*. Berlin: Springer Verlag, 1962.

Edwards, Denis. *Jesus and the Cosmos*. Mahwah, NJ: Paulist Press, 1991.

Egan, Harvey D. *Soundings in the Christian Mystical Tradition*. Collegeville, MN: The Liturgical Press, 2010.

Evans, C. Stephen. *Natural Signs and the Knowledge of God: A New Look at Theistic Arguments*. New York: Oxford University Press, 2010.

Falque, Emmanuel. *The Metamorphosis of Finitude: An Essay on Birth and Resurrection*. Translated by George Hughes. New York: Fordham University Press, 2012.

Fry, Christopher. *A Sleep of Prisoners*. London: Oxford University Press, 1959.

Ganoczy, A. "Cerveau et conscience en anthropologie théologique." *Recherches de Science Religieuse* 92, no. 3 (2004): 349–81.

Gavrilyuk, Paul, and Sarah Coakley, eds. *The Spiritual Senses: Perceiving God in Western Christianity*. Cambridge: Cambridge University Press, 2012.

Gieben, Servus. "Traces of God in Nature according to Robert Grosseteste." *Franciscan Studies* 24 (1964): 154–56.

Goulding, Stephen Jay. *Wonderful Life: The Burgess Shale and the Nature of History*. London: Penguin, 1989.

Gregory of Nyssa. *Commentary on the Song of Songs*. Translated by C. McCambley. Brookline, MA: Hellenic College Press, 1987.

Griffiths, Bede. *A New Vision of Reality*. Victoria Park, Australia: Association for the Blind of W.A., 1993.

Harris, Elizabeth, ed. *Hope: A Form of Delusion? Buddhist and Christian Perspectives*. Munich: Editions of Sankt Ottilien, 2013.

Hart, David Bentley. *The Experience of God: Being, Consciousness, Bliss*. New Haven, CT: Yale University Press, 2013.

Hart, Kevin. *Kingdoms of God*. Bloomington: Indiana University Press, 2014.

Haught, John F. *Christianity and Science: Toward a Theology of Nature*. Maryknoll, NY: Orbis Books, 2007.

Heidegger, Martin. *Discourse on Thinking: A Translation of Gelassenheit*. Translated by John M. Anderson and E. Hans Freund. New York: Harper and Row, 1969.

Heller, Michael. *The New Physics and a New Theology*. Translated by George Coyne, SJ, et al. Notre Dame, IN: University of Notre Dame Press, 1996.

Hill, William. *Knowing the Unknown God*. New York: The Philosophical Library, 1971.

Horner, Robyn. *Rethinking God as Gift: Marion, Derrida, and the Limits of Phenomenology*. New York: Fordham University Press, 2000.

Hoye, William W. *The Emergence of Eternal Life*. Cambridge: Cambridge University Press, 2013.

Hudson, Deal W., and Dennis William Moran, eds. *The Future of Thomism*. Notre Dame, IN: University of Notre Dame Press, 1992.

Hunt, Anne. "Psychological Analogy and the Paschal Mystery in Trinitarian Theology." *Theological Studies* 59 (1998): 197–218.

———. *The Trinity: Insights from the Mystics*. Collegeville, MN: The Liturgical Press, 2010.

———. *Trinity: Nexus of the Mysteries of Trinitarian Faith*. Maryknoll, NY: Orbis Books, 2005.

Hurtado, Larry W. *God in New Testament Theology*. Nashville: Abingdon Press, 2010.

Imhof, Paul, Hubert Biallowons, and Harvey D. Egan, eds. *Faith in a Wintry Season: Conversations and Interviews with Karl Rahner in the Last Years of His Life, 1982–84*. New York: Crossroad, 1990.

Jeanrond, Werner. *A Theology of Love*. London: T&T Clark, 2010.

Johnson, Elizabeth A. *Quest for the Living God: Mapping Frontiers in the Theology of God*. New York: Continuum, 2007.

Keck, David. *Angels and Angelology in the Middle Ages*. New York: Oxford University Press, 1998.

Kelly, Anthony. *An Expanding Theology: Faith in a World of Connections*. Sydney: E. J. Dwyer, 1993.

———. *Eschatology and Hope*. Maryknoll, NY: Orbis Books, 2006.

———. "God: How Near a Relation?" *The Thomist* 34 (1970): 191–229.

———. “A Multidimensional Disclosure: Aquinas’ Theological Intentionality.” *The Thomist* 67, no. 3 (July 2003): 335–74.
———. “A Trinitarian Moral Theology.” *Studia Moralia* 39 (2001): 245–89.
———. *The Trinity of Love: A Theology of the Christian God.* Wilmington, DE: Michael Glazier, 1989.
———. *Upward: Faith, Church, and the Ascension of Christ.* Collegeville, MN: The Liturgical Press, 2014.
Kelly, Anthony, and Francis J, Moloney. *Experiencing God in the Gospel of John.* Mahwah, NJ: Paulist Press, 2003.
Klubertanz, George. *St. Thomas Aquinas on Analogy: A Textual Analysis and a Systematic Synthesis.* Chicago: Loyola University Press, 1960.
Konner, Melvin. *The Tangled Wing: Biological Constraints on the Human Spirit.* New York: Harper and Row, 1982.
Lacoste, Jean-Yves. *Experience and the Absolute: Disputed Questions on the Humanity of Man.* Translated by Mark Raferty-Skeban. New York: Fordham University Press, 2010.
———. *From Theology to Theological Thinking.* Translated by W. Chris Hacket. Introduction by Jeffrey Bloechl. Charlottesville: University of Virginia Press, 2014.
———. *La Phénoménalité de Dieu: Neuf etudes.* Paris: Cerf, 2008.
Lafont, G. *Peut on connaître Dieu en Jésus-Christ.* Paris: Cerf, 1969.
Lampe, Stephen. *Thinking about God: Reflections on Conceptions and Misconceptions.* Agawam, MA: Millennium Press, 2014.
Latour, Bruno. *Inquiry into Modes of Existence: Anthropology for Moderns.* Cambridge, MA: Harvard University Press, 2011.
Lonergan, Bernard. *Method in Theology.* London: Darton, Longman and Todd, 1972.
———. *Philosophy of God, and Theology: The Relationship between Philosophy of God and the Functional Specialty, Systematics.* London: Darton, Longman and Todd, 1973.
Long, Eugene Thomas, ed. *Prospects for Natural Theology.* Washington, DC: The Catholic University of America Press, 1992.
Long, R. James, ed. *Philosophy and the God of Abraham: Essays in Memory of James A. Weisheipl.* Toronto: Pontifical Institute of Medieval Studies, 1991.
Louth, Andrew. *Maximus the Confessor.* New York: Routledge, 1996.
McCabe, Herbert. *God Matters.* London: Geoffrey Chapman, 1987.

MacIntyre, Alasdair. *God, Philosophy, Universities: A Selective History of the Catholic Philosophical Tradition*. Lanham, MD: Rowman and Littlefield, 2009.

Macquarrie, John. *Principles of Christian Theology*. London: SCM Press, 1977.

Mahoney, John L., ed. *Seeing into the Life of Things: Essays on Religion and Literature*. New York: Fordham University Press, 1998.

Marion, Jean-Luc. *Being Given: Toward a Phenomenology of Givenness*. Translated by Jeffrey L. Kosky. Stanford, CA: Stanford University Press, 2002.

———. *In Excess: Studies of Saturated Phenomena*. Translated by Robyn Horner and Vincent Barraud. New York: Fordham University Press, 2002.

———. *Reduction and Givenness: Investigations of Husserl, Heidegger, and Phenomenology*. Translated by Thomas A. Carlson. Evanston, IL: Northwestern University Press. 1998.

Milbank, John. *Theology and Social Theory: Beyond Secular Reason*. Oxford: Blackwell, 1990.

———. *The Word Made Strange: Theology, Language, Culture*. Oxford: Blackwell, 1997.

Moloney, Francis J. *Love in the Gospel of John: An Exegetical, Theological, and Literary Study*. Grand Rapids: Baker Academic, 2013.

Moltmann, Jürgen. *The Way of Jesus Christ*. London: SCM, 1990.

Monod, Jacques. *Chance and Necessity*. New York: Knopf, 1970.

Morse, Christopher. *Not Every Spirit: A Dogmatics of Christian Disbelief*. Valley Forge, PA: Trinity Press International 1994.

Nicolas, Jean-Hervé. *Synthèse dogmatique: de la Trinité à la Trinité*. Paris: Beauchesne, 1985.

Nietzsche, Friedrich. *The Antichrist*. In *The Portable Nietzsche*. Edited and translated by Walter Kaufmann. New York: The Viking Press, 1972.

Ogilvie, Matthew. "New Evolutionary Theory and Catholic Theology." *Australian EJournal of Theology* 7 (2006): 1–11. http://aejt.com.au/__data/assets/pdf_file/0003/395130/AEJT_7.4_Oglivie_Evolution.pdf.

Ombres, Robert. "God, Angels, Us." *New Blackfriars* 86 (January 2005): 48–61.

O'Meara, Thomas F. *Vast Universe: Extraterrestrials and Christian Revelation*. Collegeville, MN: The Liturgical Press, 2012.

Ormerod, Neil. "In Defense of Natural Theology—Bringing Transcendence to the Public Realm." *Irish Theological Quarterly* 71 (2007): 227–41.

———. *A Public God: Natural Theology Reconsidered*. Minneapolis: Fortress Press, 2015.

Panikkar, Raimon. *The Intra-religious Dialogue*. Revised ed. Maryknoll, NY: Orbis Books, 1998.

Plantinga Pauw, Amy. "'Where Angels Fear to Tread.'" *Modern Theology* 16, no. 1 (January 2000): 39–59.

Polanyi, Michael. *Personal Knowledge*. Chicago: University of Chicago Press, 1958.

Polkinghorne, John. *The God of Hope and the End of the World*. New Haven, CT: Yale University Press, 2002.

Pottier, B. "Note sur la mission invisible du Verbe chez saint Thomas d'Aquin." *Nouvelle Revue Théologique* 123, no. 4 (October–December 2001): 547–57.

Purcell, Brendan. *From Big Bang to Big Mystery: Human Origins in the Light of Creation and Evolution*. Hyde Park, NY: New City Press, 2011.

Rahner, Karl. *Theological Investigations IV*. Translated by Kevin Smyth. Baltimore, MD: Helicon Press, 1966.

———. *Theological Investigations XI*. Translated by David Bourke. London: Darton, Longman and Todd, 1974.

Robbins, Jill, ed. *Is It Righteous to Be? Interviews with Emmanuel Levinas*. Stanford, CA: Stanford University Press, 2001.

Rolnick, Philip A. *Analogical Possibilities: How Words Refer to God*. Atlanta: Scholars Press, 1993.

Romano, Claude. *L'événement et le monde. Épithée. Essais Philosophiques*. Paris: Presses Universitaires de France, 1998.

Rousselot, Pierre. *The Eyes of Faith and Answers to Two Objections*. Translated by Joseph Donceel and Avery Dulles. New York: Fordham University Press, 1990.

Sagan, Carl. *Cosmos*. New York: Random House, 1980.

Schönborn, Christoph. *From Death to Life: The Christian Journey*. Translated by B. McNeil. San Francisco: Ignatius Press, 1995.

Sheldrake, Rupert. *The Rebirth of Nature: The Greening of Science and God*. New York: Bantam Books, 1991.

Smith, Timothy L. "The Context and Character of Thomas' Theory of Appropriations." *The Thomist* 63 (1999): 579–612.

Spitzer, Robert J. *New Proofs for the Existence of God: Contributions of Contemporary Physics and Philosophy*. Grand Rapids: Eerdmans Publishing Company, 2010.

Steiner, George. *Real Presences*. Chicago: University of Chicago Press, 1989.

Still, Carl N. "'Gifted Knowledge': An Exception to Thomistic Epistemology?" *The Thomist* 63 (1999): 173–90.

Tanner, Kathryn. *God and Creation in Christian Theology: Tyranny or Empowerment?* Oxford: Basil Blackwell, 1988.

Te Velde, Rudi. *Aquinas On God: The "Divine Science" of the* Summa Theologiae. Aldershot, UK: Ashgate, 1996.

Thunberg, Lars. *Man and the Cosmos: The Vision of St. Maximus the Confessor*. Crestwood, NY: St. Vladimir's Seminary Press, 1985.

Torrance, Thomas F. *Trinitarian Faith*. Edinburgh: Continuum, 2003.

Torrell, Jean-Pierre. *Saint Thomas d'Aquin, maître spirituel*. Paris: Cerf, 1996.

Tracy, David. *The Analogical Imagination: Christian Theology and the Culture of Pluralism*. New York: Crossroad, 1981.

———. *Pluralism and Ambiguity: Hermeneutics, Religion, Hope*. San Francisco: Harper and Row, 1987.

Vale, Carol Jean. "Teilhard de Chardin: Ontogenesis vs. Ontology." *Theological Studies* 53, no. 2 (June 1992): 313–37.

Van Tongeren, P., P. Sars, C. Bremmer, and K. Boey, eds. *Eros and Eris: Contribution to a Hermeneutical Phenomenology; Liber Amicorum for Adriann Peperzak*. Dordrecht: Kluwer Academic, 1992.

Voegelin, Eric. *Order and History*. Volume I, *Israel and Revelation*. Baton Rouge: Louisiana State University Press, 1969.

Von Balthasar, Hans Urs. *The Glory of the Lord: A Theological Aesthetics*. Volume 1, *Seeing the Form*. Translated by Erasmo Leiva-Merikakis. New York: Crossroad Publications, 1982.

———. *The Glory of the Lord*: A Theological Aesthetics. Volume 5, *The Realm of Metaphysics in the Modern Age*. Translated by Oliver Davies et al. Edinburgh: T. and T. Clark, 1991.

Ward, Graham, ed. *The Post-modern God: A Theological Reader*. Oxford: Blackwell, 1997.

Wilber, Ken, ed. *Quantum Questions*. Boston: Shambhala, 1984.

Williams, A. N. *The Ground of Union: Deification in Aquinas and Palamas*. Oxford: Oxford University Press, 1999.

Williams, Rowan. *On Christian Theology*. Oxford: Blackwell, 2000.

Wright, Judith Wright. *A Human Pattern: Selected Poems*. Sydney: Angus & Robertson, 1990.

Wynn, Mark. *God and Goodness: A Natural Theological Perspective*. London: Routledge, 1999.

Yates, John C. *The Timelessness of God*. Lanham, MD: University Press of America, 1990.

INDEX